D0482010

CULTURE

CULTURE

THE ANTHROPOLOGISTS' ACCOUNT

Adam Kuper

Harvard University Press

Cambridge, Massachusetts / London, England / 1999

Library of Congress Cataloging-in-Publication Data
Kuper, Adam.
    Culture : the anthropologists' account / Adam Kuper.
        p.   cm.
    Includes bibliographical references and index.
    ISBN 0–674–17957–9 (alk. paper)
    1. Culture.   2. Ethnology—Philosophy.   I. Title
GN357.K87   1999
306—dc21   98–46126

FOR JESSICA

CONTENTS

PREFACE   ix

Introduction: Culture Wars   1

Part One: Genealogies

1 Culture and Civilization: French, German,
   and English Intellectuals, 1930–1958   23

2 The Social Science Account: Talcott Parsons
   and the American Anthropologists   47

Part Two: Experiments

3 Clifford Geertz: Culture as Religion
   and as Grand Opera   75

4 David Schneider: Biology as Culture   122

5 Marshall Sahlins: History as Culture   159

6 Brave New World   201

7 Culture, Difference, Identity   226

NOTES   249

ACKNOWLEDGMENTS   289

INDEX   291

My subject in this book is a particular modern tradition within the long-running, shifting, international discourse on culture. As early as 1917, Robert Lowie proclaimed that culture "is, indeed, the sole and exclusive subject-matter of ethnology, as consciousness is the subject-matter of psychology, life of biology, electricity as a branch of physics." Wild words. A whole swath of German scholarship, for example, described its field as cultural science, but not as ethnology. Followers of Matthew Arnold would have questioned whether any culture worthy of the name was to be found beyond the limits of the great civilizations. And some anthropologists protested that the true subject matter of their discipline was human evolution. But Lowie was speaking for a newly established American school of cultural anthropology, which set out to challenge the established ideas. His claims would be taken more seriously a generation later. After World War II, the social sciences enjoyed an unprecedented moment of prosperity and influence in America. The various disciplines became more specialized, and cultural anthropology was now granted a special license to operate in the field of culture.

The results were very satisfactory, at least at first, certainly for the anthropologists. Stuart Chase observed in 1948 that the "culture concept of the anthropologists and sociologists is coming to be regarded as the foundation stone of the social sciences." In 1952 the leading American anthropologists of the day, Alfred Kroeber and Clyde Kluckhohn, gave it as their considered opinion that "the idea of culture, in the technical anthropological sense, is one of the key notions in contemporary American thought." And they were confident that in "the technical anthropological sense," culture was a concept of enormous, almost limitless, scientific promise. "In explanatory importance and in generality of application it is comparable to such categories as gravity in physics, disease in medicine, evolution in biology."

Things look very different today. Few anthropologists would claim that the notion of culture can be compared in "explanatory importance" with gravity, disease, or evolution. They still see themselves as specialists in the study of culture, but they have to accept that they no longer enjoy a privileged position in the packed and diverse gallery of culture experts. Moreover, the nature of the expertise they claim has changed dramatically. By and large, they have switched their intellectual allegiance from the social sciences to the humanities, and they are likely to practice interpretation, even deconstruction, rather than sociological or psychological analysis. Nevertheless, modern American anthropologists have systematically put theories of culture to work in a great variety of ethnographic studies, and I believe that their experiments offer the most intriguing and satisfactory test of the value—and perhaps the validity—of cultural theories. The core of this book is accordingly an evaluation of what has been the central project in postwar American cultural anthropology.

My conclusion will be that the more one considers the best modern work on culture by anthropologists, the more advisable it must appear to avoid the hyper-referential word altogether, and to talk more precisely of knowledge, or belief, or art, or technology, or tradition, or even of ideology (though similar problems are raised by that multivalent concept). There are fundamental epistemological problems, and these cannot be solved by tiptoeing around the notion of culture, or by refining definitions. The difficulties become most acute when (after all the protestations to the contrary have been made) culture shifts from something to be described, interpreted, even perhaps explained, and is treated instead as a source of explanation in itself. This is not to deny that some form of cultural explanation may be useful enough, in its place, but appeals to culture can offer only a partial explanation of why people think and behave as they do, and of what causes them to alter their ways. Political and economic forces, social institutions, and biological processes cannot be wished away, or assimilated to systems of knowledge and belief. And that, I will suggest, is the ultimate stumbling block in the way of cultural theory, certainly given its current pretensions.

I hope that the substantive chapters of this book will back up these conclusions, persuade the open-minded reader, and sow doubts in the minds of true believers. However, it could reasonably be objected that I was prejudiced against most forms of culture theory before I began this project. I am a fully paid-up member of a European party of anthropologists that has always been wary of taking culture for its exclusive subject matter, let alone endowing it with explanatory power. No doubt my initial skepticism was further colored by my political views: I am a liberal, in the European rather than the American sense, a moderate man, a wishy-washy humanist; but though I am always very reasonable, I cannot claim that I am free of bias. Moderately materialist and with wishy-washy convictions about universal human rights, I am resistant to the idealism and relativism of modern culture theory, and I also have limited sympathy for social movements based on nationalism, ethnic identity, or religion, precisely the movements that are most likely to invoke culture in order to motivate political action.

Shortly before I began work on this book, I was made acutely aware that these theoretical doubts and political concerns were deeply rooted in my own background as a liberal South African. At an early stage of the recent tranformation of South Africa, after the election of F. W. De Klerk to the presidency but before the release of Nelson Mandela from prison, a moment pregnant with great historical possibilities, I received a letter from a distinguished American anthropologist. He had been invited to deliver an annual public lecture on the subject of academic freedom at the University of Cape Town. Naturally enough, he asked himself what an anthropologist might contribute to the desperately serious debates about race, culture, and history that possessed South Africa, and he invited me to provide him with some background about the state of the argument in local anthropological circles. I sent him reviews of the mainstream arguments in Afrikaner cultural anthropology, and he wrote back to say that he was very grateful. He had narrowly avoided an appalling solecism, for his first impulse had been to devote the lecture to a classical Boasian discourse about culture. He would probably have argued that race and culture were independent of each other; that culture made people what they were; and that respect for cultural difference should be the basis of a just society. A benign argument in America, in South Africa this would have come across as a last-ditch justification for apartheid.

This paradox was deeply ingrained in my consciousness, and no doubt it is one of the impulses from which this book has come. I was an undergraduate in South Africa in the late 1950s. A radical Afrikaner establishment was firmly in control of the country, and its policy of enforced racial segregation, apartheid, was being implemented with a sort of moralizing sadism. The regime appeared to be almost invulnerable, and impervious to criticism. The African opposition movements had been brutally suppressed. And yet there was one field in which it did seem that some of the regime's most dearly held beliefs might be exposed by rational argument and irrefutable evidence. Although they were often wrapped up in the language of theology, the official doctrines on race and culture invoked scientific authority: apartheid was based on an anthropological theory. It was no accident that its intellectual architect, W. W. M. Eiselen, had been a professor of ethnology.

The Afrikaner nationalists were suspicious of the "civilizing mission" that was proclaimed, with good faith or bad, by the colonial powers in Africa. Some believed that Africans could not be civilized, even that the attempt was counterproductive; or, at best, that it would take centuries to achieve this goal, and perhaps only at a great human cost. This sort of argument is often motivated by a crude racism, and racist thinking was certainly very general among white South Africans. However, some of the Afrikaner intellectuals, Eiselen among them, repudiated popular prejudices. There was no evidence that intelligence varied with race, Eiselen pointed out in a lecture in 1929, nor was any one race or nation privileged to lead the world forever in civilization. Not race but culture was the true basis of difference, the sign of destiny. And cultural differences were to be valued. Cultural exchange, even progress, was not necessarily a boon. It might come at too high a price. If the integrity of traditional cultures were undermined, social disintegration would follow. Eiselen recommended that government policy should be aimed at fostering "higher Bantu culture and not at producing black Europeans." Later, the slogan "separate development" was used. Segregation was the proper course for South Africa, because only segregation would preserve cultural differences.

The apartheid school of ethnology cited American cultural anthropologists with approval, though very much on its own terms; but its leaders were radically opposed to the theories of the British school of social anthropology, and in particular to those of A. R. Radcliffe-Brown, who was appointed to the first chair in social anthropology in South Africa, in 1921. Radcliffe-Brown did not, of course, deny that cultural differences persisted in South Africa, but he rejected the policy of segregation on the grounds that South Africa had become a single society. National institutions crossed cultural boundaries and shaped life choices in all the villages and towns in the country. Every one of its citizens (or subjects) was in the same boat. To base politics on cultural difference was a recipe for disaster. "Segregation was impossible," he told his audience in one public lecture. "South African nationalism must be a nationalism composed of both black and white."

In part as a result of his South African experience, Radcliffe-Brown was later inclined to treat all talk of culture with suspicion. "We do not observe a 'culture,' " he remarked in his Presidential Address to the Royal Anthropological Institute in 1940, "since that word denotes, not any concrete reality, but an abstraction, and as it is commonly used a vague abstraction." And he dismissed the view of his great rival, Bronislaw Malinowski, that a society like South Africa should be studied as an arena in which two or more "cultures" interacted. "For what is happening in South Africa [Radcliffe-Brown explained] is not the interaction of British culture, and Afrikander (or Boer) culture, Hottentot culture, various Bantu cultures and Indian culture, but the interaction of individuals and groups within an established social structure which is itself in process of change. What is happening in a Transkeian tribe, for example, can only be described by recognising that the tribe has been incorporated into a wide political and economic structural system."

Coming from South Africa, I was no doubt predisposed to accept arguments of this kind. Moreover, any initial prejudices I may have had were reinforced by my graduate training in the structural and sociological anthropology current at Cambridge University in the early 1960s. Certain of my contemporaries did shake themselves free of this early conditioning, however, and crossed over to the culture school. My skepticism about culture was more robust, in part because I had been so impressed by the abuse of culture theory in South Africa. But it is not necessarily a bad thing to approach a deeply entrenched theory in a skeptical frame of mind. And political inclinations do not necessarily disqualify one from appreciating the strengths and weaknesses of counter-arguments. Moreover, theories

of culture commonly carry a political charge, justifying a political critique. But while my background as a South African has informed my
inquiries into culture theory, it is my hope that this did not determine the conclusions I have reached. Whatever bias I may have
brought to this project, I have done my best to respect both the arguments and the evidence.

This is probably all one can ask of history, and of the history of ideas in particular: not to resolve issues, but to raise the level of the debate.

Albert O. Hirschman

INTRODUCTION:

CULTURE

WARS

> I don't know how many times I've wished that I'd never heard
> the damned word.
>
> *Raymond Williams*

American academics are waging culture wars. (Not many
dead.) Politicians urge cultural revolution. Apparently a seismic cultural change is needed to resolve the problems of poverty, drug
abuse, crime, illegitimacy, and industrial competitiveness. There is
talk of cultural differences between the sexes and the generations,
between football teams, or between advertising agencies. When a
merger between two companies fails, it is explained that their cultures were not compatible. The beauty of it is that everyone under-
stands. "We tried to sell 'semiotics,' but we found it a bit difficult,"
reported a London company called Semiotic Solutions, "so now we
sell 'culture.' They know that one. You don't have to explain it."
And there is no call to sell culture short. "Culture rules the roost
in terms of motivating consumer behavior," claims the company
brochure, "more persuasive than reason, more 'mass' than psychology." There is also a thriving secondary market in cultural discourse.

In the mid-1990s, bookshops set up "cultural studies" sections in the prime positions that were once devoted to New Age religion and before that to self-improvement. The book manager at Olsson's in Washington, D.C., Guy Brussat, explained: "Somebody sees sociology, and they think, *dry, academic text.* You see cultural studies and you think, *Oh, culture!* It's a subtle, psychological thing."

Everyone is into culture now. For anthropologists, culture was once a term of art. Now the natives talk culture back at them. " 'Culture'—the word itself, or some local equivalent, is on everyone's lips," Marshall Sahlins has observed. "Tibetans and Hawaiians, Ojibway, Kwakiutl, and Eskimo, Kazakhs and Mongols, native Australians, Balinese, Kashmiris, and New Zealand Maori: all discover they have a 'culture.' " The monolingual speakers of Kayapo in the South American tropical forest use the Portuguese term *cultura* to describe their traditional ceremonies. Maurice Godelier describes a migrant laborer returning to his New Guinea people, the Baruya, and proclaiming: "We must find strength in our customs; we must base ourselves on what the Whites call culture." Another New Guinean tells an anthropologist, "If we didn't have *kastom,* we would be just like white men." Sahlins cites all these instances to illustrate a general proposition: "The cultural self-consciousness developing among imperialism's erstwhile victims is one of the more remarkable phenomena of world history in the later twentieth century."

These erstwhile victims may even develop critical discourses on culture. Gerd Baumann has shown that in Southall, a multi-ethnic suburb in West London, people "question what the terms *'culture'* and *'community'* may signify in the first place. The terms themselves become pivotal points in the making of a Southall culture." However, even anti-Western nationalists may simply appropriate the dominant international rhetoric of culture to affirm the unique identity of their own people, with no fear of self-contradiction. "We consider the main threat to our society at the present time," says a fundamentalist Iranian politician, "to be a cultural one." (But surely to speak of cultural identity is very . . . American?) Akio Morita, one of the founders of Sony, rejects pleas that Japan should liberalize its trading arrangements to permit more competition from foreign firms. "Reciprocity," he explains, "would mean changing laws to accept foreign systems that may not suit our culture." (Fortunately, selling Sony TV sets to Americans and making Hollywood movies is perfectly in accordance with Japanese culture.)

Perhaps the future of the whole world depends on culture. In 1993, Samuel Huntington announced in an apocalyptic essay in *Foreign Affairs* that a new phase of global history has begun, in which "the fundamental sources of conflict" will not be primarily economic or ideological. "The great divisions among humankind and the dominating source of conflict will be cultural." Elaborating this thesis in a recent book, he argued that we can expect a titanic clash of civilizations, each representing a primordial cultural identity. The "major differences in political and economic development among civilizations are clearly rooted in their different cultures," and "culture and cultural identities . . . are shaping the patterns of cohesion, disintegration, and conflict in the post–Cold War world . . . In this new world, local politics is the politics of ethnicity; global politics is the politics of civilizations. The rivalry of the superpowers is replaced by the clash of civilizations."

It goes without saying that culture means something rather different to market researchers in London, a Japanese mogul, New Guinean villagers, and a radical clergyman in Teheran, not to mention Samuel Huntington. There is nevertheless a family resemblance between the concepts they have in mind. In its most general sense, culture is simply a way of talking about collective identities. Status is also in play, however. Many people believe that cultures can be measured against each other, and they are inclined to esteem their own culture more highly than that of others. They may even believe that there is only one true civilization, and that the future not only of the nation but of the world depends on the survival of their culture. "The multiculturalists notwithstanding," Roger Kimball insists, "the choice facing us today is not between a 'repressive' Western culture and a multicultural paradise, but between culture and barbarism. Civilization is not a gift, it is an achievement—a fragile achievement that needs constantly to be shored up and defended from besiegers inside and out." Huntington suggests that the clash of civilizations in the post–Cold War world is but a stage on the way to the climactic struggle that is to come, "the greater clash, the global '*real* clash,' between Civilization and barbarism."

Whereas the patriots of Western Civ claim the high ground of the great tradition, the multiculturalists celebrate the diversity of America and champion the cultures of the marginal, the minorities, the dissidents, the colonized. The culture of the establishment is denounced as oppressive. Minority cultures empower the weak: they are authentic; they speak to real people; they sustain variety and choice; they feed dissent. All cultures are equal, or should be treated as equal. "So culture as a theme or topic of study has replaced society as the general object of inquiry among progressives," Fred Inglis writes, with only a touch of irony. But while conservatives reject these arguments, they agree that culture establishes public standards and determines national destiny. And when people of different nations and ethnic groups meet, whole cultures confront each other. Something must give in this confrontation.

Culture is also often used in a different sense, to refer to the high art that is enjoyed by the happy few. But it is not simply a private accomplishment. The well-being of the whole nation is at stake if art and scholarship are threatened. For Matthew Arnold, the true class struggle was not between rich and poor but between the guardians of culture and the people he called the philistines, who were in thrall to Mammon. Radical writers, however, deny that the culture of the elite spreads sweetness and light. High culture can be represented as an instrument of domination, a trick of caste. Within the elite, Pierre Bourdieu has argued, the value of high culture lies precisely in the fact that the ability to judge works of art, to make distinctions, itself confers "distinction." Culture is the gift of educated taste that marks off a lady or a gentleman from the upstart. For those in the Marxist tradition, culture has its place in the larger class war. High culture cloaks the extortions of the rich. Ersatz mass culture confounds the poor. Only popular cultural traditions can counter the corruption of the mass media.

Although there has been a striking efflorescence of culture talk, arguments of this sort are, of course, not new. They all cropped up in the course of a similar burst of cultural theorizing between the 1920s and the 1950s, as the following chapter will show. (Perhaps this long argument was simply interrupted for a generation by the ideological preoccupations of the Cold War.) Then as now, the more reflective authors cited their forerunners in the eighteenth and nineteenth centuries, recognizing that discourses on culture tend to fall into well-established categories.

A French, a German, and an English theory of culture are often loosely identified. Alternatively, and equally loosely, Enlightenment, Romantic, and Classical discourses are distinguished. These are rough-and-ready labels for complex constructs that have regularly been taken to pieces and reassembled in new patterns, adapted, pronounced dead, revived, renamed, revamped, and generally subjected to a variety of structural transformations. Yet however crude, this classification does provide an initial orientation. Even the most imaginative and original thinkers can generally be placed in one or another of these central traditions, each of which specifies a conception of culture and puts it to work within a particular theory of history.

In the French tradition, civilization is represented as a progressive, cumulative, distinctively human achievement. Human beings are alike, at least in potential. All are capable of civilization, which depends on the unique human gift for reason. No doubt civilization has progressed furthest in France, but in principle it may be enjoyed, if perhaps not quite to the same degree, by savages, barbarians, and other Europeans. According to Louis Dumont, a Frenchman will therefore "naively identify his own particular culture with 'civilisation' or universal culture." To be sure, a reflective Frenchman would readily admit that reason does not have things all its own way. It must struggle against tradition, superstition, and brute instinct. But he could rest secure in the belief that the ultimate victory of civilization is certain, for it can call to its aid science: the highest expression of reason, and indeed of culture or civilization, the true and efficient knowledge of the laws that inform nature and society alike.

This secular creed was formulated in France in the second half of the eighteenth century, in opposition to what the *philosophes* considered to be the forces of reaction and unreason, represented above all by the Catholic church and the *ancien régime*. As it took hold in the rest of Europe, its most formidable ideological opposition came from German intellectuals, often Protestant ministers, who were provoked to stand up for national tradition against cosmopolitan civilization; for spiritual values against materialism; for the arts and crafts against science and technology; for individual genius and self-expression against stifling bureaucracy; for the emotions, even for the darkest forces within us, against desiccated reason: in short, for *Kultur* against *Civilization*.

Unlike scientific knowledge, the wisdom of culture is subjective. Its most profound insights are relative, not universal laws. What is true on one side of the Pyrenees may be error on the other side. But if the cultural faith is eroded, life loses all meaning. While material civilization was tightening its iron grip on every European society, individual nations therefore struggled to sustain a spiritual culture, expressed above all in language and the arts. The authentic *Kultur* of the German people was surely to be preferred to the artificial *Civilization* of a cosmopolitan, materialistic French-speaking elite. In any case, cultural difference was natural. There is no common human nature. "I have seen Frenchmen, Italians, Russians," wrote the French counter-revolutionary de Maistre. "But as for man, I declare that I have never in my life met him; if he exists, he is unknown to me." (Henry James may have had this aphorism in mind when he wrote, "Man isn't at all one, after all—it takes so much of him to be American, to be French, etc.")

These two traditions of thinking about culture developed in dialectical opposition to each other. A central theme of Enlightenment thinkers was human progress, whereas their opponents were interested in the particular destiny of a nation. In the Enlightenment view, civilization was engaged in a great struggle to overcome the resistance of traditional cultures, with their superstitions, irrational prejudices, and fearful loyalties to cynical rulers. (Voltaire said he would rest in peace only when the last king was strangled in the entrails of the last priest.) For the party of the Counter-Enlightenment, the defining enemy was rational, scientific, universal civilization: the Enlightenment itself. Associated with material values, with capitalism, and often with foreign political and economic influence, this civilization menaced authentic culture and condemned age-old crafts to obsolescence. Cosmopolitanism corrupted language. Rationalism disturbed religious faith. Together they eroded the spiritual values on which the organic community depended.

These contrasting ideologies could fuel nationalist rhetoric, and stir up popular emotions in time of war, but even at their most envenomed they were never merely national discourses. There were French intellectuals who sympathized with the Counter-Enlightenment, if only because it came to the defense of religion against the insidious subversion of reason. After the Battle of Sedan in 1870 (won, it was said, by the schoolmasters of Prussia), the idea of a national culture penetrated a humiliated France, and "la culture Française" was increasingly contrasted to "la culture allemande," though without necessarily compromising French claims to superiority. (As late as 1938, the Dictionary Quillet noted that the term *culture* could be used ironically, as in the phrase "la culture allemande.") In Germany there was a long tradition of Enlightenment thinking, which was never completely submerged, though it sometimes took strange, almost unrecognizable forms. Nietzsche condemned his countrymen for their chaotic *Bildung,* or cultural formation, corrupted by borrowing and fashion, which he contrasted to its detriment with the organic *Kultur* of France, and he equated that in turn with Civilization itself. He opted for civilization—in other words, for France: home to "the most spiritual and refined European culture." A French dissident like Baudelaire, on the other hand, could call France "a truly barbarous country," and speculate that perhaps civilization "has taken refuge in some tiny, as yet undiscovered tribe." The First World War was fought behind the rival banners of Western Civilization and German *Kultur,* but in the war's very shadow the brothers Thomas and Heinrich Mann took opposite sides—the German and the French— in a famous debate about culture and civilization.

In both these traditions, culture or civilization stood for ultimate values. It has been suggested that these concepts spread in the eighteenth century because religion was losing its grip on many intellectuals. They provided an alternative, secular source of value and meaning. Each tradition, however, had affinities with a specific Christian outlook. The idea of Civilization recalls the universalist claims of the Catholic church. Comte and Saint-Simon created a religion of positivism for which they borrowed Catholic rituals. Its central dogma was progress, which stood for secular, this-worldly salvation. The German notions of *Bildung* and *Kultur,* characteristically expressed in a spiritual idiom, engaged with the needs of the individual soul, valuing inner virtue above outward show, pessimistic about secular progress, are in turn imbued with the values of the Reformation, and Thomas Mann suggested that the Reformation had immunized Germans against the ideas of the French Revolution.

The English, as ever, stood somewhat aloof from these Continental arguments. John Stuart Mill had tried to bring the French and German traditions together, in his famous essays on Bentham and Coleridge, but the English had their own specific preoccupations. As industrialization transformed England, intellectuals identified a spiritual crisis, a defining struggle between what Shelley called Poetry and Mammon. The technology and materialism of modern civilization represented the enemy. Against this, the liberal intellectuals pitted eternal cultural values, distilled from the great tradition of European art and philosophy. Matthew Arnold defined culture as "the best that has been known and said," an enduring, cosmopolitan canon. Acquiring culture, we acquaint ourselves with "the history of the human spirit." The possession of culture marked off the elect from the unlettered barbarians. But now this humanist legacy was under siege from the armies of industrial civilization. A great question of the day was whether the intellectual culture of the educated elite could somehow sustain the spiritual values of society. Perhaps culture would falter, overwhelmed by the Gradgrind materialism of hard-faced men who knew the cost of everything and the value of nothing. "As civilisation advances," Macaulay concluded, "poetry almost necessarily declines."

Yet it will not do to exaggerate the distinctiveness of the English tradition. Arnold drew on Coleridge, and Coleridge on the German romantics. Concerns and values overlapped. Everywhere, culture stood for the sphere of ultimate values, upon which, it was believed, the social order rested. Since culture was transmitted through the educational system, and expressed most powerfully in the arts, these were the critical fields that a committed intellectual should study to improve. And because the fortunes of a nation depended on the condition of its culture, this was a crucial arena for political action.

Modern arguments do not precisely recapitulate earlier controversies. Contemporary contexts make their mark. Each generation modernizes the idiom of debate, usually adapting it to current scientific terminology: evolutionism in the late nineteenth century, organicism in the early twentieth century, relativity in the 1920s. Tropes borrowed from genetics compete today with the jargon of contemporary literary theory. Yet even if they are expressed in novel idioms, discourses on culture are not freely invented; they refer back to particular intellectual traditions that have persisted for generations, spreading from Europe throughout the world, imposing conceptions of human nature and history, provoking a series of recurrent debates. Ancestral voices haunt contemporary writers. New formulations can be set in a long genealogy, even if they are related to the needs of the moment.

As the human sciences crystallized, competing schools of thought drew on these classic perspectives. Central themes of the Enlightenment view of the world, or of the French ideology, reemerged in nineteenth-century positivism, socialism, and utilitarianism. In the twentieth century, the idea of a progressive, scientific world civilization was translated into the theory of modernization, and then the theory of globalization. In the short run, culture was a barrier to modernization (or industrialization, or globalization), but modern civilization would in the end trample over local, less efficient traditions. Culture was invoked when it became necessary to explain why people were clinging to irrational goals and self-destructive strategies. Development projects were defeated by cultural resistance. Democracy crumbled because it was alien to the traditions of a nation. Rational choice theories could not account for what economists despairingly call "stickiness," entrenched ways of thinking and doing that persist in the face of the most compelling arguments. Culture was the fallback, to explain apparently irrational behavior. Culture also accounted for the disappointing outcome of many political reforms. Tradition was the refuge of the ignorant and fearful, or the recourse of the rich and powerful, jealous of any challenge to their established privileges.

From another point of view, the resistance of local cultures to globalization might be respected, even celebrated. This was the perspective of the heirs to the Counter-Enlightenment. The romantic, or German, tradition was also not static. It underwent its own transformations, though always exhibiting an elective affinity with idealism, relativism, historicism, a hermeneutic style of analysis, and what we now call identity politics. Richard A. Shweder has even attempted to construct a genealogy that connects the romantic movement of the nineteenth century with what he calls anthropology's contemporary "romantic rebellion against the enlightenment."

But even if they decked themselves out in the latest fashions, the classical ideas about culture did not have the field to themselves. They confronted new rivals, the greatest of which made its appearance with the publication of Darwin's *The Origin of Species* in 1859. Even the least scientific thinker could not ignore the challenge after Darwin extended his argument to human beings in *The Descent of Man* in 1871. The possibility now had to be faced that human universals and human differences could be explained in biological terms. Culture might follow natural laws. Nevertheless, Darwinian theory did not necessarily make the classical ideas obsolete. The theory that all human beings had a common origin reaffirmed the Enlightenment faith in the unity of humankind. Civilization might still be celebrated as the defining human trait. The evolution of life might also provide a model for the evolution of civilization. Human beings were an advance on the apes, and higher races—or higher civilizations—were in the same way an advance on lower races and their civilizations. Darwin himself shared this view, but some of his followers were recruited to the cause of the Counter-Enlightenment. Cultural difference might be an expression of more fundamental racial differences. Racial purity could be a political imperative, linked inextricably to the defense of a cultural identity. History might be written in blood, its theme the struggle for survival between races.

The challenge of a biological theory of human progress and human difference provoked the development of what was in some ways a new conception of culture. Culture was now conceived of in opposition to biology. It was culture that marked human beings off from other animals, and nations from other nations. And it was not inherited biologically, but learned, acquired, even borrowed. Christopher Herbert has argued that this notion of culture has, again, an origin in a religious controversy. He associates it with the early nineteenth century Evangelical revival in Britain, which propagated a notion of original sin that he calls "the myth of a state of ungoverned human desire." The idea of culture offered the countervailing hope of secular salvation: culture was our defense against human nature. Human beings raised themselves from their fallen condition by the grace of taboos and laws. Herbert argues that "one can think of the ideas of culture and of free desire as two reciprocal, complementary elements of a single pattern of discourse, albeit a conflict-laden and necessarily unstable one." Perhaps Herbert is right, and this conception of culture first took shape in response to religious concerns, but it came to maturity in reaction to the Darwinian revolution, which threatened to give scientific authority to something like the doctrine of ungoverned human desire.

Nowhere was the cultural argument against Darwinism formulated with greater urgency and power than in Berlin in the 1880s. The leading Darwinian in Germany, Ernst Haeckel, adduced political conclusions from Darwinian theory that made Darwin himself rather uneasy. According to Haeckel, Darwin provided irrefutable, scientific arguments for free trade and against hereditary aristocracies. His theory could also be used to demonstrate the superiority of the Prussian race and to underwrite the politics of Bismarck, which demonstrated the wonderful effects of struggle and selection.

Haeckel's dogma appalled his former teacher, Rudolf Virchow, who was the leading medical scientist in Germany, a prominent politician of liberal views, and the guiding spirit behind the Berlin Society of Anthropology. Methodologically, his objection was to premature theoretical closure. The multitudinous accidents of evolutionary change could not yet be reduced to laws. Substantively, he was especially hostile to Haeckel's racial determinism, and to the cultural nationalism with which it was associated. Races were unstable categories, with shifting boundaries, and racial mixing was widespread if not universal. Biological traits cut across the conventional racial classifications, which were in any case influenced by local, environmental factors. Cultural difference was not a sign of racial difference. Race, culture, language, and nationality did not necessarily, or even usually, coincide. The Huguenot refugees, Virchow insisted, "are Germanised, just like the numerous Jews, whom we accept from Poland or Russia, and [who] . . . have become a powerful ferment of cultural progress for us."

Virchow's associate, Adolf Bastian (who became the first director of the great Berlin museum of ethnology in 1886), attempted to demonstrate that, like races, cultures are hybrids. There are no pure cultures, distinctive and enduring. Every culture draws on diverse sources, depends on borrowings, and is in flux. Human beings are very much alike, and every culture is rooted in a universal human mentality. Cultural differences were caused by the challenges presented by the local natural environment, and by the contacts between human populations. Borrowing was the primary mechanism for cultural change. And since cultural changes were the consequence of chance local processes—environmental pressures, migrations, trade—it followed that history has no fixed pattern of development.

This liberal Berlin anthropology has been characterized as a blend of Enlightenment and Romantic ideas, but it is actually based on a double rejection. If cultures are open, syncretic, and unstable, then obviously they cannot express unchanging, essential identities, or an underlying racial character. And if cultural changes are the consequence of chance local factors, then it must follow that there are no general laws of history. Above all, however, the Berlin school insisted that culture works in a very different way from biological forces—and might even override them.

Franz Boas, a student of Virchow and Bastian, introduced this approach into American anthropology. As American anthropology developed into an organized academic discipline at the beginning of the twentieth century, it was defined by the epic struggle between Boas and his school and the evolutionist tradition, represented in the United States by the followers of Lewis Henry Morgan, whose triumphalist narratives of progress borrowed the metaphors of Darwinian theory. The Boasians were skeptical about universal laws of evolution. They also repudiated racial explanations of difference, a matter of enduring political importance in the United States. The fundamental Boasian thesis was that culture makes us, not biology. We become what we are by growing up in a particular cultural setting; we are not born that way. Race, and also sex and age, are cultural constructs, not immutable natural conditions. The implication is that we can be made over into something better, perhaps learning from the tolerant people of Samoa, or the perfectly balanced Balinese.

This was a powerfully attractive idea in twentieth-century America, but the alternative, racial understanding of cultural difference remained a potent challenge. The idea of culture could actually reinforce a racial theory of difference. Culture could be a euphemism for race, fostering a discourse on racial identities while apparently abjuring racism. Anthropologists might fastidiously distinguish between race and culture, but in popular usage "culture" referred to an innate quality. The nature of a group was evident to the naked eye, expressed to equal effect in skin color, facial characteristics, religion, morals, aptitudes, accent, gestures, and dietary preferences. This stubborn confusion persists. In the 1980s Michael Moffatt, an ethnographer studying white and black students who shared a dormitory at Rutgers University, reported that the students virtuously refused to talk about race but believed that talking about cultural differences was up-to-date and politically correct. In practice, however, they drew a line between whites and blacks, despite the fact that these students seem to have differed mainly in their tastes in pop groups and fast food.

Culture is always defined in opposition to something else. It is the authentic, local way of being different that resists its implacable enemy, a globalizing, material civilization. Or it is the realm of the spirit, embattled against materialism. Or it is the human capacity for spiritual growth that overcomes our animal nature. Within the social sciences, culture appeared in yet another set of contrasts: it was the collective consciousness, as opposed to the individual psyche. At the same time, it stood for the ideological dimension of social life as against the mundane organization of government, factory, or family. These ideas were developed by the founding fathers of European sociology and were introduced into a traditionally empiricist and utilitarian American sociology by Talcott Parsons.

In the 1950s and 1960s, the social or "behavioral" sciences were better funded, better organized, and generally in better spirits than ever before (or since), certainly in America, and their leaders were convinced that the future—which could only be better still—lay with large scientific projects that would deliver a rational plan for an even better world. Talcott Parsons, the great figure of social science in America in the period, insisted that further progress required a more efficient division of labor, in the social sciences as in any modern enterprise. The psyche was, of course, studied by psychologists. The social system, politics, and the economy were being dealt with by appropriate specialists, which was satisfactory as long as all concerned accepted that sociology had priority. Culture, however, had been entrusted for too long to the amateurish hands of the humanists. From now on it was to be allotted to the anthropologists, who might make a science of it at last, if only they could be persuaded to concentrate on the task at hand and to abandon their picturesque hobbies.

Not every anthropologist was best pleased with this prospect. Some regarded it as a definite come-down to be a culture maven rather than, say, the expert on every aspect of a tribal community, or even an authority on the whole story of human evolution. Moreover, demarcation disputes with other social scientists persisted. Nevertheless, it came to be generally accepted in the 1950s that culture was a matter of scientific concern, and that the anthropologists were its specialists. In 1952 the twin deans of American anthropology, Alfred Kroeber at Berkeley and Clyde Kluckhohn at Harvard, published a magisterial report on the scientific, anthropological conception of culture, confident that it was poised to render the traditional approaches obsolete. Two decades later, Roy Wagner could introduce an essay on culture with the observation that the concept "has come to be so completely associated with anthropological thinking that . . . we could define an anthropologist as someone who uses the word 'culture' habitually." By the 1990s, culture talk has become so pervasive that on Wagner's definition practically everybody who writes about social issues would have to be counted as an anthropologist. However, a commentator could still remark that "a modern anthropologist disbelieving in culture is something like a contradiction in terms."

But before anthropologists could investigate culture scientifically, they had to agree what they meant by the word. Kroeber and Kluckhohn made an exhaustive search of the literature and finally had to agree that Parsons had hit upon the correct definition of culture, for the purposes of science. It was a collective symbolic discourse. What it discoursed on was knowledge, beliefs, and values. It was not equivalent to the high arts, as the humanists believed, for every member of a society had a share in its culture. It was also quite distinct from the universal human civilization that had given the world science, technology, and democracy, for every community had its own culture, with its specific values, that marked it off from all others.

If this was culture, then how important was it? According to Parsons, people fashion a symbolic world out of received ideas, and these ideas impinge on the choices they make in the real world. Nevertheless, he was quite sure that ideas on their own seldom determine action. Similarly, collective symbols enter into the individual consciousness but do not take it over completely. However, the more the anthropologists committed themselves to their new specialism, the more convinced they became that culture was much more powerful than Parsons made it out to be. People not only construct a world of symbols; they actually live in it. The leaders of the next generation of American anthropologists, Clifford Geertz, David Schneider, and Marshall Sahlins, created a gallery of native types of unparalleled spirituality. Their subjects appeared to live only for ideas, whether they were Hawaiian priests, or Balinese courtiers, or middle-class citizens of Chicago. In Geertz's *Negara,* the play's the thing—or rather, what he calls court operas are the epitome of the whole way of life. Politics and economics are merely noises off-stage. For Schneider, kinship is a matter of the ideas that people have about procreation. Biology is in the mind, or it is nothing. For Sahlins, history is the endless acting out of an old script, a saga in performance. Earthquakes, the rough intrusion of conquistadores, even capitalism, must be translated into cultural terms, mythologized, before they can affect peoples' lives.

The next question was how to go about the investigation of culture. Parsons himself offered little practical guidance on this matter, but in mid-century America two models presented themselves, one old, one new. The first recommended the sympathetic exploration of a native world view, its translation and interpretation. Weber's name was evoked, the word *Verstehen* pronounced reverently, if not always accurately. Geertz chose this course, which he identified initially as Parsonian, then as Weberian, and later as a form of hermeneutics. Gradually he became less eager to claim that it was a scientific procedure, having come to the conclusion that while culture could be interpreted, it could not be explained (and certainly not explained away). There were no general, cross-cultural, laws of culture. You could, perhaps, work out what a symbolic performance meant to an audience, but you could not detach it from its vernacular meaning and treat it as a symptom of a more fundamental and culture-free biological or economic cause, of which the patient was unaware.

The alternative approach was, in contrast, scientific, reductionist, generalizing. It began with the premise that culture—a symbolic discourse—was very like language. Accordingly, the study of culture should follow the path that was being blazed by modern linguistics, which was on the verge of discovering the universal laws of language. "For centuries the humanities and the social sciences have resigned themselves to contemplating the world of the natural and exact sciences as a kind of paradise which they will never enter," Claude

Lévi-Strauss remarked at a conference on linguistics and anthropology at Bloomington, Indiana, in 1952. "All of a sudden there is a small door which is being opened between the two fields, and it is linguistics which has done it." This door led beyond language and culture to their ultimate source. There was, he told the conferees, an "uninvited guest who has been seated beside us during this Conference, and that is *the human mind.*" If a new science of culture was to follow the lead of linguistics, then together these sciences would ultimately establish the deep structure that all languages and cultures shared, and that was (surely) etched in the brain itself. A scientific, Cartesian anthropology was waiting to be born.

This was all very exciting, but it had to be admitted that the linguists themselves were not in agreement on the best route to their great goal. Lévi-Strauss had been introduced to linguistics during his wartime exile in the United States by a fellow exile, Roman Jakobson. His model was accordingly the structuralist phonology that had been developed by the Prague School. This he applied first to systems of marriage, then to modes of classification, and finally to myths. The American structuralists preferred to take their lead from the transformational grammar of Chomsky. The Yale school of Lounsbury and Goodenough (which recruited a number of graduates of the Harvard Department of Social Relations) launched a formal, scientific investigation of the underlying structures that generated kinship terminologies, botanical classifications, symptoms of illness, and other folk taxonomies that constituted specialized semiotic domains.

These structuralist programs flourished for a while, producing remarkable accounts of specific bodies of native thought, but at some point in the late 1960s (precisely in May 1968, Lévi-Strauss has suggested) French structuralism lost its fashionable appeal. It gave way to a variety of "poststructuralisms" of a decidedly relativist cast. Their adepts abandoned the scientific ambitions of classical structuralism, insisting upon the ultimate indeterminacy of words and symbols. American ethnoscience fell out of fashion at much the same time, but some former enthusiasts discovered an alternative scientific promise in cognitive science. Computer models of the brain processes, knowledge schemas, and connective networks were now sought instead of the grammatical rules in which the practitioners of the new ethnography had previously put their faith. Another faction seized upon fresh developments in linguistics, and determined to adapt pragmatics, or discourse theory, to the study of culture.

The Geertzians were consistently dismissive of any suggestion that there could be a science of culture. Culture was indeed rather like language, but their preferred model of culture was the text. Accordingly, they drew upon literary theory rather than linguistics. It was this approach that prospered, and interpretivism became the orthodoxy in mainstream American cultural anthropology. Although the younger Geertzians rebelled against the father, they did not opt for a more scientific project, but moved in the same direction as the French poststructuralists. A culture could not be so readily understood by a sympathetic outsider as Geertz had suggested. Culture may be a text, but it is a fabricated text, a fiction written by the ethnographer. Further, the clear message of deconstruction is that texts do not yield up unequivocal messages. Discordant voices dispute the official line. Culture is contested, as the new slogan says. As there is no canonical text, so there are no privileged readers. The postmodern anthropologists prefer to imagine the realm of culture as something more like an unruly democracy than a theocratic state or absolutist monarchy. Uneasy about the totalitarian overtones of the term *culture,* some prefer to write about habitus, or ideology, or discourse, although, as Robert Brightman points out, the net effect of these rhetorical strategies is to "(re)construct an essentialized culture concept in the antipodes of contemporary theoretical orientations." The assumption remains that people live in a world of symbols. Actors are driven and history is shaped by (perhaps unconscious) ideas. Mainstream American cultural anthropology, in short, is still in the grip of a pervasive idealism.

Idealism has been in the ascendant more widely in recent decades, together with its handmaiden, relativism. Each culture was founded on unique premises. Generalization was impossible, comparison extremely problematic. A similar tendency was evident in philosophy, which greatly emboldened the anthropologists. Even fashionable Marxism became obsessed with ideology. ("La fantaisie au pouvoir," chanted the Parisian students of '68, as they hurled paving stones at the *flics.*) Nevertheless, the idealists and the culturalists did not have everything their own way. On the contrary, they felt that they were besieged by the great battalions of their rivals, who marched behind the familiar banners: The Market Decides, The Ruling Class Rules, We Are Our Genes. Culturalist arguments had to be pitted against the established models of economic rationality and biological determinism, but a growing if motley collection of aesthetes, idealists, and romantics agreed that Culture Makes Us.

Part One

GENEALOGIES

Chapter 1

CULTURE AND CIVILIZATION:

FRENCH, GERMAN, AND ENGLISH

INTELLECTUALS, 1930–1958

> *Civilisation* nâit à son heure.
> ([The word] "civilization" was born at the right time)
>
> *Lucien Febvre*

"To reconstruct the history of the French word 'civilisation,'" remarked the historian Lucien Febvre, "it would be necessary to reconstitute the stages in the most profound of all the revolutions through which the French spirit has passed from the second half of the eighteenth century to the present day." This was the topic he chose for his address to a weekend seminar he convened in 1929 on the theme "Civilisation: Le mot et l'idée" (the word and the idea, not, it should be noted, the thing itself). It was very much the issue of the day. As the storm clouds gathered over Europe for the second time in a generation, intellectuals were moved to think again about the meaning of culture and civilization, and their relationship to the destiny of their nations. The German sociologist Norbert Elias was drawn to these questions at the same time, and he remarked that while theories of culture and civilization had been current (with the words themselves) since the second half of the eighteenth century,

[23]

they became matters of general concern only at certain historical moments when "something in the present state of society finds expression in the crystallization of the past embodied in the words."

Febvre (1878–1956) was educated at the École Normale Supérieure, where he specialized in history and geography. During World War I he saw active service with a machine-gun unit, and when peace came he took up an appointment at the University of Strasbourg, reestablished as a French university in 1919 when Alsace was returned to France. The brilliant young faculty members recruited to the university included some of the leading social scientists and historians of the next generation, among them Maurice Halbwachs, Charles Blondel, Georges Lefebvre, and, along with Febvre himself, the historian Marc Bloch, with whom he began a long collaboration that was to transform French historiography. In 1929 they founded the journal *Annales,* which became the forum of a school of historians closely allied to the social sciences. Cultural, psychological, and social themes were to be brought back into a historiography that had been dominated by the study of politics, diplomacy, and war, and intellectual history was revived.

Opening the seminar on "Civilisation," Febvre began by noting that a dissertation had recently been presented at the Sorbonne on the "civilization" of the Tupi-Guarani of South America, whom, he remarked, an earlier generation would have called savages. "But for a long time now the concept of a civilization of non-civilized people has been current." (He added the barbed comment that one might imagine an archaeologist "coolly dealing with the civilization of the Huns, who we were once told were 'the flail of civilization.'") Yet while now ready to grant that the Tupi-Guarani, and even the Huns, had a civilization, the French nevertheless still tended to believe that there was progress in civilization. Apparently the word had come to designate two quite different notions. One of these Febvre characterized as the ethnographic usage; it referred to the set of characteristics that an observer might record in studying the collective life of a human group, an ensemble that embraced material, intellectual, moral, and political aspects of social life. This usage implied no judgment of value. In the second sense, the word connoted our own civilization, which was highly valued, and to which some individuals enjoyed privileged access. How could a language known for being clear and logical have arrived at two contradictory usages for one word?

Febvre had been unable to find a source that used the term *civilisation* in either of its modern senses before 1766. *Civilisation* had previously occurred only as a technical legal term, referring to the conversion of a criminal prosecution into a civil matter. However, the terms *civilité, politesse,* and *police* (meaning law-abiding) go back to the sixteenth century. Throughout the seventeenth century, the terms "savage" and, for more advanced peoples, "barbarian" were current in French for people who lacked the qualities "of civility, courtesy, and, finally, administrative wisdom." In time, *civilisé* displaced the term *policé,* but by the eighteenth century, Febvre suggested, there was a need for a new substantive term, to describe a new notion. Born at its hour, in the 1770s the neologism *civilisation* "won its papers of naturalization," and in 1798 it forced the doors of the Dictionary of the French Academy.

This was a time of great scientific activity in all fields, and daring theoretical syntheses. The enormous range of materials on exotic cultures and the ancient past brought together in the *Encyclopédie* provoked reflections on the great pattern of history. The growing literature on exploration at first tended to reinforce belief in the superiority of civilization. French intellectuals began to conceive the outlines of a universal history in which savagery led to barbarism, and barbarism to civilization. This model of cultural development imitated Lamarck's representation of the relations between the species in his version of the great chain of being. Soon, however, this triumphalist history of progress began to be questioned. Not only levels of civilization but even states of civilization were gradually distinguished. The immense empire of "la Civilisation" was divided into autonomous provinces. It was admitted that distinctive ways of being civilized had been developed in different parts of the world. In 1819, according to Febvre, the plural form, *Civilisations,* was first introduced.

Febvre dated this relativization of the notion of civilization to the half-century from 1780 to 1830, noting that it represented the climax of a long and patient effort of documentation and reasoned inquiry. There was a simultaneous transition in biology, history, ethnography, and linguistics from the universalism of the eighteenth century to a more relativist perspective. Lamarck's theory now also came under fire. Cuvier insisted that there was not one great chain of being but many separate ones. These changes in scientific thinking reflected a more general shift in the intellectual mood. The optimism of the revolutionary period had waned. The survivors of the revolution had learned something new: that a civilization may die. ("And they did not learn this simply from books," he remarked.) Faith in a philosophy of progress and the perfectibility of humanity was eroded. There was renewed sympathy for the pessimism of Rousseau and for his concern with the ills of civilization.

With the restoration of the monarchy, the optimistic belief in a progressive civilization returned, with fresh force. It was presaged most powerfully in Guizot's *De la civilisation en Europe* (1828) and *De la civilisation en France* (1829). Febvre quotes Guizot's bald statement of faith: "The idea of progess, of development, seems to me to be the fundamental idea contained in the word civilization." Progress could be measured both on the level of society and that of the intellect, though these did not necessarily go together. In England, according to Guizot, there had been social progress, but not intellectual; in Germany, spiritual progress had not been matched by social progress; only in France had both advanced hand in hand.

Febvre noted that a different line of thinking had developed in Germany. Initially, the German notion of culture was very similar to the French idea of civilization, but in time a distinction came to be drawn between the external trappings of civilization and the inward, spiritual reality of culture. Alexander von Humbolt, for instance, had suggested that a savage tribe could have a civilization, in the sense of political order, without a high level of "culture de l'esprit"—and, indeed, vice versa. Nevertheless, both traditions of thought posed a similar philosophical problem. Is a relativist appreciation of the differences between cultures compatible with "the old concept of a general human civilization"? The question was left hanging in the air.

In a companion paper, delivered at the same seminar under the title "Les Civilisations: Éléments et formes," the sociologist Marcel Mauss outlined the conception of civilization that he and Emile Durkheim had expounded for many years in the *Année Sociologique*. He passed quickly over what he termed vulgar usages, in phrases such as French civilization, or Buddhist or Islamic civilization. What was at issue in these cases was particular modes of thought, specific casts of mind, for which he preferred to use the word *mentalité*. Nor should civilization be restricted to mean only the arts, or be equated with *Kultur*, in the sense of cultivation. These were folk representations, of no scientific value.

From the point of view of a sociologist, civilization is, first of all, collective and distinctive. But it is not equivalent to what the Durkheimians called the "collective consciousness" of a society, because it is not confined to any particular population. Moreover, in contrast to purely local cultural traditions, civilization is rational and universal, and above all progressive. For that reason, it was spreading irresistibly across the whole world. With the international diffusion of science and of new technologies like the cinema, the phonograph, and the radiotelephone, a new world civilization was coming into being, which "penetrates all forms of music, all accents, all words, all the news, despite all the barriers. We are just at the beginning [of this process]." As civilization advances, it will impose sacrifices. There is no guarantee that it will promote individual happiness or advance the common good. "But the capital of humanity increases in any case . . . all nations and civilisations are in fact tending to become *more—more powerful, more general,* and *more rational.*"

Febvre had begun his essay with the famous comment that time spent in discovering the origin of a word is never wasted. His example inspired later French scholars to extend his inquiry. In 1954 the linguist Emile Benveniste noted that patient research had traced the first use of the term *civilisation* to the physiocrat Mirabeau, in 1757. This use was in the sense of *policé*, of political order, but in the 1760s the term was generally used to mean "the original, collective process that made humanity emerge from barbarity, and this use was even then leading to the definition of *civilisation* as the state of civilized society." He also observed that before the revolution few French words ended in *-isation*.

In an essay published in 1989, Jean Starobinski points out that *civilisation* was just one of many nouns formed in those revolutionary years with the suffix *-ation* from verbs that ended in *-iser*. In 1775 Diderot had defined the new term in relation to another *-ation* coinage: "Emancipation, or what is the same thing by another name, civilization, is a long and difficult work." Regarding Diderot's usage, Starobinski comments that "already there are abundant signs that civilization might well become a secularized substitute for religion, an apotheosis of reason."

The new noun assimilated related notions of polish and refinement, and of intellectual and political progress. But whereas Febvre argued that the word *civilisation* had come into being in order to designate a new idea, albeit one only vaguely perceived at first, Starobinski makes the word the precursor of the idea. "Not surprisingly, as the term gained currency due to its synthetic powers, it, too, became a subject of theoretical reflection." This reflection was stimulated by the fact that the word became current at the same time as the word "progress" in its modern sense: "The two words were destined to maintain a most intimate relationship." Reflecting on these twin neologisms, the *philosophes* concluded that they "describe both the fundamental process of history and the end result of that process . . . The action suffix *-ation* forces us to think of an agent. If that agent is confounded with the action itself, it becomes autonomous."

But the word did not suggest just one idea. "No sooner was the word *civilisation* written down . . . than it was found to contain a possible source of misunderstanding." Mirabeau himself had written of "false civilization" and "the barbarity of our civilizations." The term could refer both to extant modern societies and to the ideal of a civilized condition of social life. "The critique thus took two forms: a critique of civilization and a critique formulated in the name of civilization." In either sense, the term implies a contrary; but the contrary—natural, savage, or barbarous—might appear to be preferable. Civilization may be decadent, and the remedy may be re-Christianization, as Benjamin Constant would argue, or re-barbarization, so that Rimbaud demanded "new blood . . . pagan blood." But normally civilization was valued, and identified with progress. In general usage, the term took on a sacred aura. To represent something as contrary to civilization was to demonize it.

A few years after Febvre's seminar, Norbert Elias, a German Jewish exile writing in London on the eve of the Second World War, compared the evolution of the German notion of *Kultur* and the French idea of *Civilisation.* Elias (1897–1990) was born in Breslau and studied sociology in Heidelberg under Karl Mannheim and Alfred Weber. Alfred's brother, Max Weber, had recently died, but his legacy was very much alive in his old university. In 1929 Mannheim was called to the chair in sociology at Frankfurt, and he invited Elias to accompany him as his academic assistant. Here Elias became associated with the inner circle of the "Frankfurt School," a creative group of Marxist scholars that included Theodor Adorno, with whom Elias established a close bond, though he was always skeptical about Marxist theory.

Elias once noted that the Jews, although outsiders politically, were "at the same time carriers of German cultural life." "I was steeped in German *Kultur*," he remarked, at the end of his long life, but emphasized that "one can identify oneself strongly with the German cultural tradition—as I still do—without thereby being, let's not say a patriot, but a nationalist." However, as a Jew (associated, moreover, with the radical Mannheim), he was obliged to leave Germany after the rise of Hitler. After a spell in France he moved to England and spent the immediate prewar years in the Reading Room of the British Museum, working in isolation on his masterpiece on the civilizing process, which was published in German in 1939. Recognition came very late, and it was only during his prolonged retirement, first in Bielefeld, in Germany, and then in Amsterdam, that he became an iconic figure for a new generation of European sociologists.

Alfred Weber and Karl Mannheim stood for two opposing approaches to the study of culture. For Alfred Weber, culture represented the self-contained world of art and religion, which had no external, rational ends to serve, and which was opposed to the material world of civilization. This was the orthodox view of culture in Heidelberg, and the philosopher Karl Jaspers encouraged the young Elias to write a seminar paper on the debate between Thomas Mann and the despised *Zivilisationsliterat*. For Mannheim, in contrast, cultural productions were rooted in social situations, and they were to be understood as expressions of particular political and economic interests.

In the first volume of *The Civilizing Process*, Elias explored the relationships between the German notion of culture and the French idea of civilization. In the French tradition, civilization was conceived of as a complex, multifaceted whole, encompassing political, economic, religious, technical, moral, or social facts. This broad concept of civilization "expresses the self-consciousness of the West . . . It sums up everything in which Western society of the last two or three centuries believes itself superior to earlier societies or 'more primitive' contemporary ones." To the Germans, however, civilization was conceived of as something external and utilitarian, and in many ways alien to their national values. Civilization moves forward over time and transcends national boundaries, in contrast to *Kultur*, which is bounded in time and space and is coterminous with a national identity.

When Germans expressed pride in their achievements, they spoke not of their civilization but of their *Kultur*. This term "refers essentially to intellectual, artistic, and religious facts," and the Germans typically "draw a sharp dividing line between facts of this sort, on the one side, and political, economic, and social facts, on the other." *Kultur* was not only national but personal. The term had been introduced into modern discourse by Herder, and he had taken the term from Cicero, who wrote metaphorically of *cultura animi,* extending the idea of agricultural cultivation to apply to the mind. *Kultur* therefore implied cultivation, *Bildung,* a personal progression toward spiritual perfection. A French or English person might claim to be "civilized" without having accomplished anything on his own account, but in the German view every individual had to achieve a cultured state by way of a process of education and spiritual development.

The notion of *Kultur* developed in tension with the concept of a universal civilization that was associated with France. What the French understood to be a transnational civilization was regarded in Germany as a source of danger to distinctive local cultures. In Germany itself, the threat was very immediate. *Civilisation* had established itself in the centers of political power, in the French-speaking and Francophile German courts. In marked contrast to French and British intellectuals, who identified with the aspirations of the ruling class, German intellectuals defined themselves in opposition to the princes and aristocrats. In their eyes, the upper class lacked authentic culture. The civilization of the French-speaking elite was borrowed; it was not internalized but was a matter of forms, and of outward show. The moral principles of the aristocracy derived from an artificial code of honor. Excluded from the circles of power, German intellectuals chose to emphasize the claims of personal integrity and of scientific and artistic accomplishment. The individual achievement of spiritual growth was esteemed above inherited status and the artificial trappings of courtly style. The base of the intellectuals was the university, "the middle-class counterweight to the court," and here they fostered a literary and philosophical culture that was German, achieved, inward.

Following Mannheim, Elias identified social reasons behind these ideological differences. The concept of a universal civilization appealed for obvious reasons to the dominant classes in imperial states, like France and Britain, while "the concept of *Kultur* mirrors the self-consciousness of a nation [like Germany] which had constantly to seek out and constitute its boundaries anew, in a political as well as spiritual sense." Bound up as they were with political circumstances, these ideas ebbed and flowed with historical changes. In the aftermath of the French revolution, the antithesis between a false, aristocratic civilization and a genuine national culture was projected into an opposition between France and Germany. This antithesis was renewed with fresh vigor after the defeat of Germany in the Great War, a war that had been waged against them in the name of a universal civilization. The idea of *Kultur* was brought into play in the subsequent struggle to redefine the identity and destiny of Germany. *Kultur* and *Zivilisation* summed up the competing values that (in the view of some Germans) divided Germany and France: spiritual virtue and materialism, honesty and artifice, a genuine morality and mere outward politeness.

But in contrast to Mannheim, Elias did not believe that ideas were merely ideological productions, instruments of domination that were degraded by their uses. Whatever their origins, and however they had been manipulated, concepts such as culture and civilization might have an analytical value. Like Marcel Mauss, Elias therefore put the idea of civilization to work, and the second volume of his study illustrated what he called the civilizing process in European history. The European courts gradually refined their manners, subjecting the body and its functions to a series of cumulative checks. The "social constraint towards self-constraint" grew in force, and the "threshold of embarrassment" was raised. This argument was further developed in *The Court Society*, first published in German in 1969 but also largely written in the thirties. In both these studies, Elias chose to illustrate the classic German view of the civilization process as external, merely customary, imposing formal rules on what had been expressive or instinctual acts, a process he linked to the extension of control by the state.

Elias remarked that at the time he was working on his book he was more influenced by Freud than by any sociologist, even Mannheim. Freud had recently published two books on culture or civilization: *The Future of an Illusion* (first published in German in 1927) and *Civilisation and Its Discontents* (1930). Here Freud spoke of "human civilisation, by which I mean all those respects in which human life has raised itself above its animal status and differs from the life of beasts—and I scorn to distinguish between culture and civilisation." This disavowal perhaps excused his English translator, who systematically used the term *civilisation* where Freud used *Kultur*, but in any case the central opposition that Freud proposed was that between the cultivated human being and the instinctual animal. Culture makes a mere human into a god (if, he joked, a god with a prosthesis). But this power is dearly won. The process of human cultivation is conceived of as purely external, impressed by force. Just as the individual makes the anguished sacrifice of Oedipal fantasies, so "every civilisation must be built on coercion and the renunciation of instinct." Sublimation fosters cultural creativity, but it imposes great sacrifices of sexual freedom and requires the control of aggression.

Perhaps the rise of Fascism impelled central European Jewish intellectuals like Freud and Elias to question the saving power of personal culture. When the crunch came, the frail, external, human controls that civilization had fabricated were powerless to restrain the uncivilized masses, who, Freud wrote, are "lazy and unintelligent; they have no love for instinctual renunciation." The masses will accept the sacrifice of an animal freedom only if they are compensated by improvements in their material circumstances. "If the loss is not compensated for economically, one can be certain that serious dangers will ensue."

In contrast to Elias and Freud, the right-wing, nationalist writers preferred to identify instinct and culture. They reserved their suspicion for civilization. The growth of culture is organic, that of civilization artificial. Culture and civilization will tend to conflict as their forms of growth diverge. Civilization eventually becomes an empty material shell, devoid of animating spirit, and collapses. This theme—an old one—was revived by German conservatives as the optimism of the Hegelians was checked by the catastrophe of the First World War. An extreme exponent was Spengler, who drew a moral diametrically opposed to that of Freud and Elias, excoriating "the bloodless intellect whose criticism gnaws away everything that is left standing of the genuine—that is, the naturally grown—Culture." Like a number of German intellectuals, Spengler welcomed the Nazis as the harbingers of a cultural renewal of the race, and as the enemies of an artificial civilization.

Although Elias emphasized the role of the universities in the development of this discourse on culture and civilization, he did not discuss in any detail the academic disciplines that developed in Germany to study the products of culture and the human spirit, the *Geist* (the *Kulturwissenschaften* and the *Geisteswissenschaften*). Fritz Ringer, in *The Decline of the German Mandarins* (1969), extended Elias's analysis to embrace the development of these fields of study in the critical years that followed the Franco-Prussian war. Germany enjoyed a period of rapid but turbulent economic growth, which accelerated from about 1890. The intellectuals, fearful of materialism and what Weber was to call the rationalization of public life, faced what they saw as a renewed but more powerful challenge to culture from a soulless civilization, and they reacted by drawing upon the resources of philosophical idealism and of romanticism, and by encouraging national pride. Rational, universal civilization threatened the spiritual culture of a *Volk*, and infringed on the inner freedom of the individual. Nations should not allow their unique values to be swallowed up in a common civilization. The world is made up of "contending national spirits . . . qualitatively different cultures."

Scientific materialism was the most insidious agent of civilization, corroding moral values, devaluing spiritual insights, contemptuous of traditional wisdom. The mandarins rejected the notion that ideas are imprinted on the mind by sensations, that values have a material origin. *Geist* was not to be treated as if it were part of nature. The science of the spirit was completely different from a natural science. In the 1880s, Dilthey adapted the Hegelian notion of the "objective Geist." The work of the collective spirit was made manifest and public in documents and forms of language, and so it was available for study, but only by way of a subjective, intuitive approach, leading to an empathetic understanding. The methods of the natural sciences were not appropriate. A furious debate developed between the positivists and Dilthey and his sympathizers, coming to a head in a great methodological controversy, the *Methodenstreit,* which began in 1883 and which eventually led to the development of a new cultural history. It also provoked Max Weber to set out the principles of his cultural sociology in a series of methodological statements that appeared between 1903 and 1919.

Weber defined culture as "the endowment of a finite segment of the meaningless infinity of events in the world with meaning and significance from the standpoint of human beings." Its most characteristic expression was in religious life. Although culture was a matter of ideas, often implicit, that could be grasped only by a sympathetic exercise of the imagination, Weber insisted that "beliefs and values are just as 'real' as material forces" and that they may "transform the nature of social reality." Culture was vulnerable, however. Its foundations were being undermined by civilization, by the irresistible and corrosive forces of science, rationalization, bureaucratization, and materialism. In its defense, culture can muster only the chaotic chances of charismatic renewal and the defensive work of the intellectual.

More recently, Woodruff D. Smith has refined Ringer's genealogy in *Politics and the Sciences of Culture in Germany, 1840–1920* (1991). He extracts a specific line of liberal academic reflection on culture, a *Kulturwissenschaft* that was distinct from the *Geisteswissenschaften* of the hermeneutic tradition. This was a way of thinking with closer affinities to French and British liberal ideas; and Smith suggests that Herder and Humboldt were more sympathetic to the Enlightenment than they appear to be from some other accounts. The academics in the liberal tradition approached culture in a scientific spirit, seeking laws of development. They defined culture, Smith remarks, in an anthropological sense: "That is to say, they were interested primarily in the patterns of thought and behavior characteristic of a whole people rather than the intellectual and artistic activities of the elite." The fortunes of this liberal tradition—and of the more conservative hermeneutic tradition—fluctuated with the fortunes of the liberal and nationalist movements in German politics. The years 1848 and 1870 were watersheds for both traditions of thought, and Smith traces the revival of a somewhat chastened liberal, scientific concern with culture in the ethnological school that was built up by Rudolf Virchow in Berlin in the 1870s and 1880s.

In Britain, as in France and Germany, the European political crisis of the 1930s provoked renewed, anxious debates on the questions of culture and civilization. However, intellectuals drew more directly on a very English tradition of reflections on the place of high culture in the life of a nation; its point of reference was Matthew Arnold's thesis, presented most famously in *Culture and Anarchy* (1869). Culture, they believed, was under threat from two sides: from material civilization, on the one hand, and mass culture on the other.

After the humiliation of Munich, T. S. Eliot found himself stirred not so much by a revulsion against the particular policies of the Chamberlain government as by something more profound, "a doubt of the validity of a civilization." (When Eliot wrote of materialism, or of finance and industry, he used the term "civilization" in preference to "culture.")

> Was our society, which had always been so assured of its superiority and rectitude, so confident of its unexamined premisses, assembled round anything more permanent than a congeries of

banks, insurance companies and industries, and had it any beliefs more essential than a belief in compound interest and the
maintenance of dividends?

Reflecting on these issues in the immediate aftermath of the war,
Eliot was moved to rethink the whole question of culture. By culture,
he told a German audience,

> I mean first of all what the anthropologists mean: the way of life
> of a particular people living together in one place. That culture
> is made visible in their arts, in their social system, in their habits
> and customs; in their religion. But these things added together
> do not constitute the culture . . . a culture is more than the as-
> semblage of its arts, customs, and religious beliefs. These things
> all act upon each other, and fully to understand one you have to
> understand all.

In his *Notes Towards the Definition of Culture* (1948), Eliot contrasted this anthropological idea of culture ("as used for instance by
E. B. Tylor in the title of his book *Primitive Culture*") with the conventional humanist view, which has to do with the intellectual or
spiritual development of an individual, or of a group or class, rather
than with the way of life of a whole society. The traditional literary
notion of culture was inadequate, for "the culture of the individual is
dependent upon the culture of a group or class," and "the culture of
the group or class is dependent upon the culture of the whole society." Each class "possesses a function, that of maintaining that part of
the total culture of the society which pertains to that class." Eliot's
image of society was hierarchical but organic. "What is important is a
structure of society in which there will be, from 'top' to 'bottom,' a
continuous graduation of cultural levels."

In short, culture "includes all the characteristic activities and
interests of a people." It was not confined to a privileged minority, as
Matthew Arnold believed, but embraced both grand and humble,
elite and popular, sacred and profane. By way of illustration, Eliot offered an indicative list of English cultural traits: "Derby Day, Henley

Regatta, Cowes, the twelfth of August, a cup final, the dog races, the pin table, the dart board, Wensleydale cheese, boiled cabbage cut into sections, beetroot in vinegar, nineteenth century Gothic churches, and the music of Elgar." Again in contrast to Arnold, Eliot was not out to denigrate the soulless pleasures of the philistines. Rather, he was illustrating the diverse constituents (for Eliot, a necessary diversity) that make up a national culture.

This national culture was an integrated whole. Arnold, Coleridge, and Newman had—from different points of view—all insisted that a culture is bound up with a religion. "We may go further," Eliot wrote, "and ask whether what we call the culture, and what we call the religion, of a people are not different aspects of the same thing: the culture being, essentially, the incarnation (so to speak) of the religion of a people." (Consequently, he suggested, "bishops are a part of English culture, and horses and dogs are a part of English religion.") Culture and religion may serve the same great purpose: "any religion, while it lasts, and on its own level, gives an apparent meaning to life, provides the framework for a culture, and protects the mass of humanity from boredom and despair." But it is also the function of culture to imbue life with purpose and meaning. "Culture may even be described as that which makes life worth living."

In the aftermath of the world war, Eliot adopted a qualified relativism. It was true that civilization had become more complex, social groups more specialized, the arts more sophisticated, but there had not been any obvious moral progression. Moreover, he insisted that other cultures must be treated on their own terms. "We can also learn to respect every other culture as a whole, however inferior to our own it may appear, or however justly we may disapprove of some features of it: the deliberate destruction of another culture as a whole is an irreparable wrong, almost as evil as to treat human beings like animals." The very diversity of cultures is to be valued. The ideal of a common world culture is therefore a monstrous notion: "a world culture which was simply a *uniform* culture would be no culture at all.

We should have a humanity de-humanised." Rather, "we must aspire to a common world culture which will yet not diminish the particularity of the constituent parts." He also warned that cultural variety would provoke conflict. "Ultimately, antagonistic religions mean antagonistic cultures; and ultimately, religions cannot be reconciled."

———

A decade later, in 1958, Raymond Williams produced a genealogy of English theorists on culture (parallel to the essays of Febvre on the French tradition, and of Elias on the German). Dismissing Eliot's appeal to a specialized, anthropological approach, he placed him squarely within the English tradition of thinking on culture, a tradition that he insisted was quite distinct from the German and French traditions.

Raymond Williams (1921–1988) came from a working-class, socialist milieu on the Welsh border. He went up to Cambridge University to read English, but his studies were interrupted by the outbreak of World War II, in which he saw active service. Briefly a member of the Communist Party before the war, he was nevertheless greatly influenced by the theory of literature and culture that had been developed by a charismatic but profoundly (if quirkily) conservative dissident in the Cambridge English faculty, F. R. Leavis.

Despite very different political sympathies, their approaches had much in common, and E. P. Thompson's description of Williams as "a moralist wearing a literary habit" could be applied just as well to Leavis. In 1948 Leavis had published *The Great Tradition*, in which he defined a canon of texts in modern English literature that offered a "life-enhancing" cultural alternative to the values of modern, mass, industrial society. In *Culture and Society, 1780–1950*, published in 1958, Raymond Williams constructed a parallel tradition of literary intellectuals (including both Leavis and Eliot) who had authored *theories* about the saving role of culture in industrial society—or, more precisely, in modern England.

In an introduction to a new edition of the book in 1983, Williams said that his argument had been based on "the discovery that the idea of culture, and the word itself in its general modern uses, came into English thinking in the period which we commonly describe as that of the Industrial Revolution." The term had entered into English discourse together with other new words: "industry," "democracy," "class," and "art." The notion of culture was shaped by its relationship to these other ideas. In particular, the idea of culture had developed in tension with what Carlyle called "industrialism."

According to Williams, the English discourse on culture was initiated by Romantic poets, particularly Blake, Wordsworth, Shelley, and Keats. While he recognized that many of their themes could be found in Rousseau, Goethe, Schiller, and Chateaubriand, Williams insisted that there was a specific English cast to their thinking, forged by the reaction of the poets to the Industrial Revolution. Their slogan was Shelley's: "Poetry, and the Principle of Self, of which money is the visible incarnation, are the God and Mammon of the world." But Williams argued that this Manichean opposition between art and commerce could not be sustained. "The positive consequence of the idea of art as a superior reality was that it offered an immediate basis for an important criticism of industrialism. The negative consequence was that it tended . . . to isolate art . . . and thus to weaken the dynamic function which Shelley proposed for it."

Coleridge and Carlyle developed a more sophisticated critique of industrial civilization. Civilization meant modernity, materialism, industry, and science: the world of progress celebrated by the utilitarians. It touted positive science as the only reliable basis of knowledge. Carlyle denounced the view that "except the external, there are no true sciences; that to the inward world (if there be any) our only conceivable road is through the outward; that, in short, what cannot be investigated and understood mechanically, cannot be investigated and understood at all." Coleridge proclaimed in thunderous italics *"the permanent distinction and occasional contrast between cultivation and civilisation."*

> But civilisation is itself but a mixed good [Coleridge wrote], if not far more a corrupting influence, the hectic of disease, not the bloom of health, and a nation so distinguished more fitly to be called a varnished than a polished people, where this civilisation is not grounded in cultivation, in the harmonious development of those qualities and faculties that characterise our humanity.

Matthew Arnold provided the most influential statement of the opposition between the values of culture and the values of modern civilization. Industrial civilization was "to a much greater degree than the civilisation of Greece or Rome, mechanical and external, and tends constantly to become more so." The philistines are content with the material progress that civilization delivers. But:

> Culture says: "Consider these people then, their way of life, their habits, their manners, the very tones of their voice; look at them attentively; observe the literature they read, the things which give them pleasure, the words which come out of their mouths, the thoughts which make the furniture of their minds; would any amount of wealth be worth having with the condition that one was to become just like these people by having it?"

Williams noted sorrowfully that Arnold imbued the tradition with a new priggishness and spiritual pride, reacting to vulgarity in a way that was itself vulgar. In his view, Arnold was infected with "largely self-regarding feelings of class." And if he despised the philistine bourgeoisie, Arnold trembled in the face of the common people. Despite his progressive concern with popular education, he stood ready to call on the state for protection against the threatening masses, toward whom "the lovers of culture may prize and employ fire and strength."

Arnold might be dismissed as a reactionary, but Williams believed that in general the great English theorists had failed to grasp the permanent importance of industrialism, and the nature of the civilization it had created. He devoted a long chapter to the two essays by John Stuart Mill on the ideas of culture and civilization in the philosophies of Bentham and Coleridge (essays that had been edited by Leavis). Mill had attempted to find a way of synthesizing the science of practical life, represented by Bentham, with what he called "the philosophy of human culture," whose spokesman was Coleridge. But Mill's synthesis inevitably fell short, because he wrote generally of "Civilisation" when he should have addressed specifically the question of "Industrialism" (by which Williams really intended, capitalism). Because Mill did not grasp the nature of the changes in England, he did not recognize that Coleridge's reaction to industrialism transcended the bounds of Mill's own "humanized Utilitarianism."

Coleridge, according to Williams, had foreshadowed a more radical critique of capitalist society, and Coleridge's insights were developed by Ruskin, Carlyle, and William Morris. Williams identified Morris in particular as "the pivotal figure of the tradition" because he began to articulate a proto-socialist critique of industrialism, suggesting the possibility of a popular cultural revival. Later, D. H. Lawrence was to be a more explicit spokesman for a popular sensibility, a witness to the liberating possibilities in the working-class experience. Eliot, in contrast, represented a conservative position on culture, but he was original and important because he analyzed the place of culture in a class society. ("We can say of Eliot what Mill said of Coleridge, that an 'enlightened Radical or Liberal' ought 'to rejoice over such a Conservative.' ") Williams also praised Eliot for his anti-individualist perspective, even if his ideal of an integrated society could not be reconciled with the reality of the atomized, individualist society that capitalism inevitably produced.

Nevertheless, Williams insisted that Eliot's approach to culture was firmly situated within the English literary tradition. For Eliot, the main components of culture were religion and the arts, as they had been for Coleridge and Arnold, and its enemy, as ever, was modern civilization. Williams played down the significance of Eliot's introduction of the idea of "culture" as "a whole way of life." He admitted that the use of the term in this sense "has been most marked in twentieth-century anthropology and sociology," but insisted that even the anthropological usage was not new.

> The sense depends, in fact, on the literary tradition. The development of social anthropology has tended to inherit and substantiate the ways of looking at a society and a common life which had earlier been wrought out from general experience of industrialism. The emphasis on "a whole way of life" is continuous from Coleridge and Carlyle, but what was a personal assertion of value has become a general intellectual method.

Williams was not familiar with the social sciences, but his wife, who had studied anthropology at the London School of Economics, "got him to read the sociologists on the LSE syllabus of the 1930s" while he was writing *Culture and Society*. However, he was prepared to concede that two lessons may be learned from the anthropologists. The first was that change may be positive, but it cannot be piecemeal: "one element of a complex system can hardly be changed without seriously affecting the whole." The second lesson was that there are other alternatives to industrial civilization besides the medieval world evoked by so many English writers on culture. But this was "perhaps of more doubtful value," since neither primitivism nor medievalism represented a realistic option in our own case.

The true importance of what Eliot had to say lay, for Williams, in his argument that culture varies from class to class in complex societies. An elite culture cannot flourish in isolation, but neither can it be stretched across the classes without adulteration. This suggests a very different issue. Must popular culture contaminate a higher, or more authentic, culture—or could it be a source of renewal? Leavis had addressed the same issue in his book *Mass Civilisation and Minority Culture* (1930). However, Leavis accepted Arnold's view that "it is upon a very small minority that the discerning appreciation of art and literature depends." This small elite

> constitute the consciousness of the race (or a branch of it) at a given time . . . Upon this minority depends our power of profiting by the finest human experiences of the past . . . In their keeping . . . is the language, the changing idiom, upon which fine living depends, and without which distinction of spirit is thwarted and incoherent. By "culture" I mean the use of such a language.

Williams suggested that where Arnold confronted Industrialism, Leavis recognized and challenged another monster, which had emerged from the smoke and grime of the satanic mills: Mass Culture. It was represented for Leavis by the popular press and even the intellectual weeklies, and was epitomized by Middletown, a community in Illinois that had been described by two American ethnographers, Robert and Helen Lynd, in a book boldly subtitled *A Study in Contemporary Culture*. Leavis was frankly appalled at the picture the authors presented of small-town life in the Midwest. Judging by the culture of Middletown, the contemporary world was in a very bad state indeed. "*Middletown* is a frightening book," Williams agreed, but he insisted that the manufactured culture of suburbia must be distinguished from the genuine culture that emanates from the experience of working-class people, an experience that fosters opposition to established standards and prefigures the values on which a better society might be established. Williams was accordingly impatient with Leavis's nostalgic references to a golden age when, he imagined, English culture had rested firmly on the base of an organic communal life. A socialist, he could not join Leavis in mourning the "momentous change—this vast and terrifying disintegration . . . which is commonly described as Progress."

The authors in Williams's canon had developed a distinctive national discourse on culture. In contrast to the German intellectuals, they did not appeal to a specifically national culture (and perhaps this would have been problematic, for what would they have made of Welsh, or Scottish, or Irish culture?). Unlike the French, they were not inclined to celebrate the universal values of a scientific, rational civilization. They wrote instead of a high culture that was at once European and English. Their central problem—the relationship between high culture, popular culture, and material progress in industrial society—was recast by Williams in Marxist terms, as a dimension of a more fundamental class conflict.

In the introduction to a new edition of his book, published in 1983, Williams remarked somewhat defensively that critics had asked why he ignored non-English writers on culture. A biographer notes that he "couldn't read German, and didn't read French for fun," but Williams was in any case convinced that the English discourse on culture had emerged from a very particular historical experience. The industrial revolution had begun in England, and its effects were first appreciated there.

> At the beginning, and indeed for two or three generations, it was literally a problem of finding a language to express them. Thus though it is true that comparable changes happened in other societies, and new forms of thought and art were created to respond to them, often in equally or more penetrating and interesting ways than in these English writers, it is nevertheless of some permanent general importance to see what happened where it happened first.

This is not a persuasive argument, if only because priority does not guarantee superior insight, and by the late nineteenth century the English experience of industrialism was widely shared. In any case, the writers with whom Williams was engaged were often profoundly influenced by Continental debates. Wordsworth was possessed by the language and ideas of the French revolution; Coleridge was steeped in German philosophy (indeed, Mill wrote of the "Germano-Coleridgian school"); Mill was perhaps the most sophisticated commentator on Comte's positivism; Carlyle wrote extensively on Goethe and the German Romantics; Arnold was insistently European, a scourge of English cultural insularity; and Eliot drew on the ideas of the right-wing French Catholic writer Charles Maurras.

Williams's own project must surely be seen as a contribution to the wider European debate in the middle decades of the twentieth century about the origins and meaning of *culture* and *civilization.* His account parallels those of Febvre and Elias; and, as Williams himself later came to recognize, the arguments he made were similar to those that had been developed by the Frankfurt School in Germany, and by Gramsci in Italy. As Europe endured its greatest crisis, a long-standing European discourse on culture had suddenly burst into life again. Throughout Europe, the same themes recurred in the most diverse debates, drawing in radicals and reactionaries—and also both humanists and social scientists.

Chapter 2

THE SOCIAL SCIENCE ACCOUNT:

TALCOTT PARSONS AND THE

AMERICAN ANTHROPOLOGISTS

> We suggest that it is useful to define the concept *culture* for most usages more narrowly than has been generally the case in the American anthropological tradition.
>
> *Alfred Kroeber and Talcott Parsons (1958)*

Febvre, Elias, and Williams constructed genealogies for particular traditions of thinking about culture and civilization, which they identified as French, German, and English, respectively. In 1937, in the United States, Talcott Parsons published a parallel intellectual genealogy, *The Structure of Social Action,* which, however, featured only social scientists. But he was not content to trace the history of an idea. Like John Stuart Mill, Parsons reviewed both the French and the German traditions, which he identified as the positivist and idealist discourses, and like Mill he offered his own synthesis.

Born in 1902, Talcott Parsons was educated at Amherst College (where he majored in biology); at the London School of Economics, to which he was attracted by the socialist thinkers Laski and Tawney, but where he came under the influence of the anthropologist Bronislaw Malinowski; and at Heidelberg (at the same time as Norbert Elias), where social theory was still dominated by the legacy of Max Weber, who had died in 1920. Parsons wrote his dissertation on German theories of capitalism, paying special attention to Marx, Weber, and Sombart. In 1926 he accepted a position at Harvard, to teach economics, and began to consider the interconnections between economic and sociological theories. The initial task he set himself was to review the long debate between the two embattled parties of European theorists of modernity, the positivists and the idealists, heirs respectively to the traditions of the Enlightenment and the Counter-Enlightenment, the French and the German philosophies of history.

The most sophisticated positivists within the social sciences were the utilitarians, and they dominated the field of economics. They were convinced that with the application of scientific methods it would eventually be possible to uncover law-like regularities in human behavior. These would be laws of individual behavior and motivation, for their approach was atomistic and individualistic (a heritage, Parsons suggested, from Protestantism). Finally, they were rationalists, and they believed that most other people were also rationalists, who made rational and efficient choices about important matters.

The idealist tradition was to be understood as a response to these utilitarian assumptions. The idealists denied that there were general laws of human behavior. Every historical period has its own laws, each culture its particular dynamics. Moreover, cultures shape individuals to their ends. "Against mechanism, individualism, atomism, it has placed organicism, the subordination of the unit, including the human individual, to the whole." Finally, where the positivists argued that individual strategies were rational and profitable, the idealist view was that people are driven by ideas that are often irrational, even mystical.

The debates between the positivists and the idealists had much in common with the wider controversies between the proponents of a progressive, rational, material civilization and the defenders of culture, but Parsons insisted that there was one critical difference: the social scientists put their theories to the test. Theories were measured against what Parson robustly termed *the facts*. This dialectical interplay of theory and empirical research, "the reciprocal interaction of new factual insights and knowledge on the one hand with changes in the theoretical system on the other," provided the crucial impetus for scientific progress. Because their ideas were tested against reality, social scientists were not condemned to going round and round in circles, like the philosophers and the literary theorists. And since the social scientists were addressing the same great issues, and given that the same facts were available to everyone, Parsons believed that they would inevitably tend to converge on the same, improved theories.

Each school started out from one true observation about human action. For the utilitarians, "the central fact—a fact beyond all question—is that in certain aspects and to certain degrees, under certain conditions, human action is rational." Parsons agreed that this is indeed a fact, and one that the idealists ignored to their great disadvantage. However, he pointed out, the utilitarians themselves ignored two other equally indisputable facts. One is "the fact that the phenomena are in fact 'organic,' a fact obscured by the 'atomistic' tendencies of utilitarian and positivist social theories." The idealists recognized this, making organicism a central tenet of their theories. They also faced up to another fact, to wit "that men entertain and express philosophical, i.e., nonscientific 'ideas' " and that they "subjectively associate these ideas in the closest way with the motives they assign to their actions." People do not always behave rationally, often pursuing goals that have no utilitarian value. This too was "a fact beyond dispute," but although it might be conceded in principle by the utilitarians, they did not know how to incorporate it into their theories. By and large, they concluded that ultimate preferences are not susceptible to scientific inquiry. The economist simply had to accept the goals that people set themselves to maximize.

But Parsons identified three positivists who were prepared to confront these stubborn "facts": Marshall, Pareto, and Durkheim.

Marshall agreed that the economist had to take account of moral values. For example, he pointed out that a belief in freedom is necessary for the operation of markets. Pareto recognized that choices might be determined by values which were irrational, but which nevertheless provided internally coherent guides to action. He also pointed out that the hidden hand of the market does not necessarily reconcile the means and ends of the individual with those of the society. He gets high marks from Parsons: "Pareto's development, which at first sight has close affinities to positivism, was definitely in the direction of a voluntaristic theory of action."

Like Pareto, Durkheim broke with the traditional rationalist view that the individual should be treated in isolation, as though acting alone, seeking his own satisfactions as best he could. Society has its own interests, and it imposes its goals on the individual by means of ritual and symbolism. Parsons's gloss is that "ends and norms are no longer merely individual but also social." Indeed, Durkheim was driven to recognize the extent to which society, like a parasite, colonizes the individual consciousness and makes its life there, "explicitly stating that society exists only in the minds of individuals."

And so, facing facts, the high priests of positivism were forced to pull the temple down around their own ears. "In this breakdown," Parsons argued, "the sheer empirical evidence played a decisive role along with theoretical and methodological considerations. It is a process in many ways analogous to the recent internal breakdown of the conceptual framework of the classical physics." But once the critique had been accomplished, what was to replace positivism? What, Parsons demanded, "is to be built on the ruins?" The established alternative to positivism was idealism. Durkheim moved in that direction: "In fact Durkheim in escaping the toils of positivism has overshot the mark and gone clean over to idealism." But this was no safe haven. Idealism was also cracking as it banged up against "the sheer empirical evidence," the concrete facts.

Germany was the Fatherland of idealism, and Parsons identified its point of origin in Kantian dualism. Kant's theory required the separation of biological nature and spiritual life, "a hiatus which still persists in the rigidity of the line customarily drawn between the natural sciences and the sciences of culture or of mind (Geist) in Germany." The idealists warned against reductionist and determinist assumptions in the study of the *Geist*. "A corollary of human freedom was the unique individuality of all human events, in so far as they are 'spiritual.' " It followed that there could be no general theory of the life of the mind, and no general laws of history. A person lives in a world of symbols, ideas, and values. These hang together, presenting the actor with "a complex of meanings," an "ideal toward which action is oriented." Expressed in symbols, which refer to each other rather than to some external reality, this complex of meanings can only be intuitively apprehended by the observer.

Coherent it might be, and ideologically attractive, at least to some, but there was a fatal weakness at the very core of idealism. If the positivists could not explain why people choose particular ends, the idealists had no way of accounting for the objective consequences that followed from the means they used to achieve their ends. The most impressive positivist thinkers had been obliged to borrow elements from idealism. They had to recognize that people might subordinate individual interests to collective goals, even if these were irrational from a selfish point of view. In the same way, the greatest of the idealists, Max Weber, had introduced an element of positivism into his analysis of the role of unintended but ineluctable consequences in the making of history.

Parsons devoted fully a quarter of a lengthy book to tracing the evolution of Weber's thought. As he saw it, Weber's project was to develop an anti-Marxist theory of capitalism. His particular concern was the genesis of capitalism and its partner, bureaucracy. Weber believed that a rational, material account of capitalism was inadequate because it neglected "the spirit of capitalism," the values which inform it, and which, indeed, precede it, and account for its emergence. The capitalist system was the most rational and technically efficient economic system in history, but it had first taken hold in northern

Europe only because strategically situated populations were pre-adapted to it by virtue of their Protestant religion, and in particular by Calvinism. Not that the Calvinists aspired to become capitalists; their moral principles—frugality, the spirit of vocation, and respect for law—were designed to achieve religious goals. However, their religion disposed the Puritans to save, and to work hard, and to take individual responsibility, and so, incidentally, it prepared them to become successful capitalists. The means they had chosen in pursuit of salvation brought them unsought success as entrepreneurs in this world. Other religions, which did not foster similar values, actually hindered the development of capitalism and bureaucracy.

Although they began from very different starting points, Parsons nevertheless identified "a remarkable point-for-point convergence between Weber and Durkheim." Transcending the limitations of positivism and idealism, both men ended up at the very threshold of the true, voluntarist theory of action. Unfortunately, Durkheim died before he could enter the promised land. Weber hesitated at the frontier, but, Parsons observed, he could not free himself from the German prejudice that science could not explain the work of the spirit. It was therefore left to Parsons to propose a higher synthesis of idealism and positivism. He called it, this theory in the making, the voluntaristic theory of action, or, later, the general theory of action, and claimed that its emergence represented the greatest intellectual revolution in the social sciences since the sixteenth century.

Parsons set out the central features of this new theory of action in *The Social System,* published in 1951. "It is convenient in action terms to classify the object world as composed of the three classes of 'social,' 'physical,' and 'cultural' objects." Each class of "objects" forms a system: the social system, the individual biological and personality system, and the cultural system. These three systems interact to govern the choices every actor is called upon to make, but they cannot be reduced to each other. The individual is at once a biological organism endowed with a particular personality; a citizen and a member of society; and a bit of a philosopher, whose head is full of ideas, values, and theories. As Pareto, Durkheim, and Weber had appreciated, several disciplines would have to collaborate in order to understand how these different systems combine to influence purposeful actions.

In 1946, Parsons established an interdisciplinary Department of Social Relations at Harvard, which brought sociologists, psychologists, and anthropologists together under his leadership. What he had in mind was a shake-up of the social sciences, the establishment of a rational division of labor and a more ordered and efficient academic bureaucracy. Psychology would deal with the individual, with human nature and its quirks. Sociology would take for its subject social systems. There remained what Parsons now called the cultural system. This concept did not play a central role in *The Structure of Social Action* but emerged fully-fledged in 1951 in *The Social System.* "Culture" now became an umbrella term for the realm of ideas and values. Its medium was the currency of symbols: "Cultural objects are symbolic elements of the cultural tradition, ideas or beliefs, expressive symbols or value patterns." Culture enters into action, but it also has a life of its own. "A cultural system does not 'function' except as part of a concrete action system, it just 'is.' "

But who could be charged with its scientific study? The cultural system had hitherto been left by and large to the humanists, with unsatisfactory results, but there was one marginal social science that might be able to make something more of it. A science of culture, Parsons suggested, might be "what, according to the present trend, anthropological theory is tending to become." It would be highly specialized, focusing on "the culture pattern system as such, and neither on the social system in which it is involved, nor on the personalities as systems."

What this meant in practice was that the social sciences would be rearranged on functional grounds, and anthropology would be charged with its own specialized task, the study of culture. No doubt anthropology would have to dump a lot of accumulated baggage, but this was the only hope for the salvation of the discipline. Parsons conceded that it had not yet achieved anything like the necessary level of precision. "In anthropological theory there is not what could be called close agreement on the definition of the concept of culture," he observed, in an uncharacteristic foray into irony. But in the future the anthropologists would have to acccpt a precise and strictly limited conception of culture, defined by its position in a trinity of forces that shaped action—personality, social relations, and ideas and values. "Only by some such definition of its scope can anthropology become an analytical empirical science which is independent both of sociology and of psychology."

Parsons's challenge came as a major jolt to the still small profession of American anthropology. (In 1947, there were only 408 members of the American Anthropological Association.) In the year after the publication of *The Social System*, the two most powerful figures in the field, Alfred Kroeber at Berkeley and Clyde Kluckhohn at Harvard, were provoked to publish a massive review of anthropological theories under the title *Culture: A Critical Review of Concepts and Definitions*. This was their response to Parsons on behalf of anthropology. It was by no means a cry of outrage, however. Kluckhohn, the leading anthropologist at Harvard, had been a close associate of Parsons since the 1930s. Parsons named him as one of the small set of scholars who read and commented on the manuscript of *The Structure of Social Action*. Kluckhohn was also associated from the first with Parsons's ambitious plan to establish an interdisciplinary social science department at Harvard, which would be the institutional basis for the achievement of his general theory of action, exemplifying the collaborative division of labor that the new social science required. Together with three other colleagues, Parsons and Kluckhohn had organized a "shop club" at Harvard, with the unlikely name of the "Levellers." "Meeting in each other's homes," Parsons recalled, "we discussed a whole range of problems which eventually became constitutive of the Department of Social Relations organizational experiment." Parsons and Kluckhohn had prepared the ground together, teaching an interdisciplinary course which led directly to the drafting of a charter, "Toward a Common Language for the Area of Social Science." ("Why not English?" Clifford Geertz recalls "some unreconstructed wit" inquiring.)

But while Kluckhohn was a partner from the first in this enterprise, he was not uncritical of it. Kluckhohn was in fact the sole dissident voice when the Parsons team (now further expanded, and including Edward Shils as a key figure) drafted the "General Statement" that introduced the manifesto of the Parsonians, *Toward a General Theory of Action* (1951). Specifically, Kluckhohn objected that social structure should be treated, in part at least, as an element of culture: "social structure is part of the cultural map, the social system is built upon girders supplied by explicit and implicit culture." According to Parsons, Kluckhohn was too much of a humanist to accept that social structure could be separated from culture as "an authentically independent level in the organization of the components of action."

Kroeber and Kluckhohn objected more generally that Parsons wrote of culture "in a sense far more restricted than the anthropological usage" (although they noted that more recently he "has moved in the anthropological direction"). They seemed, however, to find it difficult to identify their precise reasons for dissent, until, at last, they came clean and admitted that Parsons's definition would require anthropology to redefine itself, and in the process to abandon parts of its empire.

> Our incomplete satisfaction with Parsons probably arises from the fact that his scheme is centered so completely upon "action." This leaves little place for certain traditional topics of anthropological enquiry: archaeology, historical anthropology in general, diffusion, certain aspects of culture change, and the like . . . In particular, we are resistant to his absorbing into "social systems" abstracted elements which we think are better viewed as part of the totality of culture.

In the end, however, they found their own way to a conclusion very similar to that of Parsons.

––––––––––

Kroeber and Kluckhohn's *Culture* was the most thoroughgoing attempt to specify precisely what the anthropological conception of culture amounted to. They tabulated and classified 164 definitions of culture ("and its near-synonym civilization"). They then grouped these ideas into two broad categories: the elitist, ethnocentric, and outmoded notions of the humanists, of which they did not approve (and which Parsons had not bothered with at all), and the precise conception on which the scientists were systematically converging, and which they backed to sweep the board. In effect, their narrative traced the refinement of a modern, scientific idea of culture, an idea, they affirmed, with explanatory power, out of the woolly usages of the humanists.

Like their humanist counterparts, Kroeber and Kluckhohn constructed a genealogy for the anthropological idea of culture that they had in mind. It had first been defined by E. B. Tylor, in the opening sentence of his *Primitive Culture*, in 1871. "Culture, or Civilization," Tylor had written, "taken in its wide ethnographic sense, is that complex whole which includes knowledge, belief, art, morals, law, custom, and any other capabilities and habits acquired by man as a member of society." Culture is a whole; it is learned; and it includes practically everything you could think of, aside from biology.

But oddly enough, it had taken many years before people realized that Tylor had initiated an intellectual revolution. Kroeber and Kluckhohn noted that after Tylor there was a long pause in the development of the anthropological idea of culture. After 1871, no new definitions of culture appeared for thirty-two years. Only six could be traced to the period between 1900 and 1918, the founding years of modern American anthropology. They blamed the founding father, Franz Boas himself, for this intellectual stagnation. Not until he was seventy-two years old had he produced his first formal definition of culture. However, Boas merely slowed down the progress of science. Between 1920 and 1950 no fewer than 157 definitions of culture were created by American social scientists, most of them by anthropologists, and in this period Tylor's idea of culture had been taken up, refined, and developed.

The problem with Tylor's definition was that it threw together too many disparate elements which did not cohere. Tylor had stated that a culture formed a whole, but his idea of a whole was a list of traits, with the consequence that a culture might be inventoried but never analyzed. Kroeber and Kluckhohn believed that culture had to be treated as an integrated and structured whole, made up of connected parts. Tylor included too many elements in culture, however, and in particular he did not distinguish between culture and social organization. It was preferable to narrow down the definition, to distinguish culture from society, and to define culture as a matter of ideas, rather than of acts or institutions.

The system of ideas that constituted a culture could be observed indirectly in "their expressions, embodiments, or results." According to Kroeber and Kluckhohn, one of the most recent discoveries in the field was that cultural ideas are expressed and communicated in symbols. This realization had become central to the modern conception of culture:

> Certainly there is as of 1951 a wide recognition among philosophers, linguists, anthropologists, psychologists and sociologists that the existence of culture rests indispensably upon the development in early man of the faculty for symbolizing, generalizing, and imaginative substitution. Another decade ought therefore to see a heavier accentuation of this factor in our thinking about culture.

Finally, "those properties of culture which seem most distinctive of it and most important" are its values. "In fact values provide the only basis for the fully intelligible comprehension of culture, because the actual organization of all cultures is primarily in terms of their values." These values are "variable and relative, not predetermined and eternal." To appreciate the values of others one therefore needs to take a relativist perspective, to recognize "that every society through its culture seeks and in some measure finds values." It is this relativism that above all distinguishes the anthropological approach to culture from older approaches.

While claiming that they had no wish to add a 165th formal definition of culture to the 164 they had examined, Kroeber and Kluckhohn did finally sum up the way in which "this central idea is now formulated by most social scientists": "Culture consists of patterns, explicit and implicit, of and for behavior acquired and transmitted by symbols." And "the essential core of culture consists of traditional . . . ideas and especially their attached values."

Like the genealogies of Febvre, Elias, and Williams, Kroeber and Kluckhohn's is essentially a national one, in this case American. After the turn of the century, it also became an exclusively social science genealogy. There had been a decisive break: the social science tradition had shaken off its (European) philosophical origins and emerged as a distinctive (American) scientific discourse on culture. Kroeber and Kluckhohn regretfully remarked that many humanists still clung to their vaguer notions. Some sociologists—even American sociologists—were also still inclined to rework the old German, humanist contrast between culture and civilization, but most right-thinking American social scientists had fallen into line with the anthropological usage, which offered the correct way forward.

Foreign social scientists, however, had been slow to grasp the importance of the new idea. Even British social anthropologists like Radcliffe-Brown and Evans-Pritchard were dismissive of the notion of culture, perhaps for nationalist reasons. "The resistance appears to be stylistic, a matter of idiom, of distaste for a word usage first established in another language. Americans scrupled much less to borrow from the Germans." In France, social scientists were "even more resistive . . . Civilization, with its implications of advancement and urbanization, is still the preferred French noun for culture." Perhaps this intellectual conservatism contributed to "a certain backwardness in spots of contemporary French theoretical thinking in the social and cultural field."

In the account of Kroeber and Kluckhohn, the scientific conception of culture emerges in opposition to humanist conceptions. Tylor formulated his definition of culture as a deliberate contrast to the elitist definition that Matthew Arnold had proposed two years earlier, in *Culture and Anarchy*. Yet Tylor's conception had nothing like the same impact as Arnold's, at least for many years. "A generation or two later," Kroeber and Kluckhohn lamented, "a hundred speakers of English would still have accepted Arnold's definition to one that even knew of Tylor's directly or at second-hand." While Arnold's definition quickly entered the OED, that of Tylor was cited for the first time in the 1933 Supplement.

This myth of origin has been challenged by a historian of anthropology, George Stocking. He argued that Tylor's "idea of culture was perhaps closer to that of his humanist near-contemporary Matthew Arnold than it was to the modern anthropological meaning. And insofar as their usages differed, it can be argued that in certain ways Arnold was closer than Tylor to the modern anthropological meaning." After all, Matthew Arnold was more inclined than Tylor to take a relativist view of culture, since he distinguished culture from mechanical civilization, and argued that while Britain might lead the way in industry its culture might nevertheless be flawed, falling below the level achieved by other cultures at other times. Nevertheless, Arnold remained faithful to the European ideal, and as Stocking remarks, he would have considered the term "primitive culture" to be an oxymoron. For his part, in contrast to Arnold, Tylor subscribed to the Enlightenment faith in progress. His anthropological thought "was part of the nineteenth-century positivist incarnation of the progressionist tradition." Both Arnold and Tylor "had contacts with German thought. But the taproot of Tylor's thinking is in the tradition of the French Enlightenment and British empiricism."

In Stocking's judgment, neither Tylor nor Arnold had anticipated modern, anthropological thinking about culture. "Prior to about 1900, 'culture' both in the German and in the Anglo-American tradition still had not acquired its characteristic modern anthropological connotations." The person who was responsible for introducing the "modern anthropological connotations" of the word culture was Franz Boas. Stocking shied away from making the explicit claim that Boas "invented" it, but "far from hindering the development of the anthropological concept," as Kroeber and Kluckhohn had suggested, "Boas played a crucial role in its emergence." It was true that Boas did not go in for theoretical dissertations on the nature of culture, but implicit in many of his writings are "a number of central elements in the modern anthropological culture concept—historicity, plurality, behavioral determinism, integration, and relativism." These elements, Stocking concludes, "can be thus seen emerging from older evolutionist or humanist usages in the work of Franz Boas."

Stocking identified the crucial marker of the modern, anthropological idea as the use of the term culture in the plural. Instead of Culture, anthropologists, following Boas, began to write about cultures. Stocking has since conceded that this plural usage can be found in Herder and in Humboldt, and that it was commonplace in the long tradition of German ethnology, but it is by no means evident that Boas was responsible even for introducing this plural usage into the discourse of modern American anthropology. Kroeber and Kluckhohn, who were intimately familiar with the Boasian tradition, and who harbored no grudge against Boas, suggested that it was Ralph Linton in 1936 and Margaret Mead in 1937 who first distinguished between "culture" and "a culture." This claim is itself somewhat mysterious, since Ruth Benedict had published work in the early 1930s that dealt explicitly with different native American "cultures." In any case, they also pointed out that even when Boas did write about "a culture" rather than "culture," he wavered between describing it as an accidental accretion of traits and as "an integrated spiritual totality," animated by the "genius" of "a people." Boas's acolyte Robert Lowie took a similar view. As far as Boas was concerned, "a cultural phenomenon is intelligible only from its past; and because of the complexity of that past, chronological generalizations, like those of physics, are as impracticable as are timeless generalizations." Cultural changes were the result of chance contacts, or they were generated by the creative response of individuals to inherited tradition, under the stimulus of environmental challenge. It followed that cultures did not constitute integrated systems.

It is surely significant that although Lowie, Kroeber, and Kluckhohn were steeped in the thinking of Boas, they did not attribute the new anthropological conception of culture to him. Had they done so, however, they would have been obliged to trace the origins of his ideas back to the conceptions of the Berlin school of ethnology, in which Boas's thinking was formed. "Most English and American historians of anthropology tend to avoid dealing in depth with the influence of German thought on ethnology," Woodruff Smith has observed, and they have in consequence neglected the extent to which Boas was a product of the liberal Berlin school. But Boas, who had entered the Berlin circle in 1882, worked closely with Virchow and Bastian—under whom he wrote his *habilitation* thesis—until he emigrated to the United States in 1886. The anti-racist arguments he propounded at Columbia were taken directly from Virchow. So too was his central hypothesis—characteristically, a negative one—that race did not determine culture. His ethnological project was based on Adolf Bastian's conception of the "culture area." Woodruff Smith even suggests that it was through Boas that the Berlin school survived, for in Germany it was overwhelmed by an intellectual mood that was nationalist, imperialist, and racialist in its sympathies.

In later years, Boas did occasionally suggest that cultures should be studied as working systems, as organic wholes, and that a synchronic, functionalist approach might even represent an alternative to historical understanding. However, he did not emphasize this option until 1930, and the most plausible supposition is that he was provoked into a very late and uncharacteristic shift by the brilliant young students who came to him in the 1920s, Edward Sapir, Ruth Benedict, and Margaret Mead, a close circle of friends (and lovers) for whom Sapir was the intellectual mentor.

When did a new, anthropological idea of culture break with the established discourses? Kroeber and Kluckhohn concluded that the epistemological rupture occurred in 1871, with Tylor's definition of culture. However, as Stocking pointed out, Tylor restated the established positivist, progressive idea of civilization, even if he translated it into an evolutionist idiom and called it culture. According to Stocking, the breakthrough only happened in 1911, when, he argues, Boas's thought took a new, relativist turn. As we have seen, however, Boas was a consistent exponent of the liberal Berlin ideas of the 1880s, and the Berlin school revived a German tradition that goes back to the writings of Waitz and Klemm in the middle of the nineteenth century. Moreover, it was not until 1930 that Boas expressly put forward something like a modern, anthropological conception of culture, as an integrated system of symbols, ideas, and values. It is apparent that none of these moments marks the introduction of a distinctive idea of culture that broke with competing ideas to become the organizing concept of a new science.

Kroeber and Kluckhohn noted a sudden explosion of social science reflections on culture in the 1920s and 1930s, when notions of culture "were gradually acquiring their present-day, technical social-science meaning." Perhaps it was then that a radical change in anthropological thinking occurred. If so, the obvious place to look for signs of revolution is in the work of Boas's students.

In 1917, Robert Lowie delivered a series of popular lectures under the title *Culture and Ethnology*. His argument was that culture is "a thing *sui generis* which can be explained only in terms of itself."

It is not determined by race, or by environment. Culture is what Tylor had said it was, the non-biological heritage of the species. If one looked at the whole sweep of human cultural development, there had been a secular advance.

> We may liken the progress of mankind to that of a man a hundred years old, who dawdles through kindergarten for eighty-five years of his life, takes ten years to go through the primary grades, then rushes with lightning rapidity through grammar school, high school and college. Culture, it seems, is a matter of exceedingly slow growth until a certain "threshold" is passed, when it darts forward, gathering momentum at an unexpected rate.

Ethnology should be able eventually to reveal the nature and sources of this progress, and Tylor had therefore rightly described anthropology as "essentially a reformer's science."

By 1920, Lowie showed more interest in the differences between local cultural traditions, but he explicitly rejected the idea that a culture was an integrated whole:

> Cultures develop mainly through the borrowings due to chance contact. Our own civilization is even more largely than the rest a complex of borrowed traits . . . To that planless hodgepodge, that thing of shreds and patches called civilization, its historian can no longer yield superstitious reverence.

In 1922 Alexander Goldenweiser, another Boasian, published a book entitled *Early Civilization: An Introduction to Anthropology.* Goldenweiser's target was racist ideas, and he laid out the familiar Boasian objections to a racial view of history. The variations between races are insignificant. Civilizations cut across racial boundaries, and elements of our own civilization are not always self-evidently an improvement on the practices of "primitive" civilizations. Civilizations become differentiated as a result of local historical accidents, but all civilizations have common aspects, which derive from the common psychic endowment of human beings, and from the diffusion of better practices.

Although Goldenweiser offered accounts of specimen cultures that stressed a thematic unity, in a way that reminds the modern reader of Ruth Benedict's procedure in *Patterns of Culture,* for him, as for Lowie, a culture was a motley collection of customs, techniques, and beliefs that were passed on from generation to generation, or borrowed from others. Even Kroeber, who developed a rather vague idea of cultural patterning, which his colleagues thought somewhat mystical, insisted that a culture was to be treated historically rather than as a functioning whole.

When it came, the break in the Boasian tradition was the work of a second generation of students, largely American-born, under the inspired leadership of Edward Sapir. In his seminal essay, "Culture, Genuine and Spurious," published in 1924, Sapir announced that the classical anthropological perspective on culture would have to go— that we should jettison what he termed the technical, ethnological idea of culture, Tylor's idea, and, for the most part, Boas's idea as well. For "the ethnologist and the culture-historian," culture embodies "any socially inherited element in the life of man, material and spiritual." Ultimately, culture is coterminous with humanity, for even "the lowliest savages" have culture. Periclean drama, the electric dynamo, and the techniques and beliefs of hunter-gatherers "are all, equally and indifferently, elements of culture." Sapir concluded, however, that it might be better to speak of "civilization" in this sense rather than "culture." In any case, "I do not intend to use the term 'culture' in this technical sense."

In a second sense, culture connotes "a rather conventional ideal of individual refinement." This, of course, was culture according to Matthew Arnold. Sapir observed that its exponents often exhibit a certain aloofness from ordinary life and a fixation on the past, and that their approach to culture may easily become a matter of style rather than substance, congealing into an amused skepticism or, worse, degenerating into snobbishness. Nevertheless, there was something in this idea, to which anthropologists would do well to pay attention.

There remained the third sense of culture, which "is the least easy to define and to illustrate satisfactorily, perhaps because those who use it are so seldom able to give us a perfectly clear idea of just what they themselves mean by culture." In this sense, culture combines elements of the other usages. As in the technical, ethnological usage, culture is conceived of as the heritage of a group, but it refers particularly to the elements traditionally emphasized by the humanists, "the spiritual possessions of a group," some of which are "intrinsically more valuable, more characteristic, more significant in a spiritual sense than the rest." And as the great humanists had insisted, it is these spiritual elements that give meaning to the life of the individual.

Conceived in this way, it is culture that gives "a particular people its distinctive place in the world." "Culture, then, may be briefly defined as civilization in so far as it embodies the national genius." Sapir remarked that this was very much the popular view of what culture is about, and he conceded that this association of a culture with a nation could give rise to chauvinism or racism. Nevertheless, it embodied an insight that the ethnologist and social psychologist have missed: "It remains true that large groups of people everywhere tend to think and act in accordance with all but instinctive forms, which are in large measure peculiar to it."

Sapir also distinguished between what he called genuine and spurious culture. A genuine culture is richly varied but unified and consistent: "nothing is spiritually meaningless." No mere "spiritual hybrid of contradictory patches," a genuine culture is harmonious, like the culture of Periclean Athens or Elizabethan England. Genuine culture has nothing to do with technical progress. It is an illusion that scientific progress will help us attain "to a profounder harmony of life, to a deeper and more satisfying culture." Ethnologists have recognized "the frequent vitality of cultures" even where technology is rudimentary. Moreover, art, religion, and economic life are inter-twined in primitive societies. In industrial societies the ends of life have been split apart, and the functions separated, so that "our spiritual selves go hungry, for the most part, pretty much all of the time." The cultured individual can link "self with master soul" only where the personality is joined "with that of the great minds and hearts that society has recognized as its significant creators." The genuine culture of an individual "must needs grow organically out of the rich soil of a communal culture."

It was culture in this sense that must become the subject of anthropology, but anthropologists had neglected it, though they were perhaps uneasily aware that "underlying the elements of civilization, the study of which is the province of the ethnologist and culture-historian, is a culture, the adequate interpretation of which is beset with difficulties and which is often left to the men of letters." Sapir was, in short, making the shocking proposal that the ethnologists should abandon the study of what he termed civilization, their traditional subject matter, to which Boas remained loyal, and adopt in its place a classical humanistic idea of culture, as a national *Geist*.

Ruth Benedict worked closely with Boas, but she was also strongly influenced by Sapir. Less than a decade later, in *Patterns of Culture,* her ruling image for a culture was to be an artistic style. She cited few anthropologists but appealed to a line of German thinkers from Dilthey to Spengler. She acknowledged Spengler's notion of Apollonian and Faustian cultures in Europe as the immediate source of her contrast between the cultural styles of the Pueblos of New Mexico and the native peoples of the Northwest coast, though she (and, of course, Spengler) were equally in thrall to Nietzsche's characterization of Apollonian and Dionysian types of culture, developed in his *Birth of Tragedy,* which she had read with great excitement as a student.

For Benedict, the integration of a culture was comparable to the crystallization of a personality. Cultures had their own collective personalities—the Dobuans, for example, were paranoid, the Kwakiutl megalomaniac—and they impressed a modal personality type on the individuals who were raised in that culture.

The life-history of the individual is first and foremost an accommodation to the patterns and standards traditionally handed down in his community. From the moment of his birth the customs into which he is born shape his experience and behavior. By the time he can talk, he is the little creature of his culture, and by the time he is grown and able to take part in its activities, its habits are his habits, its beliefs his beliefs, its impossibilities his impossibilities.

Sapir was skeptical about the suggestion that cultures had collective personalities. Criticizing Benedict's account of Dobu, he told his students: "A culture cannot be paranoid." He was also committed to the view that individuals could, and should, exercise creative independence, and so he was reluctant to accept any form of cultural determinism. Although individuals adapted to a culture, this did not need to involve fundamental modifications of personality. "I suspect that individual Dobu and Kwakiutl are very like ourselves; they just are manipulating a different set of patterns . . . You have to know the individual before you know what the baggage of his culture means to him."

Sapir and Ruth Benedict were Boas's most creative young associates in the 1920s, and he moved in their direction, or at least gave his blessing to the enterprise on which they had embarked. Margaret Mead, who became the most successful popularizer of "culture and personality" studies, noted that at this time Boas

> felt that sufficient work had gone into demonstrating that peoples borrowed from one another, that no society evolved in isolation, but was continually influenced in its development by other peoples, other cultures, and other, differing, levels of technology. He decided that the time had come to tackle the set of problems that linked the development of individuals to what was distinctive in the culture in which they were reared.

This is a loyalist view, which skates over the radical break initiated by Sapir and Benedict. Robert Lowie, the orthodox old-school Boasian, had no doubt that this was heresy. Sapir's essay, he wrote, had "nothing to do with anthropology, for Sapir explicity sets aside 'the technical meaning of culture,' thus dealing with something beyond the sphere of science altogether." Boas himself, by now a man in his seventies, made some concessions to the energetic, ambitious, and creative elements in his entourage, but in the textbook that he edited in 1938, *General Anthropology,* he reaffirmed his historicist view of culture as a loose and accidental assemblage of traits.

Although Kroeber and Kluckhohn were reluctant to admit the fact, it was Parsons who created the need for a modern, social scientific conception of culture, and who persuaded the leading anthropologists in the United States that their discipline could flourish only if they took on culture in his sense as their particular specialty. It was his challenge that obliged the anthropologists to reexamine their ideas about culture, and to focus them more sharply.

Kroeber and Kluckhohn dug into their own history for ancestral formulations that could be fitted more or less to the new conception, and, of course, they found some, for Parsons drew on the German romantic tradition that influenced many anthropologists, including Sapir. In the German tradition, culture was treated as a system of ideas and values, expressed in symbols and embodied in religion and art. The individual found a purpose in life, and a sense of identity, through absorbing the culture's values and making them his own. What Parsons did was to take this venerable idea and situate it within a general theory of social action. He then invited the anthropologists to study it, as their contribution to an interdisciplinary exercise.

At the same time, the anthropologists were encouraged to ignore biology, personality, social institutions, and historical questions, since these were now the subject matter of other disciplines. Kroeber and Kluckhohn protested that Parsons wanted to exclude some of the traditional interests of anthropology, notably diffusion and history. Some of the anthropologists, including Kluckhohn, were particularly reluctant to abjure the study of social structure. But this was the price that had to be paid if anthropologists were to be granted the freedom of their own domain in the brave new world of interdisciplinary social science, with its master theory, Parsons's general theory of action.

In 1957–58, Parsons spent a year at the Center for Advanced Study in the Behavioral Sciences in Stanford, California. Kroeber was nearby, at Berkeley, and the two men had a series of discussions, in the course of which they drafted a manifesto. It was published in the *American Sociological Review* in 1958, under the title "The Concepts of Culture and of Social System." The sociologist Howard Becker has compared their compact to "a jurisdictional agreement (like those by which the building trades decide how much of the work carpenters can do and where electricians must take over)." However, the image of a diplomatic accord between formerly rival powers is hard to resist. "It was a great satisfaction to me," Parsons recalled, "when Professor Kroeber, who was surely the dean of American anthropologists at that time, proposed that he and I should make a joint statement, the main purport of which would be to emphasize the distinction between cultural and social systems as concepts and to attempt to clarify their respective natures and relations to each other."

Although Parsons diplomatically allowed Kroeber to be the first author, it was the conception of Parsons that triumphed.

> We suggest that it is useful to define the concept *culture* for most usages more narrowly than has been generally the case in the American anthropological tradition, restricting its reference to transmitted and created content and patterns of values, ideas, and other symbolic-meaningful systems as factors in the shaping of human behavior and the artifacts produced through behavior. On the other hand, we suggest that the term *society*—or more generally, *social system*—be used to designate the specifically relational system of interaction among individuals and collectivities.

The two men themselves employed the language of diplomacy. Two great powers had reached an accord, even a new offensive alliance.

> We therefore propose a truce to quarreling over whether culture is best understood from the perspective of society or society from that of culture . . . The traditional perspectives of anthropology and sociology should merge into a temporary condominium leading to a differentiated but ultimately collaborative attack on problems in intermediate areas with which both are concerned.

Reflecting on this truce, in 1973, Parsons noted that it marked a new departure:

> I think it perhaps can be said that the position which Kroeber and I took was far from being generally accepted at the time on either side of the disciplinary line. I think, however, that it [*sic*] has made substantial progress in this direction in the intervening years. On the anthropological side, for example, I cite the extremely interesting, though far from identical developments, in the recent work of such authors as Clifford Geertz and David Schneider, both of whom, of course, were trained in the Harvard Department of Social Relations.

As he noted, Parsonian projects had been launched by Harvard anthropologists, often working as members of interdisciplinary teams. Kluckhohn developed a research project that was intended to demonstrate the way in which values shape lives; he directed the "Comparative Study of Values in Five Cultures," which was set in western New Mexico and ran from 1949 to 1955. Clifford Geertz's early research in Indonesia was organized as an aspect of a broader collaborative effort, as was David Schneider's fieldwork in Yap. However, Geertz and Schneider, whom Parsons had specifically named as the representative figures of the new, Parsonian generation of American anthropology, began in time to distance themselves from Cambridge HQ, and to question the Parsonian view that the study of culture was only part of a greater task, that anthropologists were mere handmaidens of a general theory of action. As time went on, the two became intent on studying culture as an autonomous system, to be investigated for its own sake.

The two young Parsonians also refined the already restricted range of phenomena that should be treated as cultural. Parsons himself introduced further distinctions, between expressive culture, cognitive culture, and values and norms. Clifford Geertz published elegant elaborations on the Parsons formula, but David Schneider eventually went further: he came to argue that culture should exclude norms. Culture was "a system of symbols and meanings." Norms were a different sort of thing altogether. Culture "contrasts with norms in that norms are oriented to patterns *for action,* whereas culture constitutes a body of definitions, premises, postulates, presumptions, propositions and perceptions about the nature of the universe and man's place in it." And so in the hands of these younger anthropologists the Parsonian distinctions became ever finer, and the notion of culture became ever more specialized, but it was also increasingly cocooned from action.

What methods were appropriate for the study of culture if it was conceived of as a symbolic world of ideas and values? Parsons himself had suggested that appropriate procedures were intuitive interpretation, the *Verstehen* of Dilthey and Weber, or, he later thought, perhaps the interpretive methods of psychoanalysis. Linguistics offered other, seductive models. The essential point, in any case, was that symbols should be treated as a self-contained system, and not as a set of labels for an external reality. The "connection between a particular symbol and its meaning is in the causal sense always arbitrary," Parsons wrote. "The only intrinsic element common to symbols and their meanings is that of order. And this can never be grasped by the isolated study of particular symbols, but only in terms of their mutual relations in systems." (And he remarked that the recognition of what he characteristically termed "this fact" was a major source of the organicism of German social thought.)

It is only a small step from there to the argument that the relationship between symbol and reality may be the reverse of what common sense assumes. "The fact of the matter is that the 'real world' is to a large extent unconsciously built up on the language habits of the group," Sapir had written. "No two languages are ever sufficiently similar to be considered as representing the same social reality. The worlds in which different societies live are distinct worlds, not merely the same world with different labels attached." The implication is that symbols may construct what we take to be real. As David Schneider put it: " 'nature' and the 'facts of life' are always a special case of the cultural definition of things; they have no independent existence apart from how they are defined by the culture." The prestige of linguistic models reinforced the notion that culture was a thing in itself, floating free, a closed and self-referential system—like a language, or at least like a monolingual dictionary, or a scientific grammar. The anthropologist was also granted the assurance that tried and true methods appropriate for the study of culture had already been worked out by linguists, or by linguistic philosophers, or by literary theorists.

Even a purely symbolic world of culture might perhaps be susceptible to scientific inquiry. After all, linguistics was, apparently, a science. Kroeber and (less certainly) Kluckhohn looked forward to a quick victory for the scientific conception of culture. Yet it was possible that there was something in the very nature of culture that made it resistant to any positivist strategy of research. Kroeber and Kluckhohn implied that the humanist and the anthropological views of culture were natural opponents, but Clifford Geertz began to argue that the anthropologists should take the idealists as their model, and concede that their goal should be interpretation rather than scientific explanation. He was in time to lead mainstream American cultural anthropology back to a view of culture that reaffirmed the humanist conceptions of the late nineteenth century.

Part Two

EXPERIMENTS

Chapter 3

CLIFFORD GEERTZ:

CULTURE AS RELIGION

AND AS GRAND OPERA

> No matter how much one trains one's attention on the supposedly hard facts of social existence, who owns the means of production, who has the guns, the dossiers, or the newspapers, the supposedly soft facts of that existence, what do people imagine human life to be all about, how do they think one ought to live, what grounds beliefs, legitimizes punishment, sustains hope, or accounts for loss, crowd in to disturb simple pictures of might, desire, calculation, and interest . . . Bent on certitude, Olympianism, or codifiable method, or simply anxious to pursue a cause, one can ignore such facts, obscure them, or pronounce them forceless. But they do not thereby go away. Whatever the infirmities of the concept of "culture" ("cultures," "cultural forms" . . .) there is nothing for it but to persist in spite of them. Tone deafness, willed or congenital, and however belligerent, will not do.
>
> *Clifford Geertz*

Clifford Geertz characteristically presents himself to the reader in the role of ethnographer, or, more modestly and specifically, in an image that recurs, as a man finding his feet in a strange town, walking, a little uncertainly, down its maze of alleyways, trying to grasp the meaning of what he sees and hears. This particular ethnographer is also an intellectual and a literary dandy, passionately interested in ritual but with a taste for markets, games, and fetes. "I grow uncomfortable when I get too far away from the immediacies of social life," he observes.

There are some earnest theoretical disquisitions in his early work, but his natural bent is to be an essayist rather than a system-builder like Parsons. His preference is for take-it-or-leave-it statements, bolstered by the invocation of powerful authorities. In later essays he came more and more to favor epigrams, parables, and extended metaphors. "Argument grows oblique, and language with it, because the more orderly and straightforward a particular course looks the more it seems ill-advised." Hardly surprisingly, there have been recurrent complaints that Geertz's ideas and methods are not systematically developed, that crucial terms are loosely defined, and that implicit contradictions are left unresolved.

And yet Geertz must surely be taken seriously as a theoretical influence. He has written with great eloquence about a particular idea of culture; he has applied this idea to the analysis of particular cases; and, in the process, he has given the cultural approach a seductive appeal, exciting the interest of many who would otherwise be quite indifferent to anthropological writings. In short, he put a new idea of culture to work. Reading his books and essays, one may trace the trajectory of the anthropological idea of culture in the second half of the twentieth century.

Not that Geertz's argument followed a necessary path, driven by the logic of an intellectual project. Geertz himself represents his professional development as a series of (largely happy) accidents. (Perhaps there is a professional deformation here. Anthropologists, professionally attuned to displacement and chance discoveries, often have a great deal of faith in their luck and their capacity for serendipity.) "I went to Antioch College in Ohio. I was in the Second World War, and after I got back, I went on the GI Bill to Antioch. Without the GI Bill I probably wouldn't have gone to college at all." On graduation—"stumbling out of an undergraduate major in English and looking for something rather more connected to the world as it was"—he was advised by his philosophy professor to consider the new Department of Social Relations at Harvard, despite the fact that he had taken virtually no social science courses, and in particular to think about studying anthropology, which was not taught at all at Antioch. By chance, a college friend was able to engineer a meeting for Geertz and his wife with Margaret Mead. "She didn't know us from Adam; all she knew was that we were two young kids from college in the Middle West wanting to go into anthropology. And she spent, I think, five hours with us, showing us her field notes from Bali, all kinds of field notes, urging us to go . . . So we left persuaded, and applied to Social Relations."

Clifford and Hildred Geertz entered graduate school at Harvard in 1949. Their first year in the experimental setup at Social Relations was stimulating, but they still had to fix on a field site for their research. At this point another godparent entered the picture:

> In the summer after my first year . . . yet another professor walked into the office in the Peabody Museum . . . He said (he was a man of few words, mostly abrupt): "We are forming a team to go to Indonesia. We need someone on religion and someone on kinship. Do you and your wife want to go?" I said, hardly knowing more than where Indonesia was, and that inexactly, "Yes, we would." I went home to tell my wife what had happened, and we set out to discover what I had gotten us into.

Their studies on religion and kinship were planned to fit into a broader team project that "was the very stamp and image of the Social Relations Idea: a well-financed, multidisciplinary, long-term team field project directed towards the study not of an isolated tribal culture but of a two-thousand-year-old civilization fully in the throes of revolutionary change." In the event, the ambitious plans for interdisciplinary, international collaboration did not work out in the field. Indonesia had declared independence from the Netherlands in 1945, but while Americans were officially welcome, in practice relations with bureaucrats were sticky, and local universities were not ready to join forces with a foreign research team. Geertz and his wife soon decided to work effectively on their own, spending two and a half years in Java, mainly in Pare (the town that is referred to in most of their publications as Modjokuto). Yet the initial interdisciplinary conception of the project left its traces in Geertz's work over the following decade, and it was reinforced by interaction with development economists at MIT at the end of the 1950s, and with sociologists and political scientists at the University of Chicago in the early 1960s. When he wrote about the problems of "revolutionary change," Geertz addressed himself to economists and political scientists as much as to anthropologists—a pioneering effort in what was, in general, a rather unworldly discipline.

After a brief but productive period back in the States (a series of publications on Java appeared quickly), Geertz and his wife returned to Indonesia, where they spent a further year, in 1957–58. The initial idea had been to make short studies of Hindu, Christian, and Islamic areas in Indonesia, beginning with Bali. However, civil disturbances enforced a change of plan, and the Geertzes spent the year in Bali. "In that sense it was a failed plan, though I think we were lucky; I don't think it would've worked. It was unrealistic. And my work in Bali would've been quite insufficient if I had just had the four months."

Back once more in the States, there were evidently no problems about jobs. After a year at the Center for Advanced Study in the Behavioral Sciences at Stanford, Geertz moved to a position at Berkeley ("which I suppose Clyde [Kluckhohn] had arranged"), but he soon went on to join a new program at the University of Chicago. This was the Committee for the Comparative Study of New Nations, which was led by Parsons's vicar in the Midwest, Edward Shils. Geertz was to spend the 1960s attached to this committee, and to the Department of Anthropology at the University of Chicago, where he participated (with, among others, David Schneider, another Parsonian) in the creation of a new, Parsonian course in the anthropology department. Known as the "systems" course, it followed the Parsonian formula, covering the three systems of social structure, culture, and personality.

In 1965, the brief period of democracy ended in Indonesia. A bloody confrontation in the capital precipitated a chain reaction of massacres throughout the country. Hundreds of thousands of people were killed, including many hundreds in the towns in Java and Bali where Geertz had done fieldwork. His research in Indonesia in 1957 had been restricted by political unrest, and he had begun to contemplate a change of field, but the coup marked the end of a chapter. Again, he was impelled on his way by a chance contact, a stray word. Attending a conference in England, in Cambridge, in 1963,

> at some intermission in some pub or other, I poured out my "where next?" anxieties to one of the younger and less over-socialized British participants . . . and he said, "You should go to Morocco: it is safe, it is dry, it is open, it is beautiful, there are French schools, the food is good, and it is Islamic." The logical force of this argument, bereft as it was of scientific argumentation, was so overwhelming that, immediately the conference ended, I flew to Morocco rather than returning to Chicago.

He and his wife and a series of graduate students then worked intermittently in Morocco between 1965 and 1971. Geertz drew on this experience to write a comparative study of Islam in Java and Morocco, *Islam Observed* (1968).

In 1970 Geertz was invited to establish the School of Social Science at the Institute for Advanced Study in Princeton, the legendary research center once graced by Einstein, von Neumann, and Gödel. He accepted, partly because it was a chance to start something new, partly to gain time for writing, and here he created a small school in his own image, dedicated to an interpretive approach, dismissive of positivist social science. A quarter of a century later, he is still there. At the Institute he published, among other works, two influential collections of essays, *The Interpretation of Cultures* (1973) and *Local Knowledge* (1983); a study of a classical Balinese state, *Negara* (1980); and two meditations on anthropology, *Works and Lives* (1988), which is about some other anthropologists, and *After the Fact* (1995), which is about his own work.

Clearly Geertz took his chances, but it seems evident that there is a pattern in this chapter of accidents. His career falls into two phases. He came into anthropology at the moment when America, in the full flush of victory in World War II, was financing the reconstruction of Europe and promoting the independence of the European colonies in Asia and Africa. It was widely hoped, even expected, that American social science would play its part in delivering a better world, and do its bit to prevent poor countries from slipping into the hands of communists. ("There had been a time, in those Fifties," says a John Updike character, recalling the "soc-rel" majors at Harvard, "when sociology, combining psychology, anthropology, history, and statistics, seemed likely to save the world from those shaggy old beasts tribalism and religion.") In this phase of his career, Geertz was a Parsonian—and thereby a Weberian, at least according to the Parsonian recension of Weber. His central preoccupation was one that Parsons attributed to Weber: the connections between ideas and social processes, more specifically the feedback between religious belief and political and economic development.

In the second half of the 1960s, Geertz began to change course. The confused but promising initial period of Indonesian independence had come to a bloody end. Elsewhere, too, nationalist, anticolonial movements were losing their gloss as they established themselves in power. Few of the new governments showed much enthusiasm for western democratic institutions, and not many seemed to be on course for sustained economic development. And the role of the United States was now less quixotic. The Cold War introduced new priorities. America became embroiled in Southeast Asia, no longer as a liberator but as a quasi-imperial power. The war in Vietnam escalated. It was now that Geertz moved his field site from Indonesia to Morocco, where the politics were stable, if not very interesting or attractive to the democrat. At home, a civil war began to take hold on the campuses, from which Geertz was alienated. (In 1964, he described his "general ideological . . . position" as being "largely the same as that of Aron, Shils, Parsons and so forth . . . I am in agreement with their plea for a civil, temperate, unheroic politics.") At the height of the crisis in academe, in 1970, he left the campus for the ultimate Ivory Tower of the Ivy system, the Institute for Advanced Study, where no students—not even graduate students—intruded.

The Parsonian project was now also losing momentum. The disciplines that had been brought together in the Department of Social Relations reasserted their distinctive identities. After all, social science faculties elsewhere were still based on single-discipline departments, and graduates had to make their careers within a discipline. Parsonian sociology was also a particular target of the New Left critique of American society. Alvin Gouldner wrote a polemic entitled "From Plato to Parsons: The Infrastructure of Conservative Social Theory." Radicals accused Parsons of pandering to the false consciousness of the bourgeoisie, ignoring dissent and promoting a comforting illusion of social consensus, emphasizing social equilibrium and refusing to recognize the forces making for change.

Geertz himself had become discontented with a very different aspect of the Parsonian program. Parsons had identified idealist and positivist traditions in social theory and tried to foster a middle course, urging social scientists to pay attention to social constraints and to ideologies. But Geertz was turning away from sociology. He detected—and welcomed—a move in American social science away from positivism and behaviorism and toward interpretation. Natural science models were being abandoned. There was instead, he wrote in 1973, "an enormous increase in interest, not only in anthropology, but in social studies generally, in the role of symbolic forms in human life. Meaning . . . has now come back into the heart of our discipline." Ten years later, in his next collection of essays, *Local Knowledge*, he described a new interdisciplinary configuration, in which an interpretive, symbolic anthropology was linked to philosophy and literary theory. Sociology was abandoned, hard psychology dismissed.

For those social scientists who were moving with the times, "the analogies are coming more and more from the contrivances of cultural performance than from those of physical manipulation—from theater, painting, grammar, literature, law, play." In interpreting cultures, the social sciences would join up with the humanities. The distinctions between the old genres were being creatively blurred. In his recent memoir, *After the Fact,* Geertz reflected that "the move toward meaning" had "proved a proper revolution: sweeping, durable, turbulent, and consequential."

In the first decade of Geertz's career, his theoretical statements were routinely, almost ritually, legitimized by the invocation of Parsons/Weber. In the early 1970s, Parsons (and Weber too, though less completely) began to slip out of his texts and even out of his footnotes, to be replaced by a new set of references. To begin with, the literary critic Kenneth Burke, the idealist philosopher Susanne Langer, and the French philosopher Paul Ricoeur were cited as fellow travelers in the realm of symbolism, meaning, and hermeneutics. Langer and Burke agreed that the central, defining feature of human beings was their capacity for symbolic behavior. *"Man,"* as Kenneth Burke defined him, in italics, *"is the symbol-using animal."* According to Langer (who was also given to italicizing the reader into attention), this meant that the empiricist conception of knowledge was flawed: "the edifice of human knowledge stands before us, not as a vast collection of sense reports [by which she apparently meant observations], but as a structure of *facts that are symbols* and *laws that are their meanings.*" What Geertz took from Ricoeur was the idea that because human actions conveyed meanings they could (and should) be read in much the same way as written texts. The point about actions was their symbolic content, not their more mundane consequences. At a later stage, Wittgenstein, Ryle, and Rorty were called upon for pithy endorsements of theoretical propositions, usually of a relativist sort; and the works of poets and novelists were mined for epigrams.

But despite the contrasts, real enough, between Early Geertz and Later Geertz, there is a central, continuing thread in his intellectual career, one long argument that I shall try to trace through his writings. In a series of case studies, he attempted to work out the implications of treating culture (by and large this was still culture as defined by Parsons, a symbolic system, a universe of meanings) in isolation from social organization. In principle, this was only a first stage, eventually the parts would be fitted together, but that end point, the ultimate moment of Parsons's last instance, tended to recede from view. In Geertz's writings it is a sophisticated but hermetic notion of culture that works itself out, engaging a variety of discourses in the humanities, and shaped by (and shaping) field experiences in Indonesia and North Africa.

───────────

In the monographs on Indonesia that he published in the 1960s, Geertz pressed forward on several fronts at once. He was a leading figure in a generation of ethnographers who were moving from classical tribal or island studies to the analysis of the large, complex, rapidly changing societies of Asia, with their richly documented histories. These societies were caught up in a turbulent transition from colonial rule to political independence. Politicians were calling on economists and political scientists for help with analysis and planning. These specialists were in turn impatiently demanding explanations for the cultural roadblocks that apparently stood in the way of progress. New questions were urgently being posed. Was there an indigenous platform for rationalization and modernization? Would the peasant social order disintegrate as economic changes eroded old loyalties? Could different ethnic and religious traditions find a political accommodation, or would there have to be a partition, on the lines of that between India and Pakistan?

A Parsonian was primed to enter into discussion with economists, and Parsons had always been especially interested in the problem of capitalist development. The Parsonian program was being adapted to the study of newly independent states by the Committee on the New States that had been established at the University of

Chicago by a leading Parsonian, Edward Shils. Reviewing the stance of the Chicago group, the political scientist David Apter explained that its members rejected the economic determinism that was current in development studies at the time, in both its orthodox and Marxist forms. The Committee asked larger questions about political and economic change, and drew on British social anthropology, on Durkheim and Weber, and above all on Parsons. Their starting point was the proposition that traditional societies had become disordered by the processes of urbanization, economic specialization, and secularization. The aim of policy in the new states should be to foster a modern social and intellectual order. It was up to the anthropologists to specify the cultural problems involved—or at least it was up to the two anthropologists who were members of the Committee, Lloyd Fallers and Clifford Geertz. They were expected "to find in the contrast of tradition and modernity, tribe and state, sacred communities and secular ones, those contradictions which would help explain both the ability or readiness to change and the inhibitions placed by a community upon change." And this is, indeed, a fair summary of Geertz's initial project.

Geertz's first major publication, *The Religion of Java*, based on his doctoral study, was essentially descriptive, and it addressed these issues of change only in a final chapter that was added to the dissertation. But almost from the first he took up the problems of social and political transformation that had been defined by Weber: the role of religious ideas in economic development and in social change, and the crisis of political legitimacy in times of transition. Innovative, argumentative, ambitious, the monographs he published in the 1960s represent the most significant contribution made by any anthropologist to what was then one of the great questions of the day, the prospects of the New States.

It is important to remember that Geertz began his studies in Indonesia, as he has remarked, "just after a successful political revolution seem[ed] to have opened up a vast range of new possibilities." Dutch colonial observers generally argued that in societies like Java economic progress was blocked by the pre-logical mentality of the people and by obsolete social arrangements. The Dutch economist J. H. Boeke had accepted, however, that the depressed state of the Javanese peasantry was in part the effect of Dutch colonial policies. Traditional society stagnated, deliberately cut off from the forces of modernization, and traditional leaders lost the capacity to organize large projects. But fatalist, anti-entrepreneurial values lived on. In consequence, people did not react to economic incentives in what economists considered to be a rational manner. There was accordingly little prospect of healthy economic or social development.

This analysis presented a challenge to more optimistic observers of newly independent Indonesia. Boeke was criticized by some economists for relying on outmoded economic models. Perhaps the Javanese were making rational choices after all, but the economists had misunderstood their economic situation. Others argued that old ideas were indeed a barrier to progress, but that they would be swept away by modernization. Geertz took a very different line. It was true that the colonial authorities had deliberately prevented the Javanese from making use of opportunities to profit from the development of new commercial crops and markets. Yet, though locked out of the modern economy, they had found ways to cope with the constraints imposed upon them. There were also indications—if one looked for them in the right places—that traditional forms of organization and established value patterns might serve as a basis for economic modernization.

Agricultural Involution, published in 1963 but based on a report written in 1956, set up a contrast between two ideal types of agriculture, each of which Geertz associated, in bold terms that were to attract criticism, with two broad regions, Inner Indonesia (mainly Java, Bali, and Lombok) and Outer Indonesia. The difference between these regions was at bottom ecological. (Always alert to new currents of thought, Geertz also borrowed some of the concerns of the cultural ecology movement that was fashionable in American anthropology at the time.) The economy of Outer Indonesia, relatively sparsely populated, dominated by forest, was traditionally reliant on slash-and-burn farming. Here the Dutch had successfully introduced large commercial plantations. The smallholders in the Outer Islands had been stimulated by the establishment of tobacco, coffee, and rubber plantations to grow these crops themselves. Some had prospered, and Geertz discerned a spread of "frank individualism, social conflict and cultural rationalization." In short, in this region there was modernization, if at a cost.

The ecology of Inner Indonesia favored the development of intensive, irrigated agriculture. In these areas, a densely settled population was dependent on wet rice cultivation. The Dutch had established a few plantations in Java, but had not allowed the native peasantry to grow cash crops or to profit from trading opportunities. The Javanese had been forced to intensify their irrigated field agriculture to support a growing population, but at the cost of steadily diminishing returns. The outcome (in the words of the Dutch economist Boeke) was "static expansion."

Always on the lookout for a striking neologism, Geertz borrowed the term "involution" from the Boasian theorist Alexander Goldenweiser to describe Boeke's "static expansion." What Goldenweiser meant by involution was a sterile elaboration, which did not deliver any real progress. As examples of involution he pointed to the development of some artistic styles (citing the Gothic and the Maori) that had ceased to innovate but were characterized by "progressive complication, and variety within uniformity, virtuosity within monotony." Geertz himself defined involution as "culture patterns which, after having reached what would seem to be a definitive form, nonetheless fail either to stabilize or to transform themselves into a new pattern but rather continue to develop by becoming internally more complicated." Involution characterized not only the economic strategies of the Javanese peasants but every aspect of social and cultural life. The outcome was what Geertz described, evocatively if imprecisely, as "a richness of social surfaces and a monotonous poverty of social substance" (qualities which he also identified in the life of

American suburbs, although these were hardly characterized by involution).

Agricultural Involution has generated a whole literature on Javanese rural sociology—"I danced for rain," Geertz remarks, "I got a flood"—but in the context of Geertz's intellectual career, the striking aspect of the book is that it provided a novel take on the problem of cultural and economic development. The Javanese system had stagnated, but people were not stuck in their old ways out of passivity, or because they were deficient in rationality. Prevented from modernizing by the Dutch, constrained by land shortages and the limitations of their irrigation techniques, the Javanese made the most of long-established forms of organization and traditional agricultural practices. The consequence, however, was that people ended up treading water, but had to kick faster and faster just to remain afloat.

Given the involution of agriculture in Inner Indonesia, a pessimistic view of the economic prospects of the region seemed to be indicated. Or was there some basis for economic "takeoff"? (This spaceship metaphor was much favored at the time. Those were the days!) Geertz was initially optimistic:

> Indonesia is now [he wrote in 1963], by all the signs and portents, in the midst of such a pretake-off period. The years since 1945, and in fact since about 1920, have seen the beginnings of a fundamental transformation in social values and institutions toward patterns we generally associate with a developed economy.

One way of looking at the matter—a very American way—was to seek out the entrepreneurs, the pioneers of modernization. In *Peddlers and Princes* (1963), Geertz again made his argument by contrasting two ideal types—two towns, one in Java and the other in Bali, both of which served as nodes of cultural contact "between 'East' and 'West,' 'traditional' and 'modern,' and 'local' and 'national.'" In a town in Java (again Pare, alias Modjokuto), economic leadership was on offer from new men, Muslim merchants, practitioners of a strictly orthodox Islam, who had moved in from the north coast. Their puritanical ethic was fitted to the development of commerce. (Geertz hints that they might come to play the role of the Puritan pioneers of European capitalism, in Weber's account.) However, their social base was insecure, for "the more traditional social loyalties [have] not wholly dissolved and the more modern ones not wholly crystallized." In consequence, they lacked the means to organize great enterprises.

The contrasting town in Bali was run by the old aristocracy. Operating now as entrepreneurs, they were able to mobilize the workers by manipulating a traditional communal ethic. Geertz concluded that various social and cultural arrangements might prepare the way for rational and efficient economic projects, and establish an ethical framework by which enterprises could be organized. Entrepreneurs were active on both cultural and economic fronts. *"The function of the entrepreneur in such transitional but pretake-off societies is mainly to adopt customarily established means to novel ends."* As the Dutch sociologist W. F. Wertheim commented in 1964, it was nevertheless somewhat romantic to expect peddlers or princes to become the agents of capitalist transformation, and it was definitely eccentric to exclude the prospect that entrepreneurs would emerge rather from the ranks of the educated bureaucrats, or from among the established Chinese wholesalers and financiers, or (one remarks with the benefit of hindsight) from within the immediate family of top politicians.

When he moved from economics to consider questions of political change, Geertz attributed a rather different role to traditional ideas, represented paradigmatically by religion. In the *ancien régime*—vaguely specified, of uncertain duration—religion had given meaning to life and supported social and political arrangements. During a period of rapid social change, traditional ideas no longer sustained an adequate design for living. In the new urban settings, religious differences actually exacerbated social and political tensions. The problem in the towns was not stagnation. Rather, there was the danger that change would take destructive forms, and instead of fostering a new value system might spawn a deadening anomie.

In *The Religion of Java* Geertz had set up a series of ideal types, corresponding to the varieties of religious orientation in Modjokuto. Each was associated also with one of the "three main social-structural nuclei in Java today: the village, the market, and the government bureaucracy." The religion of the ordinary village folk, even after they moved into town, was syncrctic. Their theology dealt mainly with spirits, and they were much concerned with curing, sorcery, and magic. The merchants, who came largely from north Java, practiced an orthodox, reforming Islam. The bureaucratic elite derived from a class of government servants in the old Javanese courts, but they had taken on new roles under the Dutch. They favored the Hinduized rituals of *prijaji*.

Following a Durkheimian model, Geertz suggested that each religious orientation sustained the values and social interests of its congregation. The central ritual of the village folk or *abangan* was the *slametan*, "the Javanese version of what is perhaps the world's most common religious ritual, the communal feast, and as almost everywhere, it symbolizes the mystic and social unity of those participating in it." Or again: "The *slametan* concentrates, organizes, and summarizes the general *abangan* ideas of order, their 'design for living.' In a subdued dramatic form, it states the values that animate traditional Javanese culture." The Muslims, though divided between traditionalists and modernizers, insisted on their place in a wider Islamic community. Their lives were organized by Islamic institutions: Muslim political parties, religious schools, the Islamic courts, and the mosques and prayer-houses. The observances of the urban bureaucratic elite were "organized around rather different types of social structure and expressive of quite different sorts of values." They prized literacy, etiquette, aesthetic standards, hierarchy, tradition, and stability.

Up to a point, then, Geertz offered paradigmatic examples of Durkheimian—or Parsonian—integration, of social groups tied together by the expression of shared values. This is, indeed, a fair summary of the first twenty-one chapters of the book, but before publication Geertz had added a final chapter to his original dissertation, in which he pointed out that there were not three societies in the town, but three elements of one community. If Modjokuto (or Java?) was a single social field, the fact that there were three religious communities might foster conflict and social disintegration, and invite political scapegoating.

There were countervailing forces. The townsfolk shared a sense of a common culture, which was fostered by Javanese and Indonesian nationalism. Some forms of conflict might ultimately be contained by new higher-level institutions. Cross-cutting ties might promote broader allegiances and contain conflict. Finally, Geertz drew attention to the pan-Javanese rituals that spanned these divisions, in particular the *Rijaja*, "the most truly nationalist of their rituals," which perhaps as such "indicates the reality and the attainability of what is now the explicit ideal of all Indonesians—cultural unity and continuing social progress."

The book closed on that optimistic note. Five years later, however, he adopted a more somber tone in his *Social History of an Indonesian Town*, which appeared on the eve of the collapse of the first Indonesian republican regime. He had revisited Indonesia in 1957–58, and it must have been evident that the value-integration to which *The Religion of Java* looked forward was not progressing well. Although he was still describing Modjokuto as it was up to 1954, Geertz now argued that the townsfolk were suffering from a breakdown in values. Modjokuto lacked identity. "The search for a viable form is in fact the leitmotif of Modjokuto urban history . . . it proved rather easier to dissolve older forms than to stabilize new ones." Every traditional principle of organization "soon gave way to another in a bewildering whirl of directionless change. The town and its environs became stranded, rather like the country as a whole, in a state of continuous transition . . . the recent phases of the town's history come to constitute an unbroken advance toward vagueness."

This characterization is itself remarkably vague. Literary theorists have accustomed us to consider the significance of an absence, but what is "an unbroken advance toward vagueness"? Yet Geertz did not hesitate to extend the diagnosis to Indonesia as a whole. The entire country was suffering from vagueness.

> From one perspective, and without neglecting the dynamic allure of wealth, power, and prestige, it is possible to see all recent Indonesian social processes as importantly shaped by a sense of intellectual, moral, and emotional disorientation—by, if not a sense of meaninglessless, at least a very thorough confusion of meaning.

Apparently, the vagueness was a result of a confusion of values, a babble of tongues, an absence of signposts. People no longer knew where they were headed, or what was the purpose of the journey. In the most general terms, Geertz argued that a disjunction had grown up between social structure and culture.

To illustrate this mismatch between ritual and social change, Geertz offered a case study of a funeral in Java. The people involved were simple folk, Geertz's *abangan*. Like other *abangan* rituals, an *abangan* funeral was normally a syncretic affair. The relatives organized a feast, a *slametan*, for the neighbors, whoever they were; and a Moslem functionary was called upon to oversee certain preparations of the corpse, and to make a prayer at the burial. In this particular instance, the normal arrangements broke down: the cleric withheld his services. He was active in an Islamic political party, and there was tension locally between his party and an *abangan* anti-Islamic party. The relatives of the deceased were active in this *abangan* party, and the minister was intent on making a political point. Accordingly, he refused to do his part unless they made a public statement of adherence to Islam. Eventually, after a serious delay in the ritual, the crisis was resolved by a negotiated compromise.

At one level, then, this was an incident in a party-political competition. Evidently it was quite exceptional, for Geertz does not suggest that there were other similar cases. The neighbors, including Muslim shopkeepers and tradesmen, were made uneasy by the confrontation, and they were eager to see the ritual properly concluded. Apparently only the Muslim functionary acted as though a matter of principle was at stake. Geertz, however, represented the breakdown in this ritual as a sign that the old religious practices no longer coincided with the social realities of mixed neighborhoods in an urban setting. Rituals could no longer carry the old message of neighborly solidarity. This may have been apparent to the observer, but there is no sign that the ritual itself had lost its coherence from the point of view of the participants. With the sole and crucial exception of the Muslim cleric, the congregation did not accept that the ritual was now inappropriate. Everyone else wanted the thing to be done properly, as it had always been done, and they could not see why it was going wrong now.

Geertz's broad proposition was that the ritual resources of Java's towns could no longer cope with the social experience of the townspeople. "The investigation of Modjokuto's progressive malaise comes down to an investigation of the reciprocal interplay between the evolving forms of human association (social structure) and the no less changing vehicles of human thought (cultural symbols)." The solidarity that once existed between rural neighbors had been eroded in the towns by religious and political polarization. The religious communities had become rallying points for new intercommunal rivalries. Thus the social groupings of the town were politicized: once "a collection of estates," they had become "a mélange of factions." Rituals that had promoted unity in the kampong now fomented divisions. The old political institutions could not cope, and in any case they were undermined by the competition for support generated by national political developments.

The political factions corresponded closely but not perfectly to the three religious orientations described in *The Religion of Java*. Geertz claimed that he was simply formalizing native social categories, but these ideal types were criticized by Indonesian scholars for simplifying a much more complex reality. According to the distinguished Indonesian anthropologist Koentjaraningrat, the terms *santri* and *abangan* were used in various ways in Java, but the key reference was to the degree of participation in Islam, not to a merchant/peasant opposition. The term *prijaji* referred to an occupational class of civil servants rather than to a religious orientation, and members of this class might be Islamic, syncretist or rather secularized, and they were often much influenced by Dutch models. Recent studies have also brought out the regional variation in all these matters within Java.

In any case, Geertz now represented the Islamic/non-Islamic distinction as the main source of social and political polarization in the town. The educated Islamic elite provided leadership for unsophisticated *santri* Muslims. On the other side of the growing divide, the syncretist *abangan* folk followed the lead of the bureaucratic elite. "The terms *abangan* and *santri* had now come to stand for two alternative adaptations to urban society, and rituals originally designed to integrate rural society now were hastening its demise." After the anti-colonial revolution, these factions had themselves split between modernizing and traditionalist wings, each allied with a national political tendency—Islamic, Communist, or Nationalist.

What Geertz's analysis boiled down to was the proposition that the cultural conceptions and rituals of the Javanese were no longer adequate to make sense of, to give meaning to, their rapidly changing social experience. The only way forward for the Javanese was to adjust their cultural symbols. And as a community emerged from the disparate elements that had been forced into association in modern Modjokuto, the townspeople had in fact started to construct a new model of its social organization. "This model is essentially a symbolic structure, that is, a system of public ideas and attitudes embodied in words, things, and conventionalized behavior . . . social action was not only understood in terms of this symbolic structure but also, in part and to a degree, judged and regulated."

The elements of this new cultural paradigm (as Geertz termed it) were drawn from the religious orientations of the past. But light updating was not enough. A modernizing nationalism sought to replace traditional values and allegiances, and to provide a fresh sense of purpose. However, precisely because the town was not a closed society, but was open to national currents of thought and to manipulation by outside politicians, local solidarity was liable to be undercut by religious and political differences. "With each tremor at the national level local equilibrium was disturbed and all the hard-earned agreements, arrangements, and understandings were dislodged to be reconstituted in some other, slightly—sometimes radically different—form."

Geertz's one hope was that the religious factions would find a common cause, that they would be brought together by a modernizing, national ideology, a secular religion. This hope was soon betrayed by events. In 1965, after initial disturbances in the capital, local activists in Java massacred tens of thousands of people who were identified as "Communists." Geertz commented in 1972 that the massacres "brought to open view the cultural disarray fifty years of political change had created, advanced, dramatized, and fed upon." The massacres were repeated in Bali, and in this instance Geertz suggested that they expressed a deep, suppressed lust for violence that he had discerned in the Balinese cock-fight. At the national level, Sukarno's theory "that the native eclecticism of Indonesian culture would yield easily to a generalized modernism . . . was definitely disproved."

Yet treating a small Javanese town as a microcosm of Indonesia was obviously problematic. Local interpretations of these terrible events were perhaps at best auxiliary, and at worst redundant. The crisis began in the capital, at a time of hyperinflation, an international diplomatic crisis, and military confrontation with Malaysia. Army officers sympathetic to the Indonesian Communist Party, which President Sukarno favored, assassinated six generals on September 30, 1965. The army, under Sukarno's rival, General Suharto, then orchestrated countrywide massacres in which between half a million and a million "communists" died. A further one and a half million were imprisoned. Suharto then took over as effective dictator of Indonesia, with the support of the army.

There was also significant foreign intervention. From the viewpoint of the White House, according to W. W. Rostow, who was there,

> a great deal was going on in Asia in 1964–5 [in addition, of course, to the escalating crisis in Vietnam]. Sukarno left the United Nations on January 7, 1965, and allied with Hanoi and Peking. Within Indonesia, he worked closely with Aidit, head of that country's Communist party. He launched the confrontation with Malaysia just as the first North Vietnamese regulars infiltrated South Vietnam.

When the coup occurred, Max Frankel reported in the *New York Times,* "the Johnson Administration found it difficult today to hide its delight at the news from Indonesia . . . After a long period of patient diplomacy designed to help the army triumph over the Communists, officials were elated to find their expectations being realized." There is little doubt that much of that "patient diplomacy" had been carried out by the CIA.

Geertz was certainly aware of these external forces, but his analytic framework could not cope with the interplay of local, national, and international politics. These matters were beyond the scope of "local knowledge." The "coup" in the capital is still imperfectly understood, but it had little to do with the local cultural and political trends that were evident in Modjokuto. Nor can the violence that it triggered even in remote areas be explained purely in local terms. Geertz's own account of an election in Modjokuto suggests that leaders on the spot could cut effective deals, and were prepared to work around ideological differences. The massacres began only after the soldiers had spread across the country and encouraged violence, even supervising the killings. They exploited local hatreds, and found willing collaborators, but there would have been no countrywide massacres without their intervention. Moreover, returning to the town years later, Geertz found that the crisis had passed.

> If in 1971, six years after the event, all this was but a bad memory, by 1986, twenty-one years after, it hardly seemed a memory at all, but a broken piece of history, evoked, on occasion, as an example of what politics brings . . . in general, the town was like a pond across which a terrible storm had once swept, a long time ago, in another climate. For someone who had known it before the storm, the place seemed to have exchanged the gathered-up energies of politics for the scattered-out ones of trade.

More generally, these terrible events expose the limits of a cultural analysis of politics. Introducing a set of essays on Indonesian politics, in 1972, Geertz wrote approvingly that the authors adopted a cultural perspective, bringing out "the structure of meaning through which men give shape to their experiences." This was the correct course because "politics is not coups and constitutions, but one of the arenas in which such structures publicly unfold." If politics is redefined as an arena in which "men give shape to their experiences," then one must ask, which men (and which women too)? And which experiences? Diplomats and politicians in the capital city, soldiers in their barracks, poor townspeople in country districts—all were surely moved by different experiences, and had different capacities to shape politics to suit their purposes.

Parallel to the monographs that appeared with striking regularity through the 1960s were Geertz's essays, many of them collected in *The Interpretation of Cultures* (1973). The monographs were problem-oriented, concerned with questions of political stability and economic modernization, the urgent issues of the development debate in the first flush of postwar decolonization. The tone was brisk, the subject matter empirical, the emphasis on the facts of the matter. The anthropologist engaged the economist, the agronomist, the technicians of development, urging them to consider local habits and traditions: the cultural factor. This was not a peripheral matter, of interest only to aesthetes or antiquarians. Culture, in the concentrated form of religion, inflected economic and political change, as Weber had argued.

Three polar oppositions—three pairs of contrasted ideal types—dominate the monographs on Indonesia. The first opposition is between culture and social structure. The second is between a traditional state, in which culture and social structure form a single, mutually reinforcing system, and modernity, where old ideas and values no longer match new social contexts and are challenged by new ideologies. Finally, the epitome of culture in traditional society is religion, whereas in modern society it is ideology. This bald summary is no doubt unfair to a subtle author. Occasionally the main propositions are presented in bold terms, but more often they are qualified by nesting sets of parentheses, or spun out in evocative images. But this is the structure of the argument.

These ideas were worked out in the early essays, but the essays increasingly came to emphasize different theoretical issues and conceptual problems: the nature of culture and symbolic expression, and the project of translation. The essays were also structured very differently than the monographs. Each broached an answer to a philosophical question, for which Geertz offered ethnographic illustrations. The presumed readership was not the development expert or the Indonesian planner but an ideal intellectual audience made up (more and more exclusively, as time went on) of humanists, with whom Geertz shared references to literary theorists, the more literary philosophers, and contemporary American and (generally rather earlier) European poets and novelists.

The essential Parsonian proposition is that social action has many ingredients, of which one is "culture." Each ingredient should be extracted and studied, in the first instance, by the appropriate kind of scientist. In that grand share-out, the anthropologist would be awarded culture. But the study of culture was still poorly developed and demanded refinement. Geertz wrote in 1973 that "this redefinition of culture has been perhaps my most persistent interest as an anthropologist." The first requirement was "cutting the culture concept to size, therefore actually insuring its continued importance rather than undermining it." Following the direction of Parsons, anthropologists should hone "a narrow, specialized, and, so I imagine, theoretically more powerful concept of culture to replace E. B. Tylor's famous 'most complex whole.'" ("The Parsonian theory of culture, suitably emended, is one of our most powerful intellectual tools.")

Geertz offered a series of more or less consistent definitions. Culture is "an ordered system of meaning and symbols . . . in terms of which individuals define their world, express their feelings and make their judgments"; "an historically transmitted pattern of meanings embodied in symbolic forms by means of which men communicate, perpetuate, and develop their knowledge about and attitudes toward life"; "a set of symbolic devices for controlling behavior, extrasomatic sources of information."

Because culture is a symbolic system, cultural processes must be read, translated, and interpreted.

> Believing, with Max Weber, that man is an animal suspended in webs of significance he himself has spun, I take culture to be those webs, and the analysis of it to be therefore not an experimental science in search of law but an interpretive one in search of meaning. It is explication I am after, construing social expressions on their surface enigmatical.

The symbolic language of culture is public, and consequently the analyst does not have to pretend to achieve insights into the dark corners of individual minds. The symbolic function is universal, and human beings could not manage without this second code, which operates alongside the genetic code itself. Indeed, to be human is to be cultured. But there is no point in pursuing (with the structuralists or formalists) universal principles that might underlie all cognition, for the key fact is that all cultures are different. "To be human here is thus not be Everyman; it is to be a particular kind of man, and of course men differ."

The symbols that constitute a culture are vehicles of conceptions, and it is culture that provides the intellectual ingredient in the social process. But symbolic cultural propositions do more than articulate what the world is like; they also provide guidelines for action in it. They provide both models *of* what they assert to be reality, and patterns *for* behavior. And it is as a guide for behavior that they enter into social action. It is therefore essential "to distinguish analytically between the cultural and social aspects of human life, and to treat them as independently variable yet mutually interdependent factors."

Particularly in the early essays, Geertz was concerned to answer the criticism that cultural analysis might explain very little—even that it was a luxury, a diversion from real life. It was objected that the cultural analyst was too readily seduced by aesthetic qualities, and was inclined to shy away from the grave issues of survival, or the worldly realities of power, or the ineluctable but often hidden constraints of biology. In response, Geertz sometimes took a Parsonian line. Culture was one of the constraints on action, and the cultural perspective was a necessary ingredient in a larger analysis, which was bound to be interdisciplinary in character. Obviously, any particular contribution was partial. But even considered in its own terms, culture was not mere decoration. People everywhere grapple with the big issues of life, death, fate, and so forth. Each culture addresses the human condition itself, a subject large enough in all conscience.

A more vexing issue had to do with the inescapable limits of "local knowledge." The ethnographer was accused of remaining too close to the ground, of not paying attention to long-term changes and outside influences. Occasionally Geertz accepted, even gloried in, the specific, local, situated nature of ethnographic knowledge. Yet he often strained to expand its reference. In his early monographs, he was ready to generalize from the town of Modjokuto to Java or even to Indonesia, and often suggestively (though, of course, he was constantly met by the cry, "But not in the South . . ."). Yet when he analyzed political and economic processes in the town, he was patently unable to build bridges—to demonstrate the links—between Modjokuto and Jakarta.

But even if these objections could be countered, the original Parsonian challenge still had to be met. If culture could be defined, marked off, and studied by appropriate means, there remained the problem—insistently posed by Parsons—of how the relationships between culture and the social process were to be established. How did culture work as a model for action? Was culture a pure, independent element that weighed in with other elements (institutional and psychological) to produce social action? If so, how could the cultural element be abstracted, since it was observed only in the course of social action? The matter was even more complex in that culture was itself shaped by social and political processes.

Geertz was often content with very broad statements about the relationship between culture and social structure, usually citing Parsons and Shils for authoritative support. ("Culture is the fabric of meaning in terms of which human beings interpret their experience and guide their action; social structure is the form that action takes, the actually existing network of social relations. Culture and social structure are then but different abstractions from the same phenomena.") In practice, he elected religion to represent an epitome of culture, and he tried to describe the effect of religious conceptions and practices upon particular political, social, and economic processes (a Weberian project). Religion had to be treated as a cultural system, but it was also a privileged aspect of culture, culture raised to its highest point, at its core "a cluster of sacred symbols, woven into some sort of ordered whole." (What symbols are sacred? Working in societies where world religions dominate, Geertz is content to give the terms *sacred* and *secular* rather conventional meanings, corresponding roughly to what he calls "religion" and "common sense.")

Like cultures more generally, religions have a dual character, telling us both what the world is like, and how we should act in it. Religious symbols assure us that the world is orderly, and so they satisfy a fundamental need to escape the chances of an absurd and irrational universe. There is a hidden meaning in loss, suffering, injustice, and death. In short, sacred symbols construct a world that makes sense, and in understanding the world we learn how to conduct ourselves. But religious symbols can work in this way only to the extent that they are accepted and absorbed. The "essence of religious action" is to impose authority on a complex of symbols, "the metaphysic they formulate and the style of life they recommend." This is the task of ritual, which at the same time symbolically presents "an image of cosmic order—a world view" and induces "moods and motivations," thus, for the moment, fusing an image of the world, an ethos, and a model for behavior. Rituals alter "the whole landscape presented to common sense . . . in such a way that the moods and motivations induced by religious practice seem themselves supremely practical, the only sensible ones to adopt given the way things 'really' are."

In systems that are in equilibrium, religion, social structure, emotions, and conventional forms of action mesh and reinforce each other. There is an efficient, Durkheimian process of feedback. But as Parsons and Shils had insisted, this isomorphism is a special case. In situations of social change, sacred symbols can no longer speak so clearly to social realities. Geertz describes in his essay "Ritual and Social Change" (1959) how formerly rural people living in Modjokuto tried to make sense of things in the old terms. Their efforts were doomed: "the difficulty lies in the fact that socially *kampong* people are urbanites, while culturally they are still folk." The social and political divisions in the town undermined the intention of the ritual, which was to assert that the world is orderly and the community united. The urbanized villager could no longer get by with the help of his folk ritual. The old ideas might still seem comforting in the dark watches of the night, but they were no longer adapted to cope with the business of the day.

In the New States, the problem of coping with modernization was most acutely experienced at the national level. Particularistic demands come up against the national interest, and they become the basis for political conflicts. The center must generate new loyalties, fashion an appeal that transcends local attachments. "The new states are, today [Geertz was writing in 1963], rather like naive or apprentice poets or composers, seeking their own proper style, their own distinctive mode of solution for the difficulties posed by their medium." Some will fail, and "there are *manqué* states as there are *manqué* artists, as France perhaps demonstrates."

Passing over this curious reference to France, which, after all, provided the modern world with most of its ideologies, Geertz proceeds to argue that the New States require a Weberian charismatic leader, who will design a new model of legitimacy: an ideology. Ideology has most of the characteristics of religion. Like a religion, an ideology is to be understood culturally, as a symbolic system, and therefore, in Geertz's recurrent image, as an art form. Deploying figurative language, ideology creates "novel symbolic forms" and offers "maps of problematic social reality and matrices for the creation of collective conscience." It is a form of religion apt for troubled times, and for a disenchanted modernity. Ideological ferment characterizes societies in the throes of change, from revolutionary France to the post-colonial states. Struggling to institutionalize new ways of doing things, leaders of these states promote unifying symbols and invent national rituals. Ideology alone will not resolve the problems of a country like Indonesia, but it is a necessary ingredient in any solution.

Yet the rise of ideology is not to be understood simply as a solution to political and social problems. Perhaps the most general presumption among social scientists in the twentieth century has been that the modern world is disenchanted. Secularization undermines established beliefs, and religion loses its monopoly as a framework for cosmology and morality. Fortunately, there is an alternative source of meaning, which Geertz calls common sense. Among the least well defined elements in Geertz's conceptual apparatus, common sense is culturally specific, infiltrated by religious notions, but still a sort of practical wisdom, fitted to deliver certain kinds of goods. "Most of the time men, even priests and anchorites, live in the everyday world and see experience in practical, down-to-earth terms—they must if they are to survive." Yet while common sense may be a necessary guide to operating in the market, or dealing with the police or with a neighbor, it cannot aspire to answer the big philosophical questions, or to rule on matters of morality. That is the province of religion. But with modernization comes secularization, bringing with it a direct challenge to religious accounts of the world. Common sense, along with its epitome, science, creates the need for something else, and also offers the materials for constructing a secular alternative to religion, an ideology. Ideologies are characteristically modern substitutes for religion.

Geertz developed this argument in *Islam Observed*, a comparative study of Islam in Indonesia and Morocco, published in 1968. ("They both incline toward Mecca, but, the antipodes of the Muslim world, they bow in opposite directions.") Religious faith in traditional societies is sustained "by symbolic forms and social arrangements." These pillars are "coming unstuck" in the New States in general, and in particular in Indonesia and Morocco. Orthodox beliefs are no longer taken for granted, and the "classical religious symbols" no longer suffice "to sustain a properly religious faith." This is a very widespread phenomenon. "So too, I think, is the major reason for this loss—secularization of thought; so, too, the major response to it—the ideologization of religion." Secularization is a triumph for common sense, or rather for a "trans-commonsensical cultural perspective . . . positive science." Traditional common sense left room for religious ideas, but the practical reason of science is insatiable, denying that any questions are ultimately too sacred or too mysterious to yield to its methods. Today, this is apparent even to "the humblest peasant or to the shepherd." Everywhere there is a war between science and religion, a "struggle for the real."

The world religions have faced scientific and philosophical challenges for many centuries, and Geertz argues that their favored strategy is simply to deny a platform to secular challenges. This generalization does scant justice to the history of the early modern state in Europe, but in any case Geertz emphasizes another process that promotes secularization in the New States. Because they were stuck with multi-ethnic populations, with conflicting religious loyalties, post-colonial rulers had to develop a secular ideology that would foster national unity under their leadership. They were therefore driven to undermine the monopoly of established religion. Revolutionary nationalism promoted "a kind of all-embracing secular religiosity" in Indonesia, and "a radical disjunction between personal piety and public life" in Morocco. In both cases, the legitimacy of science is advanced, directly or indirectly, and the authority of religion is eroded. Secularization undermines faith, and ideology replaces it. (There are many criticisms one might make of this account, but it certainly proved a poor indicator of the importance that fundamentalist Islam was to achieve in the following decades.)

If the special subject matter of anthropology was culture, then how should it be studied? In his first book, *Religion of Java,* Geertz was content with what reads today as an almost quaint empiricism:

> One of the characteristics of good ethnographic reporting . . . is that the ethnographer is able to get out of the way of his data, to make himself translucent so that the reader can see for himself something of what the facts look like and so judge the ethnographer's summaries and generalizations in terms of the ethnographer's actual perceptions.

But by the early 1970s he was grappling with methodological issues in a more sophisticated fashion. Method is the subject of his most influential essay, "Thick Description: Toward an Interpretive Theory of Culture," which was written as an introduction for his collection *The Interpretation of Cultures.*

Geertz's most consequential assumption was that the crucial data of ethnography are not synthesized from raw observations. Only naive behaviorists believe that. People's actions are considered, and they are processed through the filter of interpretation. Actions are artifacts, signs that are intended to convey meanings. (This is a Weberian idea, promoted in American social science in the 1960s by the admirers of the émigré phenomenologist Alfred Schutz.) The ethnographer is accordingly concerned not so much with what people do as with the meaning of what they do, and with the interpretations they make of each other's actions. His business is "explicating explications," his materials "constructions of constructions."

This is all by no means self-evident. Again and again in his work, Geertz counterposes the commentaries of actors to his own direct observations, of people priming their cocks for the fray, hustling votes and participating in elections, haggling in the bazaar. He (surely rightly) distinguishes what they say from what they do, and from what he and other (native and foreign) observers make of what is said and done. Yet he sometimes denies that the ethnographer's field notes may describe what he sees for himself: "what we inscribe (or try to) is not raw social discourse, to which, because . . . we are not actors, we do not have direct access, but only that small part of it which our informants can lead us into understanding." But why do actors alone have "direct access" to "raw social discourse"? What of the famous participant-observer? Surely the ethnographer may achieve a grasp of characters and conventions that permits an interpretation of actions comparable to that of the native, but which nevertheless differs because it is more analytical.

In place of the participant-observer, who learns to live in a foreign society, and who aims to find out how things really work behind the screen of pieties, Geertz proposes that the ethnographer should proceed in the same way as a textual scholar. "Doing ethnography is like trying to read (in the sense of 'construct a reading of') a manuscript—foreign, faded, full of ellipses, incoherencies, suspicious emendations, and tendentious commentaries, but written not in con-

ventionalized graphs of sound but in transient examples of shared behavior." The idea that a ceremonial drama like a cock-fight could be
treated as a text, an "inscription of action," was borrowed from Paul
Ricoeur, Geertz tells us, "and somewhat twisted." Ricoeur had argued that "the human sciences may be said to be hermeneutical" if
they meet two conditions: "(1) inasmuch as their *object* displays some
of the features constitutive of a text as text, and (2) inasmuch as their
methodology develops the same kind of procedures as those of *Aus-
legung* or text-interpretation." Clearly the first condition is primary.
Ricoeur claims that social actions have certain attributes of speech-
acts. A social act has a propositional content and a purpose, and it is
public and addressed to possible "readers." It may therefore be
treated like a record of speech, or a written document. "Human action . . . is opened to anybody who *can read*."

It would not be difficult to list a number of ways in which social
action may be different from a text, or even from a speech-act, but
what matters here is the use that Geertz himself made of Ricoeur's
metaphor. His best-known exercise in this genre is his representation
of the Balinese cock-fight as an "acted text." The title of this essay,
first published in 1972, is "Deep Play: Notes on the Balinese Cock-
fight." The notion of "deep play" is borrowed from reflections on the
irrationality of gambling by the utilitarian philosopher Jeremy Bentham. As a utilitarian, Bentham assumed that gambling for high
stakes was irrational, and he concluded that the weak of mind should
be protected from it. Geertz argues that when the Balinese indulge in
what Bentham called deep play, gambling for very high stakes, they
are expressing shared values that transcend the Gradgrind calculus of
material gain and loss. It is not just money that is at stake in the cock-
fights.

The owners of the fighting cocks and their relatives and neighbors place even-money bets, and in important encounters these are
very substantial. But the protagonists are making even larger wagers
than may appear. They are in over their heads, and not only finan-

cially. In fact, money is secondary. "It is in large part *because* the marginal disutility of loss is so great at the higher levels of betting that to engage in such betting is to lay one's public self, allusively and metaphorically, through the medium of one's cock, on the line." The cock represents its owner and his close associates. Consequently, status is at stake. The gamblers "put their money where their status is." Geertz's "general thesis" is that the deep cock-fight "is fundamentally a dramatization of status concerns." Bentham's analysis of "deep play" fails, because it considers only the mundane utilitarian stakes. "What makes Balinese cockfighting deep is thus not money in itself, but what, the more of it that is involved the more so, money causes to happen: the migration of the Balinese status hierarchy into the body of the cockfight."

Geertz's proposition is that status means more to the players than money, and that the cash stakes stand for status risks. But what aspect of status is in play? Geertz reminds the reader that the Balinese are very concerned with status and prestige in all sorts of contexts, but as the analysis proceeds it becomes evident that the values at play in the cock-fight are not the official values of Balinese culture at all, but deeper, unspoken fears and desires.

> What . . . the cockfight talks most forcibly about is status relationships, and what it says about them is that they are matters of life and death. That prestige is a profoundly serious business is apparent everywhere one looks in Bali . . . But only in the cockfight are the sentiments upon which that hierarchy rests revealed in their natural colors. Enveloped elsewhere in a haze of etiquette, a thick cloud of euphemism and ceremony, gesture and allusion, they are here expressed in only the thinnest disguise of an animal mask, a mask which in fact demonstrates them far more effectively than it conceals them. Jealousy is as much a part of Bali as pose, envy as grace, brutality as charm; but without the cockfight the Balinese would have a much less certain understanding of them, which is, presumably, why they value it so highly.

At this juncture, what interests Geertz is the interpretation of the whole scene by the audience. "Its function, if you want to call it that, is interpretive: it is a Balinese reading of Balinese experience, a story they tell themselves about themselves." And what the Balinese say about themselves in their cock-fights is subversive, deeply disturbing: "it brings together themes—animal savagery, male narcissism, opponent gambling, status rivalry, mass excitement, blood sacrifice—whose main connection is their involvement with rage and the fear of rage."

In the final sentences of this essay, Geertz remarks that "societies, like lives, contain their own interpretations. One has only to learn how to gain access to them." But how? Geertz appeals to the example of dramatic critics interpreting productions of Shakespeare, but he does not specify the methods by which he identifies and reads the acted text of the cock-fight. Nor can he underwrite the claim that he is able to interpret the unspoken values of the Balinese (all Balinese?) as they are revealed in this spectacle. One might suppose that many Balinese would indignantly repudiate the suggestion that beneath the skin the Balinese man is an animal. Yet Geertz is confident that the dangerous emotions he reads into the drama really do seethe in the unconscious of the Balinese. The play is not a holiday from reality, or a ritual reversal, but a revelation of what is there. In the final footnote to the text, he suggests that the terrible massacres that occurred in Bali in the aftermath of the coup attempt in the capital, in December 1965, demonstrate "that if one looks at Bali not just through the medium of its dances, its shadow-plays, its sculpture, and its girls, but—as the Balinese themselves do—also through the medium of its cockfight, the fact that the massacre occurred seems, if no less appalling, less like a contradiction to the laws of nature."

Ultimately, the text reads the irrational Balinese values that lie below the surface of their official values. Geertz claims in effect to have penetrated the hidden depths of the Balinese psyche. The Balinese interpretations, like the associations of the dreamer, can only lead the reader of texts a part of the way. In the end, he must call upon the foreign insights of the psychoanalyst. And what this reading reveals is not simply the power of culture to override economic rationality, but the dark forces of human nature that lie beneath the surface, that may undermine the values of a culture. ("Every people, the proverb has it, loves its own form of violence. The cockfight is the Balinese reflection on theirs.")

For a more considered discussion of what is involved in treating culture as a text, one must return to Geertz's most self-conscious methodological essay, "Thick Description," which illustrates Ricoeur's proposition by means of a very different sort of case study. Geertz begins with Gilbert Ryle's artificial, typically Oxford-philosophical description of the many layers of meaning that may be conveyed by a simple act of body language, the wink. Geertz remarks that the ethnographer has to pick his way through precisely similar "piled-up structures of inference and implication," and proceeds to tell an illustrative story, which occurred in Morocco in 1912, when French control over some Berber areas was uncertain, and traders still had to rely (unofficially, indeed illegally) on traditional trade pacts with individual sheiks.

The gist of the story is this: a local Jewish trader named Cohen and two visiting Jewish traders were robbed by some Berbers, and Cohen's companions were murdered. Cohen requested French help to recover damages, but the marauders came from a tribe that was in rebellion against French colonial rule, and he was told, in effect, to sort it out himself. Invoking a trade pact with a Berber sheik, Cohen mobilized allies. They promptly impounded herds of sheep belonging to the tribe from which the robbers had come. This obliged the leaders of the tribe to enter into negotiations with Cohen's protectors, and he was paid compensation of 500 sheep. The commander of the French military detachment, however, suspicious of Cohen's alliance with rebellious Berbers, imprisoned him and impounded his sheep.

The text of the story is printed in small type, which seems to indicate quotation, and Geertz reveals that the account was given to him in 1968. Whose text is it? Geertz does not specify whether it records the memories of one informant, or whether he constructed the text from various sources. Instead he proceeds directly to the claim that the text is "thick"—"extraordinarily thick"—and that it shows "that what we call our data are really our own construction of other people's constructions of what they and their compatriots are up to."

Neither claim is persuasive. Is the text of the story itself "thick" (layered with implications), or is it the behavior it purports to describe—the acted text—that is so "extraordinarily thick"? For Ryle, who coined the phrase, it is a description that may be thick, and it is thick if it conveys the layers of meaning that may be read into an action. As an interpretive description, this text is surely anything but "thick." It is a straightforward action narrative, a rather breathless adventure story that packs a series of dramatic incidents into a mere six hundred words or so, and it offers a minimum of commentary. Nor does it demonstrate that the ethnographer's data are necessarily pre-cooked by informants, since this is a special case, the reconstruction of an event that occurred a generation ago. Had Geertz been present at the negotiations between the Berber elders, as he was at many Balinese cock-fights, he would not have been reliant in the same way upon "other people's constructions of what they and their compatriots were up to."

In any case, one must query what this particular text has to say, whoever authored it, however thick or thin it may be. Why did Geertz select it to serve as the exemplary instance of thick description in his most important methodological essay? He suggests that this story is mimetic of the process of ethnographic understanding, for the drama it relates is itself created by a clash of interpretations. The text presents "three unlike frames of interpretation ingredient in the situation, Jewish, Berber, and French," and illustrates a state of "systematic misunderstanding" between the parties. "What tripped Cohen up, and with him the whole ancient pattern of social and economic relationship within which he functioned, was a confusion of tongues."

Yet this is by no means a persuasive reading of the story. The account Geertz presents to the reader is admittedly sketchy, but it could equally well be read to suggest that Cohen, the Berbers, and the French weighed each other up fairly accurately. The only aberration was the French colonel's conclusion that Cohen was a Berber agent, but this was not necessarily a result of cultural misapprchension. In other comparable cases it might have been a correct induction, or might have served as a useful ploy, whatever the truth of the matter in this particular instance.

At one point, Geertz himself offers a straightforward summary which is far removed from the Tower of Babel reading of this story ("a social discourse . . . conducted in multiple tongues"):

> Cohen invoked the trade pact; recognizing the claim, the sheik challenged the offender's tribe; accepting responsibility, the offender's tribe paid the indemnity; anxious to make clear to sheiks and peddlers alike who was now in charge here, the French showed the imperial hand.

He also remarks that since "code does not determine conduct," any of the parties might have acted differently, which suggests that rational calculations might have been decisive. There do not appear to be impenetrable cultural mysteries here. This does not seem to be a story about "confusion of tongues." The reader is given a thin account of a complex historical event, and may reasonably conclude that—on the evidence, such as it is—the parties grasped the nature of the business pretty adequately at the time.

There is another point to be made about Geertz's carefully constructed example. In buttressing his argument that social processes are like texts, he has rigged the argument by instancing an *account* of an incident that is, indeed, very like a text. But this reduction of direct observations, interviews, secondary accounts of all kinds, to the status of a text remains problematic, a metaphor running away with itself. It also has a high cost, erasing distinctions that would normally be considered to have obvious significance, collapsing various kinds of data together into a single type. Geertz insists on this maneuver, perhaps, because it vindicates his preference for interpretation. "The culture of a people is an ensemble of texts, themselves ensembles, which the anthropologist strains to read over the shoulders of those to whom they properly belong." If our data take the form of texts, then they are to be read, translated, annotated, explicated. The ethnographer's work will then indeed be comparable to that of other textual scholars (who, however, generally pay rather more attention than Geertz allows in this case to the way in which a text is made up).

Even if Geertz's maneuver is accepted for the moment, it raises questions in its own terms. First, are there more and less reliable texts? Geertz comments only occasionally on this issue, and in very general terms. Nor does he debate the criteria for judging interpretations. He does not offer any guidelines, or examples, so that the reader may assess what would "warrant" (his preferred term) one interpretation rather than another. Nor does he specify his methods in any detail. Rather, he evokes briefly and without precision the procedures of hermeneutics, or, alternatively, the case-by-case pragmatism of clinical medicine. These matters are particularly troubling where the ethnographer adds a further level of interpretation, as Geertz does when he compares the Balinese cock-fight to a production of Macbeth, or when he argues that it expresses hidden, subversive aspirations and values of Balinese men. Such interpretations are not derived from any informants, and may be inaccessible to them. Translated into Balinese, Geertz's commentary would probably arouse indignation. The implication seems to be that behind the texts constructed by informants there is a deeper text that can be read only by the cosmopolitan scientist, who is equipped with other, culturally foreign expertise. If that is so, then culture resides in the text constructed by the ethnographer.

These methodological questions—consequential enough in themselves—therefore raise a further issue, which was also broached by Geertz in the essay "Thick Description" in 1973. The ethnographer not only reads that fragmentary and fleeting text over the shoulder of his informants; he also fabricates a text of his own.

> The ethnographer "inscribes" social discourse: *he writes it down.* In so doing, he turns from [*sic*] a passing event, which exists only in its moment of occurrence, into an account, which exists in its inscriptions and can be reconsulted . . . "What does the ethnographer do?"—he writes.

This apparently harmless truism actually lays a new and perhaps crushing burden on the ethnographer. For if the ethnography is itself a text comparable to the account of an incident offered by a Moroccan informant, then the thing to do with it is to interpret it and to unravel its tropes, tricks, and hidden messages. In *Works and Lives* (1988) Geertz has many acute and interesting observations on the ways in which that made-up text, the ethnography, does its work. However, while he insists that there are better or worse ethnographic texts, more or less reliable, he leaves his readers without any way of judging anything besides the author's dissimulations and the critic's skill in unmasking them.

In his latest work Geertz suggests a further move, or makes explicit a technique that can be traced in many of his essays. Texts work by means of symbol and metaphor, he says, and the ethnographer's task is to find fitting metaphors with which to shape a new text.

> Asking whether Pare really is a succession of contestings or Sefrou [a town in Morocco] really is a dissolving shape is a bit like asking whether the sun really is an explosion or the brain really is a computer. The issue is: What do you say in saying that? Where does it get you? There are other figurations—the sun is a furnace, Sefrou is a bear garden; Pare is a dance, the brain is a muscle. What recommends mine?

What recommends them, or disrecommends them if they are ill-constructed, is the further figures that issue from them: their capacity to lead on to extended accounts which, intersecting other accounts of other matters, widen their implications and deepen their hold.

Once the metaphor of the text is swallowed, one can hardly strain at other metaphors. And if all is text, then relationships between Geertz's ethnographic essays and Balinese ceremonies or Berber stories are relations of intertextuality. His metaphors illuminate their metaphors, and the best ones generate new metaphors, by a chaste but fruitful process that somehow is its own justification. The poetics of culture becomes a kind of poetry in itself. The ethnographer discovers that he has been writing poetry all along.

––––––

Geertz's thinking on the role of culture, and its textual character, was pushed furthest in the most original and ambitious ethnographic monograph that he published in his years at the Institute for Advanced Study. This was *Negara: The Theater-State in Nineteenth Century Bali*, published in 1980. No mere descriptive monograph, it has been hailed by Quentin Skinner as "a work of political philosophy in its own right."

The starting point for Geertz's analysis was Louis Dumont's *Homo Hierarchicus*, an analysis of Indian religion, politics, and hierarchy that had appeared in 1967. For Dumont, the pivot of Indian ideology was a conceptual opposition between the Brahman and the secular king. Geertz proposed what was in effect a structural transformation of Dumont's model. He argued that in the Southeast Asian states—Bali being a privileged instance—the role of king and Brahman was combined. The king was himself the sacred center of the society, the apex of the status hierarchy, "the numinous center of the world, and priests were the emblems, ingredients, and effectors of his sanctity." Because the king was sacred, secular power politics had no place in the court, which was a sacred center, a temple, or a theater, mounting ritual performances. It was at a lower level in the system that the business of public affairs was carried out: warfare, taxation, the allocation of land, the organization of irrigation systems.

Thus the rituals with which the court occupied itself were not coded statements about power, or a celebration of the political order.

> The state cult was not a cult of the state. It was an argument, made over and over again in the insistent vocabulary of ritual, that worldly status has a cosmic base, that hierarchy is the governing principle of the universe, and that the arrangements of human life are but approximations, more close or less, to those of the divine.

It is an egregious error to treat the royal rituals as ideological mummery. On the contrary, they

> enacted, in the form of pageant, the main themes of Balinese political thought: the center is exemplary, status is the ground of power, statecraft is a thespian art. But there is more to it than this, because the pageants were not mere aesthetic embellishments, celebrations of a domination independently existing: they were the thing itself.

Secular power, which operated in the lower reaches of the system, was fragmented and inherently unstable. Its fields of action—land, water, temples—were distinct from each other, so that it was difficult to control followers. And secular power was quite distinct from ritual power. Indeed, the one excluded the other. As a lord rose in the hierarchy, he had to surrender secular power in order to build up his sacred power.

> The problem was that the negara changed its character from its lower reaches to its higher. At the lower, it engaged the hundreds of criss-cross village polities, praying from them . . . the bodies and resources to stage the court operas. At the higher, progressively removed from contact with such politics and the crudenesses associated with them, it was turned toward the central business of exemplary mimesis, toward staging the operas.

The Parsonian opposition between culture and social action is now realized in a new fashion. Culture is epitomized by the royal rituals—what Geertz calls the court opera (high culture indeed!). The rarefied culture of the court is opposed to the mundane world in which people make their living, compete, and exercise power. The argument is that "culture came from the top down, while power welled up from the bottom." Bali was "a society stretched taut between cultural paradigms conceived as descending from above and practical arrangements conceived as rising from below." In old Bali, at any rate, culture ruled. Civil society bought tickets to its theatricals. But the theatricals were not mere by-products of real politics. The court theatrics gave meaning to everything else, just as culture more generally is supposed to give meaning to social action. "The dramas of the theater state, mimetic of themselves, were, in the end, neither illusions nor lies, neither sleight of hand nor make-believe. They were what there was."

In a recent study J. Stephen Lansing argues, contra Geertz, that the lower, more practical levels of public action were also highly ritualized. But even if the court rituals were of paramount importance, it is not easy to understand how the court could maintain control purely through ritual means. This is partly because the evidence is thin. As Geertz conceded, "careful, detailed descriptions of much Balinese ritual life, and especially of royal ceremonies, are lacking." This admission, buried in a footnote, deserves attention. If it is true, we cannot know how the rituals worked their magic, supposing that they did indeed move ordinary people. The public had to buy tickets to the spectacles, but why they did so remains a mystery.

Another, equally puzzling, issue is the absence of normal politics at the top of the system. Hierarchical societies are not usually entirely free from competition or dissent. And as a Dutch historian, Schulte Nordholt, points out, "the concept of the theater state leaves little room for the conflicts and the violence inherent in Balinese society." If conflict and violence were inherent in the system, then presumably the court could not remain aloof from secular affairs.

Drawing on a close study of Balinese texts, Nordholt argues that in nineteenth-century Bali the king had to provide political leadership, including leadership in war; that irrigation was not, as Geertz argues, a local affair, but rather an arena in which lords and commoners had shared interests; and that the court was vitally concerned with questions of trade and taxation. (A nineteenth-century European observer insisted that in Bali, "money is the nerve of power.")

It is more plausible to suppose that as colonial control was tightened the powers of the king were eroded, and the courts turned perforce to a symbolic politics. These adaptations in turn colored perceptions of the past. Something of the sort happened in Java, where the royal elite lost political power after 1830. "With no real room or will for political manoeuvre," M. C. Ricklefs comments, "the royal elite turned its energy towards cultural affairs . . . The courts . . . degenerated into an effete formalism, an elaborate and antiquated artificiality." Rather than representing "degeneration," this cultural politics may have been the only manner in which the aristocracy could express their resistance to colonialism.

On comparative grounds, it is difficult to believe that a hierarchical, large-scale political system could have survived for millennia simply in order to provide circuses, or even operas: and not once, but in many places, for Geertz regards Bali as a type-case for Southeast Asia. (Authorities on comparable systems elsewhere in the region are skeptical, and Stanley Tambiah specifically questions Geertz's distinction between ritual and political power in Southeast Asian states.) Even leaving aside the questions raised by regional specialists, *Negara* is an implausible model for a new kind of political theory, despite Quentin Skinner's endorsement of Geertz's grandiose claims to that effect in the final chapter of the book, "Bali and Political Theory." At best, the study may inadvertently draw attention to a particular strategy of anti-colonial resistance. However, his analysis of the *negara* does serve as an illuminating metaphor for Geertz's own mature theory. He depicts a society whose true life is governed by ideas, expressed in symbols, enacted in rituals. The ethnographer need only read the rituals, and interpret them. There is nothing outside the text, and if the texts pass over politics and economics in silence, then those matters can safely be ignored.

Geertz's mature writings have a central place in modern American anthropology, and they have fascinated scholars in cultural history, literary theory, and philosophy. They offer a coherent notion of "culture," defined as a domain of symbolic communication. They teach that to understand culture is to interpret its symbols. Geertz illustrated what he had in mind with intrinsically fascinating and also suggestive case studies that described exotic complexes of ideas and elaborate ritual performances. From time to time, he claims that a cultural perspective will lead to a revolution in moral philosophy or political theory, and this promise has surely encouraged some desperate characters in those overpopulated fields, in which involution has often led to shared poverty.

Yet his mature work does not offer what was promised in the original prospectus, a development of social theory. Rather, Geertz returns his readers to a tradition of interpretation that is familar to humanists. A professor of literature, Vincent Pecora, observes that "literary studies have appropriated Geertz's insights about as readily as Geertz himself borrowed literary tools." A historian, Donald Walters, remarks that "both [Geertz's] starting point and the distance he has traveled from it have an air of familiarity to historians." However, "coming from a supposedly more theoretical discipline," he did offer analytical clarity, a fresh vocabulary, and the timely promise (for the archives were as overpopulated as Javanese paddy fields) that if one paid close attention to apparently marginal practices one might learn some interesting things about the wider society.

And yet Geertz has been hailed as a theorist, and not only by anthropologists but by historians and literary scholars. When in 1977 a group of leading American intellectual historians met to discuss "new directions" in their field, Geertz—absent in the flesh—was pronounced "virtually the patron saint of the conference." In 1990, Robert Darnton proclaimed in general terms that "anthropology offers the historian what the study of *mentalité* has failed to provide, a coherent conception of culture," and he indicated that he meant in practice the anthropology offered by Geertz. "Reading Geertz," Ronald Walters remarks, writing of historians, "appears to be one of the few things shared by people who seldom read each other," and on the whole they do not read him to learn about Indonesia or Morocco, but to pick up ideas. Geertz is routinely cited on matters of culture, symbolism, meaning, and relativism by literary theorists, and in other fields by such luminaries as Jerome Bruner in psychology or Richard Rorty in philosophy. In cultural studies, he has become a guru for the less *marxisants* practitioners.

What Geertz offers in the end is an elegant endorsement of the project of interpretation, and he lends to this project the legitimacy of something that may be a science, and that is, at least, magically exotic in its range of reference. Some historians are reassured that they have been writing ethnographies all along, and cultural historians have been encouraged by Geertz's example to separate themselves from social and economic historians. As Geertz has distanced himself from social scientific approaches, he has come out as a traditional humanist. His references, his interests, his manner, and even the matters with which he deals have addressed, increasingly, what was once called high culture, and before that simply culture. Geertz's manner is also sympathetic: aphoristic, self-consciously literate, full of high cultural allusions and knowing references to Wittgenstein, Lionel Trilling, Kenneth Burke, and Richard Rorty. Finally, Geertz is himself something of a ruler in the most sacred groves of American academe. All in all, it is not surprising that humanists have been inspired by his example to explore the otherness of Jane Austen's world-view, or the charivari of eighteenth-century French tradesmen, or the elaborate ceremonials of the court at Versailles.

Within anthropology, there are two broad critical responses to Geertz's intellectual trajectory. One view holds that he abandoned the true path when he shifted from his concern with social history, economic change, and political revolution and began to treat culture as the prime mover in human affairs—and, in the end, as a sufficient field of study in itself. Authors of this persuasion dispute the dominant role Geertz attributes to culture. They argue that cultural models serve the political purposes of particular constituencies. Culture—or ideology—is contested and not simply swallowed. The other charge is that Geertz took the right path but stopped short. He did not dare to work through the implications of his insight that ethnographies were cultural constructs rather than straightforward attempts to tell it as it is. Though he is no positivist, he remains convinced that ethnography is in some sense a scientific pursuit.

The one party prefers the early Geertz, the other prefers the mature Geertz. But each underplays the central concern of his work. He sharpened and refined the definition of culture, and then treated it in its own terms—or in terms that he attributed to it—as a symbolic system, working by way of metaphors, a mélange of texts. Ultimately, culture came to mean for Geertz something very like the culture of the old humanists: the epitome of the values that rule in a society, embodied most perfectly in the religious rituals and the high art of the elite. These shifts in emphasis are mirrored in the growing ornateness of Geertz's own style, and by references that signal allegiance to the highest high culture to hand.

Above all, Geertz's message is that culture is the essential element in the definition of human nature, and the dominant force in history. *Negara* is his ultimate answer to the question posed by Parsons, about the role of culture in social action. Culture rules: indeed, *high* culture rules. It is a coherent vision, even if, under pressure, Geertz sometimes formulated it more loosely, and in weaker, less shocking terms. Notwithstanding his protestations to the contrary, the fact of the matter is that Geertz became an extreme idealist, and he is accordingly vulnerable to the familiar critique of ideological theories of history. The Parsonian program may have been overambitious, and Geertz's own early studies on Java illustrated some of the problems that arise when the elaborate Parsonian apparatus is taken into the field. Yet Parsons addressed the concerns of Weber, Marx, and Durkheim, and he was quite clear about the limitations of an idealist historiography or sociology. Geertz remained faithful, after his fashion, to Parsons's idea of culture and also to his critique of behaviorism, but he lost interest in sociological issues, though without explaining or justifying his shift. He merely illustrated it. In *Negara*, society is the mucky realm of the peasantry. Time stands still at the court, the true center of the world, for Balinese and anthropologist alike.

"I am going to revel in culture-specific accretions, pore over processes of ratiocination, and plunge headlong into symbolic systems," Geertz told an audience at the Yale Law School in 1981. "That does not make the world go away: it brings it into view." Yet part of the world does go away. National politicians, Indonesian soldiers, CIA operatives, overseas Chinese entrepreneurs are lost to view. The world that we are introduced to in Geertz's later work seems to be very different from the world in which we are accustomed to live. It is also less complex, less *lived-in,* than the world of Indonesian villagers and townsfolk that is described in Geertz's early monographs. A world *has* been lost, and it is not evident that another world has been gained.

Chapter 4

DAVID SCHNEIDER:

BIOLOGY

AS CULTURE

> There are only cultural constructions of reality . . . In this sense, then, "nature" and the "facts of life" . . . have no independent existence apart from how they are defined by the culture.
>
> *David Schneider*

In 1973 Talcott Parsons had picked out Clifford Geertz and David Schneider as the up-and-coming anthropologists of the new school, but if Clifford Geertz was to end up as the establishment anthropologist, David Schneider remained always an anti-establishment man, a maverick, a trickster, something of a troublemaker, out to shock the orthodox, never at peace with his colleagues or with himself. Nevertheless it was Schneider who remained in his quirky way the more loyal Parsonian. Born in Brooklyn in 1918, he died in Santa Cruz, California, in 1995, not the only anarchist and postmodernist in that state, but probably the only one who hoped that Parsons was coming back into fashion at last.

His parents were first-generation immigrants, devout Communists, atheists, and anti-Zionist Jews. After he had displayed an alarming inability to sublimate sibling rivalry, Schneider was sent to a progressive boarding school, where "I learned to read, but I never really learned to write, and I never really learned arithmetic. And my spelling is atrocious." He later became fascinated, for a while, by Freudian theory, and it is tempting to cast him in a Freudian case-study, doomed forever to replay his unresolved conflicts with his parents and his brother. To the end of his life he had difficulties with authority figures, and was acutely rivalrous toward contemporaries; however, a good father himself, he had loving and loyal relationships with many of his students, to whom he was generally indulgent. ("I gave everybody an 'A' unless there was something which prevented me from doing so.")

Schneider attended what was in effect a poor man's premedical course at the New York State College of Agriculture at Cornell. Finding that he could not master organic chemistry, he took a course in rural sociology, in which it was said that everyone could get A's. A further, unanticipated, benefit was an introduction to anthropology at the hands of R. Lauriston Sharp, who had recently completed his doctorate at Harvard. Easily diverted from agricultural bacteriology, and by now a married man, Schneider progressed to Yale as a graduate student in anthropology.

Yale had established its own interdisciplinary social science institute, the School of Human Relations, but in contrast to the Parsonians at Harvard its members were generally committed to a positivist approach that they called "behaviorism." George Peter Murdock, who presided over anthropology at Yale, put great faith in numbers, while Schneider's unfortunate inability to learn arithmetic at school left him unable to pass even the most elementary qualifying examinations in statistics. Murdock was also a New England Christian gentleman, a type to which Schneider was antipathetic. He recalled that he "didn't like [Murdock], couldn't get along with him, and did not like his anthropology." As soon as he had an offer of a suitable job, he told Murdock that he was withdrawing from the program. "And he, in the first sign of any humanity that I had ever seen, stood up from his desk, put his hand awkwardly on my shoulder, and said, 'I know you will be a success at something, David, but it isn't anthropology, is it?' I said, 'No, sir, I am quitting anthropology forever.' "

The job had been arranged by a sympathetic English anthropologist at Yale, Geoffrey Gorer, via Margaret Mead. It was based in Washington, with the Division of Program Surveys, an agency of the Department of Agriculture. He rapidly got into trouble. ("So I was not very tactful about telling Riley that he didn't know his ass from his elbow . . .") After being drafted into the army, where he served as a clerk (soon in trouble again), he decided upon demobilization to return to academic study. Margaret Mead helped him to find a place in Kluckhohn's department at Harvard in 1946, a favor she was to repeat three years later for Clifford Geertz.

Almost thirty by now, Schneider found that the brand-new Department of Social Relations offered a sympathetic intellectual milieu, and one in which his raw, self-destructive outbursts were tolerated. Parsons was an acceptable father-figure, for reasons that remain obscure. (Perhaps he was rather a sort of grandfather.) Schneider's own explanation was that "I liked him a great deal because I thought he was very clear," though perhaps he was joking. ("And he seemed to be raising and answering a host of questions which I had only thought about vaguely, but which were clearly ones that I wanted to be concerned with.")

He did not regard Kluckhohn with the same awe—"Clyde had parties at his house. He talked to us by first name. There was a lot of fun and joking"—and characteristically he elected to challenge Kluckhohn at his Ph.D. qualifying examination. Something of a Freudian at this stage, Schneider was working in the (still fashionable) culture and personality field. The original theory, popularized by Ruth Benedict and Margaret Mead, was that each culture is associated with a specific personality type. This rather general proposition could be elaborated in one of two ways. Benedict herself argued that a culture could exhibit all the characteristics of a personality:

there were paranoid cultures, manic cultures, buttoned-up anal-retentive cultures, and so on. Margaret Mead was intrigued rather by the impact of culture on personality development. But whatever specific form it took, the cultural approach played down biological constraints on personality, and at Schneider's oral examination Kluckhohn accordingly asked a question about the relationship between biology and psychology.

> I told him that to the best of my knowledge, and to the best of anybody else's knowledge, biology didn't have a damn thing to do with psychology. That until they could establish some kinds of relations between the biological and the psychological that really amounted to something . . . we should proceed as if there were no basic biological considerations.

Kluckhohn was frankly appalled, and at the end of the examination Schneider returned home and told his wife that they had better start packing, because he was about to be thrown off his course of study. Kluckhohn, however, allowed him to pass. Schneider later suggested that Kluckhohn had personal reasons for wishing to believe that biology shaped human conduct. Kluckhohn was secretly gay, and according to Schneider he found it comforting to suppose that his sexual orientation was inborn. Yet Schneider did not speculate about the reasons for his own provocative challenge to Kluckhohn, and he offered no explanation for his gut antipathy to the notion that biology might be a significant factor in personality development, or, as he later came to believe, in kinship. He also explicitly denied that his challenge to Kluckhohn, and his antagonism to Murdock, were rooted in an antipathy to his own father ("in fact, my relationship to my father was not antipathetic").

Once Kluckhohn had passed him, the next step was to find funds and a site for fieldwork. Ironically, the problem was solved by Murdock, who had been chosen by the U.S. Navy to supervise an ambitious series of field studies in Micronesia. The Navy had been appointed to administer the Micronesian territories that the United

States had captured from the Japanese in the course of World War II. Murdock was well placed to land the Navy's contracts for social research, since he had been commissioned as a Naval officer and supplied background materials on the region during the Pacific war, an experience that had persuaded him "of the need of selling social science by demonstrating its practical utility."

Murdock subcontracted the research, and twenty-one expeditions were eventually financed. Harvard drew Yap. That island was best known for the fact that its population had suffered a remarkable decline, from an estimated 30,000 before colonial occupation, to under 8,000 at the end of the nineteenth century, to a mere 2,582 in 1946, according to the first American census. Predictably, the general problem chosen for investigation was this extraordinary demographic collapse, and a team of four, including two biological anthropologists, a sociologist, and a cultural anthropologist, David Schneider, were dispatched to the field in 1947. (In due course, Schneider quarreled with his three associates and, inevitably, with the Navy.)

Not only was the project controlled by Murdock, but Schneider came to focus on the kinship system in Yap, and so he was engaged in a field he had learned from Murdock. Murdock had become an international leader in kinship studies with the publication in 1949 of *Social Structure,* a book that offered a positivist account of the laws of kinship systems, buttressed by cross-cultural statistical tests. The world's kinship systems were arranged into types according to their systems of classifying kin, and associations were established between forms of kinship terminology, residence rules, marriage prescriptions, and so on.

Schneider's report on kinship in Yap followed the lines laid down by Murdock; but, inevitably, it contained a challenge. He tried to demonstrate that the Yap kinship terminology could not be fitted into Murdock's scheme. Yap kin terms, he reported, did not specify genealogical relationships. They were not strictly speaking terms for kin at all, as non-relatives might be lumped together with relatives in a single category. Since Murdock's whole system of comparison rested on the classification of kinship terminologies, this was potentially a radical line of argument. If it was true, then Murdock's cross-cultural research rested on an illusion. The challenge was also somewhat reckless, since Murdock's report on the thesis was to be considered by Schneider's examiners. As it turned out, this was the only feature of the thesis on which Murdock commented in his report, and he was damning—

> saying that the material I had presented was unlike anything he had ever seen in any ethnography in his life. It was essentially unbelievable . . . Well, I stuck to my guns pretty well. Kluckhohn said, "Well, what the hell! Kinship terminology—who gives a shit!" He accepted my thesis, Parsons accepted my thesis, Doug Oliver [the Pacific specialist at Harvard] accepted my thesis, and that was it.

Parsons and Kluckhohn were perhaps quite content to let Schneider tease the rival School of Human Relations at Yale. In any case, Kluckhohn continued as Schneider's patron, conjuring up a Fulbright fellowship that allowed him to teach for two years in England, at the London School of Economics (from 1949 to 1951). Schneider was now introduced into the intimate, rivalrous milieu of British social anthropology, which was at the time focused intellectually, and with singular intensity, on the study of kinship systems. At the LSE he worked happily with two of Malinowski's most distinguished associates, Raymond Firth and Audrey Richards, and he later co-edited a collection of essays that elaborated Audrey Richards's general model of matrilineal kinship systems. However, he reacted in characteristically prickly fashion to slights, real and imagined, from other British social anthropologists. The first published volley in his campaign against kinship studies was aimed at the British leaders in the field, and with characteristic chutzpah Schneider fired it off at a conference that had been arranged specifically to promote good relations between British and American social anthropologists. In his paper, Schneider attacked most of the leading British social anthropologists. He later remarked that the occasion gave him the opportunity to dismiss, more generally, the whole field of kinship studies: "it was a good chance for me to essentially say, 'Fuck off! I've had it with that stuff.' And that was good."

When Schneider returned to the States, Kluckhohn found soft funds to employ him as a teacher at Harvard from 1951 to 1955. He now collaborated with a senior Harvard sociologist, George Homans, on a cross-cultural analysis of a form of cousin marriage. Working with a hypothesis of Radcliffe-Brown's, the aim was to provide a psychological theory of cross-cousin marriage in competition with Lévi-Strauss's structuralist theory. Like the book Schneider edited on Audrey Richards's model of matrilineal societies, and like his essays of the period on double descent on Yap, this work was based on the assumption that kinship systems in different parts of the world shared common characteristics.

Kluckhohn then arranged for Schneider to spend the academic year 1955–56 at the Center for Advanced Study in the Behavioral Sciences at Stanford. Kluckhohn and Kroeber still worked closely together, and they now set up appointments for both Schneider and Geertz at the anthropology department at Berkeley, where Kroeber, though officially retired, remained influential. Schneider was also allowed to recruit L. T. Fallers to join them. However, he quickly became thoroughly discontented with his situation. He decided that the Berkeley department "was really screwed up," and he was eager to move on. Compounding his demoralization, his new field project, another kinship study, set among the Mescalero Apache, was also not going well. He had quarreled with a key informant and then with a collaborator, and finally abandoned the whole thing. In 1960 he left Berkeley to join the anthropology department at the University of Chicago, taking Geertz and Fallers with him. Kluckhohn and Kroeber were not pleased by the ungrateful behavior of their protégés, and Schneider was left with an uneasy feeling that he had not acted with due loyalty. (Both Kluckhohn and Kroeber died during the summer of their move to Chicago. Schneider, who was undergoing psychoanalysis between 1958 and 1960, may have mused that his Oedipal challenge had been horrifyingly effective.)

At Chicago, in his forties by now, Schneider was in a position to play a leading role in a successful revolution. American anthropology departments were still generally based on the established "four fields" conception. Cultural anthropology was combined with physical anthropology, archaeology, and linguistics in a joint endeavor, which was defined as the study of human evolution, or (the Boasian view) as the history of human populations. The old structure was already anachronistic. It no longer shaped the bulk of research projects that were taking shape in the anthropology departments. In most universities, cultural anthropology had emerged as a distinct specialization, with only tenuous and often distinctly uncollegial connections to physical anthropology and archaeology. At the University of Chicago, the cultural anthropologists had established a different set of alliances. This was partly a result of their association with a school of sociology that was itself famous for ethnographic research. Robert Redfield in particular had built bridges between the "social" anthropologists and the sociologists at Chicago. The British social anthropologist A. R. Radcliffe-Brown, who had been a member of the Chicago faculty from 1931 to 1937, taught that social anthropology should be a form of comparative sociology, and he had brought the very sociological anthropologist Lloyd Warner to the department. He also became the mentor of two key Chicago social anthropologists, Fred Eggan and Sol Tax.

The young men, Schneider, Geertz, and Fallers, wanted to displace the remaining institutional vestiges of the four fields approach at Chicago, but they had little sympathy for the sociological anthropology of the old guard. Their project was to restructure the department so that it could participate in the new project of Talcott Parsons. Anthropology was to be the science of culture. "I beat the culture drum. Geertz beat the culture drum. We both got it through Parsons from Kroeber and Kluckhohn."

So we all agreed to put in a Parsonian program. There were two parallel courses, "The Human Career"—that was essentially done by the physical anthropologists doing human evolution, and the archaeologists doing what they regarded as history—and then the social or cultural side. We divided social from cultural, so you had three "systems" courses: social systems, cultural systems, and then psychological systems.

It was probably inevitable, however, that Schneider would turn against his closest associates. The immediate disagreements had to do with American policy in the Congo, where the Kennedy administration had let the CIA loose in a cloak-and-dagger operation to destabilize the government of the day. Arguments about American adventures in the Third World became more acute as military involvement in Vietnam escalated. The campuses were riven, and Schneider began to quarrel with Geertz and Fallers about the politicization of the university. On these issues, Schneider was on the left, Geertz and Fallers right of center. Schneider also resented the fact that Geertz and Fallers were associated with the conservative social theorist Edward Shils, Parsons's former collaborator, in the Committee for the Comparative Study of New Nations, a prestigious think-tank for the study of the post-colonial states. Schneider felt that he was being sidelined, and he suspected that Geertz and Fallers thought that they were dealing with really important issues and big societies, while he was just an old-fashioned, small-island ethnographer.

At the end of the 1960s the triumvirate fell apart. Fallers became seriously ill, and died young. In 1970, Geertz moved to a position at the Institute for Advanced Study. It was at this time that Schneider, who remained in Chicago, issued the work on which his reputation was to depend. He chose America for his case study, an assertion, perhaps, that he, too, was not just a small-island man. His subject was the analysis of kinship in strictly cultural terms. This was to be his mature and decisive rebellion against the orthodoxies: against the coupling of cultural anthropology with social or biological anthropology; and within cultural anthropology, against kinship theory, its sacred heart.

Despite all its internecine quarrels, anthropology had always rested on the certainty that kinship was the foundation of "primitive" social systems. Kinship was perhaps the one field in which social and cultural anthropology could claim to have booked secure advances. To the extent that anthropologists had developed a sociological theory to call their own, this was kinship theory. Schneider set out to undermine it. He intended to prove that kinship theory was founded on an ethnocentric illusion, that the basic concepts of kinship theory—genealogies, descent, the family itself—were culturally specific creations of the Europeans and North Americans. When anthropologists wrote about kinship they were simply projecting their own cultural obsessions onto other peoples.

But that was barely the half of it. Schneider's cultural relativism carried an even more radical sting in its tail. The orthodox view was that all kinship systems rested on the foundations of a universal human biology. Schneider conceded that he could not "make biology and sexual intercourse go away . . . All known kinship systems use biological relationship and/or sexual intercourse in the cultural specification of what kinship is." But so far as the cultural anthropologist was concerned, it was not biology itself that mattered, but rather what people believed to be the case about human biology. Starting from these principles, Schneider mounted the most subversive of the culturalist programs, the deconstruction *(avant la lettre)* of the ark of the anthropological covenant, kinship.

There are enough clues in Schneider's biography to prompt a psychological explanation of his choice of kinship as a subject for deconstruction. His childhood had been disrupted, and he felt that he had been rejected by his family. He may have picked up from his father something of the classic Marxist belief that kinship was part of the superstructure of capitalism, the family a bourgeois invention. His animus against any biological explanation was also deep-seated.

In any case, Schneider was not content with parricide. He embarked on a wholesale slaughter of the ancestors.

The slim volume that constituted Schneider's manifesto, *American Kinship: A Cultural Account,* was published in 1968, a vintage year for revolutionary pronouncements. Schneider introduced himself as a long-time Parsonian ("my interest in developing a theory of culture which could accord with Talcott Parsons's theory of social action started when I returned to graduate school in 1946"). As a Parsonian anthropologist, his aim was to offer a "cultural account" of kinship, as a system of symbols: "The book is about symbols, the symbols which are American kinship." It was none of his business, as a disciplined member of the anthropologists' section of Parsons's party, to treat sociological issues. Schneider accordingly paid no attention to such questions as rates of marriage, divorce, or births; household composition; or regional or class variations.

His study had initially been conceived in collaboration with Raymond Firth, the idea being that they would deliver comparable accounts of American and British kinship. Schneider said later that he had taken the project on only out of a sense of obligation to Firth, but as it turned out he found Firth's study too sociological for his taste, and he withdrew from the joint venture. To be sure, even a Parsonian anthropologist had to acknowledge that there was room for a sociological approach to kinship, and Schneider initially paid lip service to Kluckhohn's formula that symbolic constructs may provide "a model to live by." But he insisted on strict adherence to the Parsonian division of labor. What Parsons termed "social action" should be left to the sociologists. Anthropologists were students of culture. As a system of symbols, culture is quite distinct from patterns of observed behavior; indeed, "these two are to be understood as *independent* of each other." "I have chosen to assume the significance of symbol and meaning in the total pattern of action, and to go ahead and study that." Moreover, symbols were not only independent of observed behavior; they might have no anchor at all in the real world. Parsons had argued that a symbolic system was autonomous and self-contained. Schneider concurred: "By symbol I mean something which stands for something else, where there is no necessary or intrinsic relationship between the symbol and that which it symbolizes."

This was, of course, a well-established idea, endorsed by Saussure and by Peirce, the pioneers of semiology. Yet Schneider went beyond Parsons. Not only is the symbol arbitrary, but the referents, the things or the ideas for which the symbols stand, are themselves cultural constructs. They may have no objective reality at all. As an example of what he meant, Schneider offered the idea of ghosts. Informants may have all sorts of fantastic notions about ghosts, but the ethnographer has no way of knowing whether or not ghosts exist. What matters is therefore only what informants believe to be the case about ghosts. From this uncontentious observation he derived, more problematically, a general rule.

> Since it is perfectly possible to formulate . . . the cultural construct of ghosts without actually visually inspecting even a single specimen, this should be true across the board and without reference to the observability or non observability of objects that may be presumed to be the referents of the cultural constructs.

Now it is all very well to summon up the spirit of Saussure in order to assert that signs are arbitrary, but it does not necessarily follow that all signs refer to imaginary constructs, free from the constraints of reality. Ghosts may be figments of the collective imagination, but the category "rain" (for example) might refer to a fact of nature for which every language had a word. And symbolic representations are not always arbitrary. Dark clouds are universally associated with rain, and are often evoked to stand for the concept of a coming storm. Schneider insisted, however, that "a cultural unit or cultural construct must be distinguished from any other object elsewhere in the real world." It followed that the symbols of kinship must be treated as though they were arbitrary, and the concepts to which kinship symbols refer should not be confused with what we quaintly call the facts of life. Just as a religious symbol might refer to ghosts, so kinship symbols denote culturally constructed ideas.

What, then, was the core symbol of American kinship? It was, Schneider announced, *sexual intercourse*. This was a surprising, perhaps even a shocking proposition. It is not immediately obvious that the values of American kinship are summed up in sexual intercourse, nor, indeed, that sexual intercourse is best understood as a symbol, let alone an arbitrary symbol that has no intrinsic connection to the facts of procreation and parenthood. No evidence was offered to support these striking claims. Did the solid citizens of Chicago, interrogated in the early 1960s by Schneider's assistants, volunteer that kinship and the family all boiled down in the end to sexual intercourse? That seems unlikely, yet Schneider did not doubt that he had grasped the essence of the matter. "The fact of nature on which the cultural construct of the family is based is . . . that of sexual intercourse. This figure provides all of the central symbols of American kinship." (The phrase "fact of nature" was to be understood, of course, ironically. "Nature" itself was a category in an idiosyncratic system of ethnobiology.)

Not every conceivable act of sexual intercourse was an appropriate symbol. Americans apparently believe—or believed back then, when the data were collected in the early 1960s, on the eve of the sexual revolution—that sexual acts between a man and a woman should not simply be a matter of the passionate coupling of two animals. Alfred Charles Kinsey's reports on American sexual behavior, published in 1948 and 1953, indicated that Americans allowed themselves considerable latitude in their behavior. But Schneider had no doubts about the American cultural rule: sexual intercourse was proper only between a husband and wife, and even then it had to be genital to genital, with no fancy business.

And what did this approved mode of sexual intercourse stand for, symbolically? Decent sex expressed love. "Sexual intercourse between husband and wife is not only an act which specifically defines the conjugal relationship, but it is also an act which is a sign of love." Parents share a common substance with their children, and common substance gives rise to another kind of love, the love of blood relatives. There are therefore two very different kinds of love, the conjugal and the cognatic. Erotic love goes with marriage, cognatic love with blood relationship. Conjugal love "is erotic, having the sexual act as its concrete embodiment." Cognatic love "has nothing erotic about it." Nevertheless, Schneider points out that (in the American view) the blood relationship between parents and children is a product of sexual intercourse. And so, he suggests, cognatic love is also symbolized by sexual intercourse.

The proposition is, then, that sexual intercourse symbolizes love, and "love is what American kinship is all about." The simplicity of this proposition is misleading, however. Not only are there apparently two very different conceptions of love, but it turns out that love is itself a symbolic expression. "It is the symbol of love which links conjugal and cognatic love together and relates them both to and through the symbol of sexual intercourse." Love, it seems, is at once the very substance of kinship and a symbol of something else. With the best will in the world, there is no way to sort out this confusion between symbol and concept. Schneider is culpably content with a mélange in which signifier and signified are hopelessly muddled: "Sexual intercourse is love and stands as a sign of love, and love stands for sexual intercourse and is a sign of it. The two different kinds of love, conjugal and cognatic, the one erotic, the other not, are nevertheless both symbols for unity, oneness, togetherness, belonging."

So what, finally, is love? "Love," Schneider asserts, "can be translated freely as *enduring, diffuse solidarity*." Gentle reader, mock not. Certainly the question of what is love's true essence has been addressed more elegantly, but the shock of Schneider's proposition lies only partly in its insistently philistine language. He was fully aware that his definition of love would not appeal to poets, or to the lovelorn. One might object more pertinently that this idea of love seems to be very different from the native conceptions of Americans, as these were represented in American popular songs and movies of the 1960s. Reviewing *American Kinship* in the *American Anthropologist*, Anthony Wallace insisted that Americans think that falling in love, and being in love, are natural, that love is a force of nature like magnetism and gravity. It may be irresistible, riding over social barriers of "class, age, race, marital status, and even blood relationship." But however strange Schneider's definition might seem to the American-in-the-street, the language in which it was set out would have been familiar to the sociologist. Parsons had himself formulated a rather similar definition of the ideal type of romantic love as diffuse, particularistic, and affective. The terms "diffuse, enduring solidarity" all correspond to Parsonian pattern variables (the values that, Parsons believed, express cross-culturally the criteria by which people evaluate relationships). But Schneider did not reveal this particular debt to Parsons; it might have diluted the shock of this "free translation" of what Americans meant by love. His overriding aim was to bounce his readers into accepting that, in contradiction to what they intuitively believed, even sexual intercourse is a symbol, even love is a convention. The message was that kinship is not natural: it is cultural.

But this was only a preliminary move. Claude Lévi-Strauss had argued that kinship systems were all based on a universal opposition between nature and culture. Schneider proceeded to argue that the very distinction between culture and nature is a Western fabrication. Americans construct an opposition between culture and nature, and (waving away all those romantics in their literary tradition) he affirmed that they value culture above nature. Nature has some features that are good, others that are dangerous, even evil, and so nature must be brought under moral, cultural control. Human beings are themselves a mix of nature and culture, but it is their cultural identity that makes them human. Morality tames the animal beneath the skin. Nature is improved, moralized, by the application of law and reason. And, as Schneider remarked, these American notions about the order of law added up to something very like a classic anthropological definition of culture. "In America, it is the order of law, that is, culture, which resolves the contradictions between man and nature, which are contradictions within nature itself."

This culturally constructed opposition between nature and culture structures American thinking about kinship. A person may be a kinsman by nature or by culture—or, as Americans say, there are relatives by blood and relatives by law. "The rule is very simple," Schneider concluded. "A person is a relative if he is related by blood or marriage." Relatives in nature are born; relatives in law are acquired through marriage. Blood ties are natural, while the connections arising from marriage are defined by Americans themselves as relationships "in law." In contrast to blood relatives, who are given by nature, one acquires relatives by marriage in consequence of a choice of a marriage partner, a choice that may be annulled. A relationship in law is therefore established by custom, and it is guided by a conventional "code for conduct," a moral rule that expresses love.

But this neat opposition between relatives by blood and relatives by law had to be qualified. Ideally, culture humanizes nature. A person might be a relative both by blood and by "code of conduct." For example, a child born out of wedlock is called a "natural" or an "illegitimate" child. There is a blood relationship, but it is not hallowed by law. In contrast, an adoptive child is legally one's son or daughter, but is not a blood relative. Ideally, Americans feel, a child should be both natural and legitimate, born to a mother and father who are married to each other. The paradigmatic kinship relationships combine the two principles of law and nature. Relationships in nature, they are at the same time motivated by an appropriate moral "code for conduct" founded on love, which implies an ethic of diffuse, enduring solidarity.

According to Schneider, when Americans talk in shorthand of blood ties they mean both a biological relationship and a code of conduct. "[Blood] not only means the red stuff which courses through the veins, but also that combination of substance and code of conduct which those who share that red stuff, the blood relatives, should have." Whether a blood relative is treated as a relative or not is a function of genealogical distance (which calibrates the amount of common substance that the two relatives share) and social distance, which is determined by such factors as geographical dispersal, difference of social class, and so on. Genealogical links do not guarantee effective kinship. Only some relatives beyond the immediate family circle are treated as such. On the other hand, the Famous Relative, who crops up in many genealogies, illustrates the fact that distance may also be obliterated where it pays to do so.

Considering how central these concepts were to his account, it is remarkable that Schneider never unpacked the notion of "blood" or "common substance," the "natural" element in kinship. It is not evident that Americans conceived of all natural—or "natural"—relations of kinship as "blood" relationships. According to Schneider, husband and wife are not related by blood, but by law: "marriage is simply the code for conduct without the substantive (biogenetic) element." Yet he himself insisted that Americans understood the relationship between spouses to be in some sense natural. "Informants describe the family as consisting of husband, wife, and their children who live together as a natural unit. The family is formed according to the laws of nature and it lives by rules which are regarded by Americans as self-evidently natural." According to a common American view, the family could be observed among some animals and birds. It was based on a natural division of functions between father, mother, and children. Many Americans apparently also believed that love was a natural force, and Anthony Wallace suggested that in consequence Americans saw marriage as being in part natural, "the natural aspect being sexual love."

The conception of relatives in law was equally problematic. Some persons are kin despite the fact that they are not blood relations. Schneider suggested that their kinship flows from a legal agreement (such as marriage or adoption). But he observed that unrelated people might be pressed into the role of relatives by the application of an appropriate "code of conduct"—as, for instance, in the case of the family friend who is called "uncle" or "aunt." If the "code of conduct" is followed, it may be enough on its own to make a person a relative. He concluded that adopted children, parents-in-law, and honorary uncles are all the same kind of relatives: relatives in law, people who are not related by blood but who nevertheless follow the appropriate code for conduct toward kin. Yet this assortment of affines, adopted kin, and courtesy kin seem to have little in common except for the fact that they are not kin by blood, and there is evidence that Americans did not intuitively lump together adoptive children with relations by marriage. In a contemporaneous analysis of Yankee kinship terminology, Ward Goodenough found that a distinction was made between relatives by marriage, on the one hand, and adoptive relatives, on the other. (For reasons that were not explained, Schneider decided to exclude step-relatives, adopted kin, and half-kin from his genealogies.)

Nor are all relatives by marriage much of a muchness. According to Goodenough, Yankees distinguished between two categories of relations by marriage: in-laws, and aunts and uncles by marriage. When Americans speak of "aunt" or "uncle," they include in the category both blood relatives, the siblings of their parents, and relatives by marriage, the husbands or wives of these people. Schneider himself provided evidence that undermined his assertion that there are two kinds of aunts and uncles: he quoted a child who said that his uncle's divorced wife was indeed his aunt, because she was the mother of his cousin. The child's rule was apparently that the mother of a blood relative must be a blood relative. Anthony Wallace pointed out a further problem with Schneider's strict dichotomy between blood kin and in-laws: he has nothing to say about the sexual tensions between cousins, and the not uncommon phenomenon of marriage between cousins.

A still more difficult problem arises from Schneider's insistence that a code of conduct, or even the use of a kinship term of reference, is sufficient to constitute kinship. This leads him to argue that Americans do not intend any distinction when they use the term "father" for a "real" father and a metaphorical "father," such as a Catholic priest. Harold Scheffler has argued that Schneider got himself into this absurd position because he was determined, for *a priori* theoretical reasons, not to acknowledge that Americans (perhaps like most people everywhere) operate with a genealogical framework in mind. In cases where non-kin are allowed a kinship designation (the family friend who is addressed by the children as "uncle," or a fellow-Elk who must be referred to as "brother"), this may be a metaphorical extension that people recognize as such.

However, Schneider was bound by the logic of his argument to reject the view that Americans may use kin terms in a consciously metaphorical way. Metaphorical usage could be distinguished only on the condition that a kinship term had a primary meaning that referred to a genealogical position. He objected that genealogical connection is not a sufficient reason to count somebody as a relative. Americans sometimes chose to ignore distant relatives, even if they were aware of a genealogical connection. Nor is genealogical connection a necessary reason for the identification of a relative, since my mother's friend may be my "uncle." It is the "code of conduct" that is decisive. It is because a child follows the appropriate "code for conduct" that a person is to be counted as an "aunt" or "uncle." These points may be conceded, yet the conclusion does not necessarily follow. Americans may neglect some of their relatives, and may use kin terms—perhaps metaphorically—for some non-kin, and yet still treat genealogical connection as the bedrock of kinship. Schneider had himself insisted that, for Americans, red blood was more important than blood in any other sense, and the genealogical studies carried out by his team of researchers provided a good deal of evidence to suggest that their Chicago informants operated with genealogical conceptions. (It is worth noting that the published field report on

Schneider's project, *The American Kin Universe* by Schneider and Cottrell [1975], was subtitled *A Genealogical Study*.)

These are by no means the only problems raised by the analysis. In a later essay, Schneider argued that it had perhaps been a mistake to assume that American kinship constituted a distinctive domain of American culture. After all, religion and nationality also embody the values of diffuse, enduring solidarity. However, he exhibited a peculiar, almost willful, blindness to the salience of American religion, and he ignored religious values in his account of kinship. Yet is is evident that American kinship notions encode not only American ideas of biology and law, but also religious conceptions, as Schneider conceded in a throwaway passage in a later book (incidentally eliding "American," "Western," and "European" cultural themes).

> Western cultural constructs of kinship depend heavily not merely on the notion of biological relatedness, but also on the notion of creation . . . God the father, the priest as father, Mary mother of God, and so forth, are all very closely involved with ordinary fatherhood and motherhood in European culture.

Recent American controversies about abortion suggest that when Americans think about procreation they have more than the biology of reproduction in mind. A cultural account of American beliefs about procreation cannot realistically ignore ideas about the sanctity of life.

It may seem extraordinary that Schneider's analysis of American notions of kinship should have been so descriptively impoverished, but his final confessional book made it clear that he was drawing on his own experience rather than disciplining his intuitions by a close reading of what his informants told him—or rather, what they told the interviewers marshaled by his field managers (ever-changing, for there were, inevitably, quarrels).

> I read every single interview that came in, and I talked to every interviewer either about that interview or about how things were going, and we met weekly and discussed what was happen-

ing, etc. And I do not believe that anything more than minor alterations or emendations or ornamentations on my basic presuppositions arose either from the interview material or from the discussions from the interviewers that in some way changed my picture of what the hell was happening, what the schema was like.

He even boasted that when he wrote his monograph he had refused to consult his notes. This so enraged his wife, who had typed out extracts for his use, that she spent a day destroying her work.

Schneider's reliance on his own intuition was not the only problem. Another source of bias was the selection of interviewees, who were all middle-class, white Chicagoans. Had Schneider studied a more diverse sample, it would have been less easy to sustain the claim that there was a single American kinship system. Were there no class or regional and ethnic differences in the symbolism of kinship? Schneider denied their significance. Underlying superficial variations, there was a single American culture. This conclusion was soon challenged by other scholars, who believed that there was, on the contrary, considerable evidence to suggest that American family and kinship systems varied significantly among ethnic groups, social classes, and regions.

Schneider was sufficiently moved by these criticisms to undertake a special study in collaboration with his Chicago colleague Raymond T. Smith, an authority on Caribbean kinship. Comparing the kinship conceptions of lower-class (largely black) and middle-class (white) Chicagoans, they discovered substantial variation at the level of the norms. For example, middle-class whites emphasized the independence of the nuclear family, while working-class blacks did not. There was also systematic variation in the conceptions of the roles of men and women within the family. They also noted marked differences in actual behavior, determined partly by the variation in norms, but also by other factors, such as employment patterns, housing, and so on. Perhaps precisely in order to cope with these complications, Schneider now proposed a refined definition of culture that specifically, and conveniently, excluded norms, let alone practices. Given such a restricted definition of culture, he saw no need to amend his hypothesis. There was one symbolic system, one American culture. He conceded that there might be variations in the norms that people propounded. In consequence, they might make very different choices with respect to marriage, divorce, or residence. All that was irrelevant to a cultural account. The fundamental cultural conceptions about blood, marriage, family, relationship, and so forth were constant across all classes of Americans.

Schneider's central claim was that he had captured the native view of American kinship. The grounds for doubting this have been sketched. Even the most suggestible American readers may well have been surprised to learn, for instance, that sexual intercourse symbolized the love of parents and children, or that what people really meant when they talked of love was "diffuse, enduring solidarity," or that marriage was not "natural." Yet while Schneider's fidelity to American intuitions may be debatable, his account did not come out of nowhere. It clearly echoed Parsons's sociological account of American kinship. Although generously acknowledging Parsons as the father of his theoretical project, Schneider did not discuss the substantive account of the American family that Parsons offered. Yet the coincidences are remarkable, the more so since, in characteristic fashion, Parsons was concerned with "social action," precisely the realm of choice and action from which Schneider so fastidiously distanced himself.

For Parsons, the family was a product of cultural, social, and psychological forces. The peculiarities of American family structure were a consequence of modernization and secularization, functional differentiation and economic specialization, and the attendant rise of individualism. Schneider's initial summary of the nature of American kinship closely followed what Parsons had to say on the subject, even to the point of characterizing American kinship as an industrial variant of a worldwide set of kinship systems. Kinship groups in modern societies have shed the functions they typically fulfill elsewhere, in the economy and in relation to religion and politics. According to both Parsons and Schneider, it was precisely the functional specialization of American kinship that made it a privileged instance for the student of kinship systems. Parsons had written that the modern family, stripped of the functions it performed in traditional societies, presents "a kind of natural experimental situation." Schneider agreed. "It makes particularly good sense, it seems to me, to study kinship in as close to its 'pure form' as possible here in America, rather than in some other society where it is hidden beneath layers of economic, political, religious, and other elements."

But there was also a deeper sense in which Schneider's analysis was Parsonian. For a Parsonian, society was a system made up of subsystems, each with its particular function to perform. In each domain of social life the social actor plays a particular role. The set of roles constitutes the social person. Schneider adopted this model, but translated it into purely cultural terms. Each subsystem was defined not by its functions, but by its core symbol. The actor is also a symbolic construct, the *person,* whose attributes derive from various symbolic fields. "A person as a cultural unit is a composite, a compound of different elements from different symbolic subsystems or domains." Some of a person's attributes are drawn from the kinship system, others from the sex-role system, the age-role system, occupational and religious systems, and so forth, "each defined by reference to its own self-contained set of symbols from its own domain." Each of these subsystems adds its bit to the construction of the rounded person, defining who that person is, and providing "a normative guide for how such a person should behave or how such a person should act." This notion of the person was offered as a description of an American folk cultural category, on a par with American notions of family, company, city, or nation. However, it is remarkably like Parsons's notion of the actor, who must play many roles. It does not, on the other hand, match the common American idea of the self-motivated "individual."

If Schneider's book is read as a contribution to the Parsonian enterprise, it raises a curious paradox. He aimed to produce a purely cultural account of American kinship, fulfilling the specialized function allotted to anthropologists in the Parsonian division of labor. Yet the result was congruent with Parsons's account of the American family analyzed from the outside as a system of social action, the product of values, norms, and social and psychological imperatives. Schneider claimed simply to be restating the folk ideas of Americans, and yet if he was right, then it seemed that Americans were all Parsonian sociologists. The implication was that orthodox sociological theories were as American as apple pie. It followed that they were just as culturally specific. Social scientists delivered accurate, if labored, translations of American ideas. However, there was no reason to believe that American folk ideas were replicated in other cultures.

Similarly, the biological theory of kinship is also true, but again only as an account of American ideas. The anthropological distinction between nature and culture is a Western convention. Lévi-Strauss's thesis that all peoples build an opposition between culture and nature into their cosmological thinking was an ethnocentric, Western illusion. "Culture" and "nature" are not objective realities but rather historically specific cultural constructs that may not find parallels in the ideologies of other peoples. Oddly, Schneider never followed this proposition through to its logical conclusion. Had he done so, he would have had to accept that the very idea of "culture" is itself a Western construct. The question would then have arisen whether this Western folk idea could be applied to other "cultures" that may very well lack a notion of "culture."

But if the logic was not pressed to its obvious conclusion in this case, the tendency of the argument was clear. With the telling exception of the notion of culture itself, the twentieth-century orthodoxies of sociology and anthropology were exposed as expressions of American ideology. Not only the science of kinship but all of anthropology, sociology, and biology were revealed to be not false sciences but ethnosciences.

Schneider worked out these ideas in *A Critique of the Study of Kinship*, published in 1984. The central thesis of the book was that all kinship theory is just a fancy version of Western folk models. The theory "appears to fit the data—because it is the idiom in terms of which the data are described at the outset."

> I have spoken to many people who have come back from the field and been assured, most sincerely and without conscious deceit, that the people they studied really do have the constructs of kinship . . . But on close questioning I usually find that they did very much as I did when I returned to write up my material on Yap. They imposed the notions of kinship on their materials even while actually eliciting that material in the field. Their first unquestioned translations of terms and relationship "find" "mothers" and "fathers," "sons" and "daughters"—kinship— and this is then confirmed by being made consistent with their first assumptions. My own experience in this matter is most compelling, for I did just that and there is a record of publica- tions which I have been required to repudiate here.

Schneider concluded that many, perhaps most, other societies might turn out not to have kinship systems at all. Kinship may be nothing more than "a special custom distinctive of European culture, an in- teresting oddity at worst, like the Toda bow ceremony."

Half of the *Critique* makes the case that "kinship has been de- fined by European social scientists, and European social scientists use their own folk culture as the source of many, if not all, of their ways of formulating and understanding the world about them." These so- cial scientists were the products of disparate societies, at different historical periods, and they represented a variety of religious and po- litical backgrounds. However, Schneider assumed that they (and their American successors) all took for granted the concepts and values that had been made flesh in *American Kinship,* a folk view of kinship that was translated into a scientific theory. There were, admittedly, theoretical differences and heated polemics, but on the main points there was consensus. "The ideas of kinship, the kin-based society, the idiom of kinship, and the content of kinship are the received wisdom of today, as they have been almost from the beginnings of anthropology." And these ideas depended on the belief that kinship everywhere is based on a single, universal biological principle.

According to Schneider, American theorists of the 1960s and 1970s were still unable to shake themselves free from the same ancient error, the belief that a bedrock of biology—the facts of nature—underlies kinship systems everywhere. They did not doubt that people everywhere reckoned kinship on a genealogical calculus, because they took it for granted that (in Schneider's satiric phrase) Blood is Thicker than Water. "The implicit assumption in all of those discussions was that genealogy was the same the world over, at some level at least, that kinship meant the same thing in each and every culture, that kinship had the same significance in all cultures."

It was true that a number of British social anthropologists had tried, in the tradition of Durkheim, Rivers, and Radcliffe-Brown, to construct a view of kinship that did not depend on these assumptions. But if kinship was not universally defined by blood ties and calibrated by genealogical reckoning, then what exactly was it? This delicate question provoked a lively debate in the 1960s and 1970s. The philosopher-anthropologist Ernest Gellner asserted that kinship relationships are indeed normally congruent with biological relationships, and a number of his colleagues rushed to refute him. All sorts of exotic kinship practices were evoked in order to demonstrate that kinship was not universally based on biology, or even upon a common understanding of human reproduction and descent. Some experts asserted that kinship should be regarded as an ideology, a discourse, a language in which matters of politics and economics were debated. As Edmund Leach put it, "kinship systems have no 'reality' at all except in relation to land and property. What the social anthropologist calls kinship structure is just a way of talking about property relations which can also be talked about in other ways." One of the British kinship theorists, Rodney Needham, took the yet more radical position that "there is no such thing as kinship, and it follows that there can be no such thing as kinship theory." Did that mean that anthropologists should abandon the study of kinship? Even Needham hesitated to take such an extreme step, but in Schneider's view it was quite hopeless to continue searching for a universal social criterion that would mark off kinship from other sorts of relationships. "Robbed of its grounding in biology, kinship is nothing."

If kinship was not a matter of biology, or of specific social institutions, then perhaps it could only be grasped in cultural terms, that is, in terms of local native formulations. This did not necessarily mean, however, that it would prove impossible to find kinship systems in exotic societies. On the contrary, it seemed that rather similar ideas cropped up in very distant societies. For some reason, however, Schneider ignored the one radically culturalist monograph on kinship that was available to him, *Kinship in Bali*, published by Hildred Geertz and Clifford Geertz in 1975. They insisted on distinguishing the "cultural" aspect of kinship from the sociological, and confirmed that kinship operated as what British anthropologists termed an idiom, based on domestic relationships. As a system of symbols, kinship also formed part of a more general cultural system. They agreed that this conception called into question traditional approaches to kinship: "What once seemed so indubitable—that kinship forms a definable object of study to be found in a readily recognizable form everywhere . . . awaiting only an anthropologist to explore it—now seems very much less so." Nevertheless, they concluded their skeptical, cultural review of Balinese kinship with the observation that there was a system of "kinship" symbols, "arising out of the experience of living as a child, spouse, parent, and elder in a small, walled yard of pavilions, kitchens, granaries, toilets, and altars with a dozen or so familial others." This familiar set of symbols did not determine the whole culture, but "neither . . . does it leave it untouched."

Schneider's review of kinship theory can easily be faulted for its irresponsible generalizations and a disorderly and selective reading of the past, but the most problematic feature of his discursive critique was the way in which he focused on *definitions* of kinship, neglecting the substantive descriptions of "kinship systems" that had accumulated in the literature. All those accounts of family life, marriage, mother's brothers, cross-cousins, kinship terminologies, inheritance and succession, incest taboos, and so forth were swept away on the grounds that the apparent ease with which ethnographers recognized such institutions was a product simply of ethnocentricism. The families into which they were adopted, and which they described in such fussy detail, were constructs of their anthropological indocrination.

Schneider did not accept that a training in anthropology freed scholars from ethnocentric blinkers:

> The assumptions and presuppositions which the anthropologist brings to the process of understanding the particular culture he is studying are imposed on the situation blindly and with unflagging loyalty to those assumptions and little flexible appreciation of how the other culture is constituted.

It took some gall to accuse all his colleagues of ethnocentricism (the most serious sin in all of anthropology). My own impression is rather that anthropology teachers revel in the most exotic practices that the literature records, particularly relishing those that affront Western assumptions about the nature of kinship, marriage, the family, and incest taboos. But Schneider did have the grace to turn the charge against himself. His own investigations into kinship in Yap in 1947–1948 had been conducted on the model he learned from Murdock. He had forced Yap ideas into the procrustean grid of established kinship notions, translating them into a misleading code. Consequently, his initial description of a "double descent" system in Yap had raised no particular difficulties for Murdock and the British anthropologists. His eyes opened to the weaknesses of the theory, and furnished with fresh evidence, Schneider would now deconstruct his own analysis, and demonstrate that the Yap did not have a kinship system.

The opening chapters of *A Critique* summarized what Schneider termed "the first description" of Yap kinship (though some crucial observations from his own early reports were missing from this summary). This version was then made to stand for all the conventional and misleading studies of kinship, whose authors had massaged their data into the ethnocentric categories of Western science. According to Schneider's reconstructed "first description," the Yap had a system of double descent: that is, a person was a member of a matrilineal group and also of a patrilineal group. The residential and landholding unit was the *tabinau*, which Schneider rendered as a patrilineal descent group, and which he described as resting upon the father-child relationship. A person also belonged to a matrilineal clan, the *genung* of its mother. All the members of a *genung* traced their ancestors to a single ancestress, but *genung* affiliation was secret, difficult to elicit, and perhaps unknown to many people. The *genung* was dispersed and exogamous. It did not dispose of any property, but its members could call upon one another for support in times of dire need.

Although his account of the Yap *tabinau* conformed broadly to the conventional anthropological notion of a lineage, Schneider had emphasized in his first paper on Yap kinship that the *tabinau* was little more than an extended family. The most important kinship unit in Yap was not the descent group but the nuclear family. "The unit of maximum solidarity is the nuclear family," he had written. The *tabinau* itself was "a series of discrete nuclear families . . . related patrilineally . . . In Yap, the individual's identity in his *tabinau* is almost exclusively his nuclear family status." Marriage, again, was "conceived as a relationship between two nuclear families." However, Schneider now set out to question what he had himself described as "the fact that [in Yap] the nuclear family is sociologically indispensable." Sociologically indispensable it might be, but evidently that that did not make it relevant for a cultural analysis. A cultural analysis began—and ended—with what people thought. And when the thoughts of the Yap turned to their home life, it seemed that they were mysteriously purged of all interest in the family.

In fact, there could be no family, in our sense, for a reason that now appeared to Schneider to be absolutely compelling. He reported that the Yap had told him that a man had nothing to do with the conception of a child. "In 1947–48 I was told by Yapese that coitus had no role in conception." Because the Yap did not believe that there was a biological relationship between a father and a child (or rather, between a *citamangen* and a *fak*), they were therefore not kin to one another. "There is no father-child relationship unless one accepts the argument that a man is a father by virtue of his being the mother's husband at the time she becomes pregnant." Malinowski had suggested that in comparable situations in other parts of Oceania the "father" is indeed the "mother's husband," and that in practice the nuclear family coheres around a woman and her husband. A man might live with his wife and her children in a stable household, but Schneider insisted that the sociology of institutions was beside the point. Native ideas were all. Although the mother's husband might act like a father, a *citamangen* was not a father.

Nor were there mothers in Yap—or, in Schneider's more roundabout phrase, "Although the relationship between woman and child is conceived of in Yap culture as at least in part biological, the notion of genetrix is not quite accurate." The Yap did not deny that a woman actually gives birth to a child, but they said that a child is also given life by ghosts of dead *tabinau* members, which suggested to Schneider that a mother was not believed to produce a child in a straightforwardly biological fashion. He also reported that adoption was common, and that an adopted child was treated like a biological child. Nor was a mother simply a mother—or rather, what the Yap termed a *citingen* was not simply a "mother." The term *citingen* was also applied to other kin, such as the father's sister. Finally, a mother was not necessarily a *citingen* to her children forever. If a man divorced his wife and remarried, the new wife became the *citingen* of his first wife's children. For all these reasons, it was a mistake to translate the term *citingen* as "mother."

If the Yap said that a father did not beget a son, it followed that kinship ties could not be traced through the father, and consequently there could be no patrilineal descent. Similarly, a person could not claim rights to *tabinau* property on the ground of kinship ties through a father. Schneider explained that land claims were expressed in the language of reciprocal exchange. A person who worked *tabinau* land gained rights in it.

An inmarrying wife could in the same way literally work herself into membership of the *tabinau*. When the Yap said that a person belongs to a *tabinau* (which is how they put it), they were saying that he or she is attached to a piece of land, and it is the land and its products that shape the identity of a person as a member. Therefore it is misleading to translate the term *tabinau* as a patrilineal kin group. Nor is the *genung* a matrilineage, for it is not a corporate public group, which is the way in which anthropologists have conventionally defined lineages. The Yap, therefore, far from having a system of double unilineal descent, had no descent groups whatsoever.

In the field, Schneider had spent many hours coping with elaborate Yap attempts to manipulate genealogical information in order to press claims to office, or to divert his attention from transgressions of rules of exogamy. Although he did not know it, his interest in kin terms and genealogical connections confirmed the Yap suspicion that he was working for the Navy, checking up on claims to office and to land. However, while in the field he had no doubt that genealogies mattered to the Yap, and that genealogical connections marked kinsfolk off from others. "When kinship can be traced . . . that relative is treated as a kinsman, as distinguished from someone who is unrelated," he had reported in 1953. But he had now demonstrated to his own satisfaction that there are no mothers and fathers in Yap, which meant that there were obviously no brothers and sisters, and it followed that there could not be genealogies.

To sum up Schneider's analysis: because the Yap deny the role of coitus in procreation, they cannot be said to have an idea of fatherhood. Moreover, since their terms for relatives may be used to refer to some non-kin, these are not kinship terms. Since the task of the anthropologist is to study Yap *culture,* which means Yap *conceptions,* these semantic considerations must be decisive. Because there were no words that could be translated into English as mother, father, son, or daughter, then obviously there could not be families. It follows too that the Yap have no notion of kinship. Sociological features of Yap life such as the nuclear family are no business of the anthropologist.

The logic is clear, if it is accepted that the exclusive business of the ethnographer is to translate the conceptions of the natives—and if, moreover, a word is taken to mean its complete string of referents, with no allowance for contextual discrimination.

> Are we aiming to understand and analyze Yapese culture? If Yapese culture consists in *their* constructs, *their* formulations, *their* mystifications, *their* conception of conception, *their* groups and how *they* structure them, then we must abide by that aim. This is certainly my aim and the only aim that I regard as legitimate in anthropology.

Yet even if the premises of Scheider's culturalism are granted for the moment, there remain grave doubts concerning the data. His own field materials were thin by modern standards—though not, perhaps, as he later said, "lousy"—and he admitted that he had not collected adequate genealogies. By his own account, it was the publication of fresh data by other ethnographers in the 1970s that made him realize the inadequacies of his own initial account of Yap kinship, but when he treated this material he systematically glossed over the more inconvenient findings.

The essential pillar of his argument was that the Yap denied the man's role in reproduction. However, one of his own students, David

Labby, affirmed that the Yap did indeed believe that a man had to impregnate a woman in order for her to become pregnant. There was a metaphorical relationship between husbandry and procreation. "Although a woman was landless in one sense, she did have a kind of 'land'—her reproductivity—that she could exchange for the land a man held."

> A woman was said to be a "garden" *(milay')* that the man planted by introducing the seed that grew into the plant that was the child. The man was the laborer who "worked on" *(marewelnag)* the woman. One person explained that the feeling a man had in orgasm was due to the fact that the strength from all the blood vessels in his body went into the sperm and the work of implanting it in the woman . . . The ancestral ghosts *(thigith)* played an important role in this process, too, making the man's "work" on the woman's "land" productive by facilitating the conception and development of the child.

Adultery was accordingly condemned, and children born out of wedlock were termed children of a thief. Labby's statement of the Yap dogma was unequivocal: "Because the father planted the seed, the child was definitely related to him." Yet Schneider insisted that according to true Yap belief, the child was not related to the father. He suggested that the Yap had changed their ideas in the twenty years between the period of his fieldwork and Labby's, as a consequence of the influence of American teachers in Yap in the 1950s and 1960s. But in any case, according to Schneider, the Yap acceptance of the American theory of procreation altered nothing. They used the biological theory as a metaphor for what was really important: conception had to do with mundane exchanges of land and labor between husband and wife.

Concerning adoption, the data were again in conflict with the interpretation Schneider offered. Two of Schneider's students, John Kirkpatrick and Charles Broder, who did fieldwork in Yap in 1972, made a study of adoption and found that "the child eventually will discover his natural parents and establish an ongoing relationship with them." They also reported that a child was normally adopted by close relatives. Another American ethnographer in Yap, Sherwood Lingenfelter, pointed out that adoption did not cancel the original blood relationships. "The effect of adoption is not to cut off relationships, but to reinforce and extend them for both the parents and the children." None of these observations were reflected in Schneider's discussion of adoption. He continued to insist that Yap adoption practices indicated the irrelevance of blood relationships. Yet in an earlier paper he had himself remarked: "The importance of the belief that clansmen are biologically as well as socially related is illustrated by the fact that the adopted child has a dual clan affiliation and a dual set of food prohibitions, those of both the real and the adoptive mother."

Clearly Schneider was inclined to play down or explain away the aspects of ethnographic reports—his own included—that did not suit his book. To take another instance, Labby provided a detailed account of Yap kin terms. It was apparent from his description and analysis that the Yap had a Crow terminological system, very similar to that of other Micronesian peoples. Murdock would have been well content with Labby's account of Yap kinship terminology. Schneider, however, had nothing to say about Labby's demonstration, although it clearly undermined his repeated assertion that the Yap did not have a kinship terminology at all. On the other hand, he pressed into use some rather questionable features of his student's ethnography. David Labby's monograph, *The Demystification of Yap*, is a competent and professional production, but Labby himself explained that it was an exercise in Marxist analysis—as, indeed, the title suggested. "Yapese cultural constructs," Labby wrote, must be "demystified," which meant that they must be understood "ultimately as the categories of a particular material and social situation." The analyst should seek to find the driving force of Yap life not in their ideas but in their economic relations. Labby accordingly analyzed the *tabinau* as an economic corporation, dependent on the exchange of labor (the work of women and children) for capital (the land of men). Schneider treated Labby's analytical account as though it offered a straightforward translation of Yap *cultural* notions, whereas Labby's explicit purpose was rather to demystify the Yap ideology and to reveal the material interests that it disguised. Labby did not for a moment suggest that the Yap shared his Marxist analysis. On the contrary, his argument was that Yap ideology obscured these deeper realities.

Schneider endorsed Labby's Marxism, if in a somewhat gingerly fashion, in his preface to his student's monograph, but he totally ignored its implications. For Labby insisted that a Marxist perspective was diametrically opposed to a culturalist approach:

> A "cultural analysis" that attempts to define the way a people *think* but ignores the way people *live,* in the very tasks of survival that face them daily seems to me to be significantly misconceived . . . there is, properly speaking, no such thing as a distinct or separate "cultural analysis."

This was a frontal attack on Schneider's culturalism, yet Schneider proceeded without paying any attention to what Labby termed "the way people *live.*" As a matter of general principle, Schneider was willing to acknowledge that one might wish to ask how culture influenced behavior. Once he had been enough of a Parsonian to write, "This is ultimately *the* question, of course; this is what social science is for. Without that question all the rest is empty." Yet he was not really concerned at all with the impact of culture on action, or the material constraints on culture.

A Marxist account is also necessariy historical, and Labby provided some interesting observations on such matters as population pressure on the land in the pre-colonial period and the ravages of depopulation in the twentieth century. Schneider, however, assumed that the Yap cultural system had been stable in its essentials throughout the colonial period. The only time he invoked change was to explain away Labby's findings that in the 1970s the Yap did indeed acknowledge the facts of life. Yet Yap had been changing radically for a generation before Schneider's arrival, as a result of German and Japanese colonialism, as well as trade. "In the late 1940s," Ira Bashkow notes, "Yapese often told dollar-peddling American visitors that they had seen Spanish reals, Germans marks, and Japanese yen each come and go." The Yap were also shrewdly persuaded that the Americans were out to change things, though they cannot have known that the American administrator, Lieutenant Kevin Carroll, believed that they should be helped to make the great evolutionary shift from matriliny to patriliny.

Certainly the Yap were painfully aware of one great secular change, the fact that the population of the island was in rapid decline. They were desperate to have more children. At the beginning of the century they had inaugurated a new fertility cult, and appealed to Catholic missionaries for help. The Japanese had also taken up the issue, and submitted the Yap to humiliating, public examinations by doctors. Schneider did not relate these historical events to Yap beliefs about procreation, whatever these might in fact have been. Nor did he consider the effects of depopulation on kinship organization, although Labby reported that there were often problems in finding heirs to whom land could be transmitted. Other ethnographers found that adoptions declined as the population began to grow rapidly in the 1960s. Schneider, however, invoked change only to explain away inconvenient observations. Culture floated free of economic necessity, or history.

Three endnotes remain to tie up loose threads. First, the initial American study, in which Schneider participated, was designed to uncover the reasons for the secular decline in the population of Yap. Schneider suggested that infertility was a result of abortion techniques adopted by Yap women, and that the women resorted to abortions in order to free themselves for a more varied love life. As it turned out, there was a prosaic biological cause for Yap infertility: endemic gonorrhea. It was reversed when the Americans introduced penicillin after World War II. Some Yapese "attributed to the American 'gods' the reversal of the depopulation trend in the spring of

1947, when births officially outnumbered deaths." This was precisely when Schneider was in the field, collecting what he believed for some reason to be age-old Yap beliefs about procreation. The Yap themselves must have been fascinated by his opinions on this subject, since as an American he would presumably have been credited with the successful enhancement of Yap fertility.

Second, Schneider's closest associate in Yap was a man called Tannengin, with whom he developed a complex and ambivalent father-son relationship. "I first claimed [Tannengin] for a father surrogate and now he has claimed me for a son," he wrote in his fieldnotes. Tannengin, for his part, tried to press Schneider into the role of a dutiful son, to replace his own unsatisfactory children. The episode suggests that Schneider's relationship with Tannengin recapitulated the fraught relationship he had with his own father. If father-son relationships in Yap were so evocative of father-son relationships in Brooklyn, Schneider might have done well to consider whether there is something universal about family relationships after all. Or was it precisely because he had not come to terms with his own family that Schneider was so determined to deconstruct all family relationships?

Finally, the greatest irony is what happened to Schneider's model of American kinship. His students transposed it to the furthest reaches of the globe, where it appeared that the natives also had "kinship systems" predicated on a combination of ideas of "common substance" and "blood," which constituted a "person" as a "relative."

Chapter 5

MARSHALL SAHLINS:

HISTORY

AS CULTURE

> Different cultures, different historicities.
>
> *Marshall Sahlins*

Cultural relativism gained ground in American anthropology in the 1950s and 1960s, but the proponents of a symbolic anthropology did not have the field to themselves. Julian Steward and Leslie White established centers of evolutionist theory at the University of Michigan and at Columbia University. (Steward moved from Michigan to Columbia, where he taught from 1946 to 1952, White taking his place at Ann Arbor.) Around the leaders there clustered a circle of young scholars, many of them ex-servicemen, including Marvin Harris, Sidney Mintz, Roy Rappaport, Elman Service, and Eric Wolf. Marshall Sahlins was a junior member of the neo-evolutionist circle, and like several of his colleagues he moved between Columbia, where he received his doctorate in 1954, and the University of Michigan, where he had taken his first degree, and where he served on the faculty from 1957 to 1973.

The neo-evolutionists were a radical community, and they were drawn to evolutionism in part because of its links with Marxism. America's home-grown evolutionist, Lewis Henry Morgan, had been canonized by Engels, and now he was raised from the dead by Leslie White. (All this had to be admitted with some circumspection as long as Senator McCarthy was on the warpath.) The members of the circle also viewed themselves as an embattled, revolutionary party within anthropology. Boas had led American anthropology astray, they felt, with his skeptical attitude toward evolutionary theory and his insistence on the particularity of cultural identities. Latter-day Boasians had apparently abandoned science altogether. Leslie White wrote a ferociously dismissive essay on the Boasian heritage. Marvin Harris published a polemical history of anthropology, which he represented as an epic struggle between a long line of evolutionists and their anti-scientific, idealist, relativist opponents.

In a series of textbooks, the young men staked out a large territory for the new evolutionism. It was a movement, if not quite a school. Nevertheless, a significant difference could not be denied between the ways in which White and Steward conceived of evolution. Very much in the tradition of Morgan and Tylor, White argued that, taking the long view, human civilization had progressed. The more advanced a society became, the more complex was its organization. White believed that the level of energy consumption provided an objective measure of cultural advance. Julian Steward was more skeptical than White about traditional models of unilineal evolution. He urged the study of particular evolutionary processes within enduring culture areas, in which societies with a common origin were exposed to similar ecological constraints.

However, the disagreements within the evolutionist camp were played down as far as possible. In his first ambitious theoretical essay, Sahlins took it upon himself to attempt a dialectical synthesis between White's very generalized idea of universal, progressive evolution and Steward's preference for multilinear models that emphasized local processes of adaptation. These two approaches to evolution were not in competition with each other. All species evolved in response to local pressures, through the process of natural selection, but in the long run more and more complex and efficient species emerged. Studies of "specific," local evolutionary adaptations could be synthesized into larger narratives of "general" evolution. The theme of general evolution was "the character of progress itself." Cultural evolution was simply an extension of biological evolution. It "continues the evolutionary process by new means."

Anthropologists should therefore combine the evolutionary approaches of a White and a Steward. The various societies of the Pacific islands, for example, represented a laboratory of specific evolution, like the colonies of birds in the Galapagos Islands. Sahlins had himself published an analysis of a Fijian community, based on ethnographic field work undertaken in 1954–1955, which was designed to demonstrate "that Moalan culture is an adaptive organization, quite literally 'a way of life' appropriate to a particular milieu." Other ethnographers had made comparable studies elswhere in the Pacific. Taken together, these case studies of specific evolution in the region illustrated a series of stages in a common historical trajectory. Each society could be placed along a continuum of development from egalitarian communities based on kinship to hierarchical states. In the Pacific, the starting point, the degree zero of the system, was represented by the small-scale, kinship-based societies of Melanesia. Fiji was an intermediate case, in which chiefship was beginning to erode the family community. A higher form of organization was achieved by the small chiefdoms of eastern Polynesia. The pinnacle of this evolutionary process was represented by the elaborate tribal states of Tahiti, Tonga, and Hawaii.

In the small-scale, kin-based societies of New Guinea, entrepreneurial Big Men manipulated a system of reciprocal exchange to build up a power base. The Big Men could not institutionalize their power, or pass it on to their heirs. But gradually productivity was raised, and leaders began to extract more and more resources from the people. Deploying this surplus in public displays, and redistributing some resources to their followers, they augmented their power. In Eastern Polynesia, the personal and temporary authority of a few Big Men was transformed into the office of hereditary chief, but the position of the chief was unstable. Inequalities provoked rebellions. Chiefs competed and went to war against each other. In consequence, particular chiefdoms were liable to cycles of fragmentation and re-centralization. Perhaps it was only when chiefdoms confronted the challenge of colonialism that full-fledged states emerged in the region, in Hawaii, Tahiti, and Tonga. While these developments could all be traced within this one culture area, Polynesia was just an instance of a universal human development. Throughout the world, though not at the same time, societies passed through similar stages of political development as a consequence of technological progress and the accumulation of resources in the hands of a few.

This analysis of political evolution rested on a contrast between two types of economy, one based on reciprocal exchanges between kin, the other on exploitation by a ruling chief. Sahlins now turned his attention to what he called "stone age economics." In essays written mainly in the 1960s, he argued that there were two kinds of society, each with its characteristic form of economic organization. In band and tribal economies, production was carried out by the domestic group, which was also the unit of consumption. There was little exploitation, and there were certainly no classes; people were affluent in their own unambitious terms, but inefficient. In contrast, the economies of advanced societies were increasingly differentiated and productive, but a small group of haves preyed on a large population of have-nots.

Conventional neoclassical economics did not apply to the working of a stone age economy. People had few wants and ample means, and they operated according to the morality of the family and house-hold. A specially honed economic theory was therefore required to understand the economics of bands and tribes. Its elements had been sketched out by an exiled Hungarian neo-Marxist, Karl Polanyi, in a famous seminar that Sahlins had attended at Columbia University in the 1950s. Polanyi denied that the struggle for subsistence in pre-capitalist societies was organized by market principles. The actors were not businessmen; the crucial institutions were not in any way like limited liability companies; there was no market in which all values could be measured and compared; and nobody had any conception of aggregate growth. Economic activities were embedded in household and family life, and they were governed by an ethic of kinship solidarity. Most goods were produced and consumed within the households, though exchanges with neighbors and kin provided an insurance against hard times. Only a small range of products were produced specifically for exchange. Often objects of purely ceremonial value, these commonly passed in fixed cycles between established partners. In places where there were petty chiefs, they received certain goods as tribute, but recycled them in the form of feasts. Each modality of exchange was fitted to express relationships of mutuality within and between social groups.

According to Sahlins, these pre-capitalist economic processes could still be observed in extant "stone age societies." He identified the "original affluent society" with the !Kung Bushmen, happy-go-lucky hunters who were spared both want and hard labor. They represented the Marxist ideal of primitive socialism, though they also anticipated the hippie rejection of materialism. However, there was a serpent in this aboriginal Eden—or, to put it in the Marxist language that Sahlins began to favor, a contradiction lurked within the system. What Sahlins called, in a Marxist flourish, "the domestic mode of production" was undermined by the inexorable development of central leadership. As a Big Man transformed himself into a chief, he began to demand economic dues from the households, eventually forcing them to produce more than they required for their subsistence. Chiefs were restrained from ruthless exploitation since they respected the notion that the members of the tribe all belonged to one great extended family, but in the long run these values would be stretched to the breaking point. Eventually, some chiefs would repudiate the claims of kinship. Kinship would be replaced by class as the ruling principle of social organization, and the domestic mode of production would give way to a command economy.

In the 1950s and 1960s, the new school of evolutionists reclaimed the abandoned territory of Victorian social theory. It was a coherent movement, its young cadres confident that they would revolutionize the field. Marshall Sahlins was one of its rising stars. It was all the more surprising, therefore, when in the late 1960s he abruptly abandoned the evolutionist position to which he had adhered for the better part of two decades. The process of conversion remains mysterious, but his road to Damascus passed by way of Paris, where he spent two years, from 1967 to 1969. This was a time of great perturbations on the Left Bank, a heady moment in which to work out new ideas. Marxism was locked with structuralism in an epic struggle for the soul of French intellectuals—and, it turned out, for the soul of Marshall Sahlins. In the end, he was converted from a Marxist-friendly evolutionism to a variety of cultural determinism. Shortly after his return to the United States, in 1973, he left the University of Michigan for the new home of cultural relativism, the anthropology department of the University of Chicago. He launched a culturalist assault on a radical mutation of Darwinian theory, sociobiology, and he completed the manifesto of his new theoretical program, *Culture and Practical Reason,* which appeared in 1976.

While Sahlins's book was something of a polemic in favor of ideological determinism, there were continuities with his earlier materialist evolutionism, although these remained unremarked by the author (who did not directly address his past errors). In any case, Sahlins took for granted a continuity between the great Parisian conflicts and the theoretical arguments that dominated his own milieu, though he obviously found the Parisian arguments more exciting, more elevated, and more relevant politically. In *Culture and Practical Reason,* the peculiarly French confrontation between Marxism and structuralism appeared as the latest engagement in a long-running argument between materialism and idealism, universalism and cultural relativism. He read the French debates as a reprise of the American arguments between culturalists and evolutionists. However, the front line had been established in Paris, and here Sahlins took up arms in the decisive confrontation between the two classical conceptions of culture in anthropology.

The materialists, Sahlins explained, treated culture as a set of tools, a technology for the rational exploitation of nature. It followed that the history of humanity could be divided into a succession of stages that were marked by technological advances and consequent changes in the modes of production. This was the conception of Tylor and also, Sahlins suggested, of the early Marx. (This was Althusser's Paris too. Marxists were asked to choose between an early, humanist and idealist Marx, and a later Marx, positivist, materialist, and determinist.) Sahlins linked the later Marx to the neo-evolutionist position of his mentor Leslie White, who strove, though unsuccessfully (Sahlins now suggested), to combine a view of culture as a symbolic system with a theory of technological determinism.

In contrast, the contemporary idealists in American anthropology treated culture as a set of representations that shaped action and informed events. Sahlins described French structuralism as a more sophisticated version of the same approach. The core proposition of the structuralists, as Sahlins formulated it, could have been the motto of the new American school of cultural analysis: "For structuralism, meaning is the essential property of the cultural object, as symboling [Leslie White's coinage] is the specific faculty of man." However, structuralism was a profoundly European enterprise, and its development was linked inextricably with the career of Claude Lévi-Strauss. Lévi-Strauss had been influenced by Boasian anthropology during his wartime exile in the United States, but his was nevertheless a very different project. Sahlins underplayed Lévi-Strauss's universalism, his conviction that the human mind imposes invariant constraints on all cultural phenomena. Yet Geertz had repudiated Lévi-Strauss's fundamental premise, that all cultural meaning was generated by a single ordering matrix, that the logic of symbolism was a function of a universal human mind. If Lévi-Strauss was in some sense a cultural relativist, he was not an intellectual kinsman of Geertz (though perhaps he had more in common with the native American structuralists, who were influenced by Chomsky).

Shortly before Sahlins arrived in Paris, Lévi-Strauss had published his major studies of how people think, culturally or, as he said, totemically, or mytho-logically. These included *Totemism* and *The Savage Mind* in 1962, and then the first volume of his *Mythologiques* sequence, *The Raw and the Cooked*, in 1964. This extraordinary series of books had a profound influence on contemporaries, particularly in Paris. Roland Barthes popularized a version of structuralism in his essays on literature and popular culture. Jacques Lacan, "the French Freud," published his *Ecrits* in 1966, which introduced structuralist thinking into psychoanalysis. J.-P. Vernant brought structuralist methods to bear upon classical scholarship, and a new generation of *Annalistes* began to publish structuralist accounts of historical *mentalités*.

Structuralism did not, however, go unchallenged. Indeed, it soon had virulent opponents, particularly on the left. This was hardly surprising, for on the face of it structuralism was incompatible with Marxism, and Marxism was the political orthodoxy of the Left Bank intellectuals—though certainly there were fierce disputes about what precisely it was that Marx had said, let alone what he would have said had he enjoyed the good fortune to live in Paris after the Liberation. "In France," Marc Augé remarked, "the anthropological debate turns on an opposition between those who, in one sense or another, are avowed Marxists, and those who repudiate this line of descent." Lévi-Strauss sometimes suggested defensively that he was engaged in a project neglected by Marx, the construction of a science of the superstructure. He had been impressed by Marxist ideas as a young man, but the occasional concessions that he made in the 1960s to the Marxist agenda were later to be something of an embarrassment to him. While some structuralists were on the left politically, their preferred subject matter was the realm of ideas. They occasionally wrote of "ideology" or "superstructure," perhaps as a concession to the Marxist idiom of the day, but they did not describe ideologies as the self-consciousness of a particular social class, or as an instrument of power.

Radical critics also claimed that structuralism could not account for processes of change, and that it was therefore implicitly conservative, providing support for a bourgeoisie that yearned for tradition and stability. Lévi-Strauss had suggested even more provocatively that the very idea of progress was a culturally specific Western notion, one that could not be generalized. He rejected Leslie White's view that the amount of energy harnessed by a culture provides a universal measure of progress. This was an ethnocentric standard. It "corresponds to an ideal found in certain historical periods and is valid for certain aspects of Western civilization, [but] it does not apply to the great majority of human societies, for which the proposed standard would seem entirely to lack significance." Other civilizations had different criteria by which they measured societies against each other. Lévi-Strauss also pointed out that even peoples regarded in the West as primitives had surpassed us in moral accomplishment and even in some technological fields. "The cultivation of plants without soil," for example, "was practised for centuries by certain Polynesian peoples, who might also have taught the world the art of navigation, and who amazed it, in the eighteenth century, by their revelation of a freer and more generous type of social and ethical organization than had previously been dreamt of." This relativism was not welcomed by thinkers on the left. Sartre launched a wounding attack on his former friend, insisting that intellectuals must remain faithful to the Enlightenment dogma "that there is *one* human history, with *one* truth and *one* intelligibility."

Some young French anthropologists attempted to construct a Marxist account of what they termed pre-capitalist societies, an enterprise related to the project of Polanyi and the American substantivists. Maurice Godelier ventured across the Atlantic in search of new ideas, and his essays of the period were influenced by discussions with like-minded Americans, including Sahlins. Lévi-Strauss himself showed interest in Polanyi's ideas. On the other hand, some Marxist anthropologists were fascinated by the elegance and power of Lévi-Strauss's work. Godelier, in particular, aspired to construct a new synthesis between Marxism and structuralism. Sahlins too was in search of such a synthesis, in his case one that would deliver both a structuralist history and a cultural understanding of economics.

Culture and Practical Reason reads at times like a translation from the French, replete with Gallicisms, especially the favored structuralist tropes ("everything happens as if . . ."). But even though it was couched in the idiom of the Left Bank, and peppered with dollops of Left Bank vernacular, Sahlins's argument continued the long debate between the two schools of American cultural anthropology. On the one side was the evolutionist approach that he had espoused in an earlier incarnation, on the other the culturalism that was coming into its own once more, in the sophisticated hands of Clifford Geertz and David Schneider. Posing the central issue as one between material and cultural determinism, *Culture and Practical Reason* inevitably recalls Marvin Harris's *Rise of Anthropological Theory*, which had appeared in 1968, but with the not insignificant difference that Sahlins now turned Harris's argument on its head, taking the side of the culturalists against the evolutionists.

"The question that first inspired this book," Sahlins wrote in his introduction to *Culture and Practical Reason*, "was whether the materialist conception of history and culture, as Marx formulated it theoretically, could be translated without friction to the comprehension of tribal societies." The short answer was that it could not. The early Marx treated culture "as an intervention in physical nature." The later Marx dealt with meaning, but "only in its capacity as the expression of human relations"—in other words, as ideology. Marx was unfortunately ignorant of the conception of culture that would be developed in twentieth-century anthropology, as a symbolic system that imposed itself on nature and on historical events. Perhaps he would have welcomed the new conception of culture. If one read him with care, it seemed that the later Marx had pointed the way forward to the position that Sahlins now occupied. At his most prophetic, Sahlins suggested, Marx had stepped out ahead of his disciples to the verge of a new perspective, a cultural Marxism, that foreshadowed a historical structuralism: "it is Marx who here criticizes Marx, if through the medium of a later anthropology." Had Marx been living in Paris in the 1960s, he would not have been a dialectical materialist. He would have become a structuralist, like Sahlins. Marxists, however, had been unable to come to terms with the advances of anthropology. To sort out their difficulties with the conception of culture "would be of the highest service to anthropology and Marxist theory alike."

As far as Sahlins was concerned, anthropology had already established a fundamental critique of Marxism. He and others had demonstrated that there was no room in the analysis of tribal societies for the classic opposition between a material base, which underpinned the life of a society, and a superstructure of dependent institutions and mystifying ideologies that was erected upon it. "In the tribal cultures," he now wrote, summing up the argument, "economy, polity, ritual and ideology do not appear as distinct 'systems,' nor can relationships be easily assigned to one or another of these functions." Kinship bonds may be mobilized to organize, and kinship values to motivate, action that could be described as economic, political, or religious.

The French structuralists were credited with a yet more radical criticism. Vulgar Marxists deluded themselves that only material forces were real. The structuralists recognized that, on the contrary, the base, or infrastructure, of society should be understood, like the superstructure, as a system of ideas. "The so-called infrastructure appears as the manifestation of a total system of meanings in action upon the world." Lévi-Strauss had certainly never formulated such an argument, generally writing in more guarded terms about the limited independence of the ideological superstructure. Yet Sahlins insisted it was this thesis that had inevitably brought structuralism into conflict with Marxism. "The relation between productive action in the world and the symbolic organization of experience—this is the issue between Marxism and French structuralism."

Structuralism had been brought to bear mainly on primitive or tribal societies, but the proposition that people are what they think could—indeed, should—be equally applicable to ourselves. Sahlins rejected the possibility that this might be true only of primitive societies, while Marxism proper applied to capitalist society. There was room only for one theory. Culture, the symbolic order, ruled everywhere. To be sure, there were differences between tribal and modern societies, but these did not reside in their technologies or social organization. The essential difference was that they understood themselves in contrasting terms. Each type of society is defined by a privileged source of symbolism. Tribal society is based on the metaphor of kinship; chiefdoms have their symbolic focus in state religions; while "in Western culture the economy is the main site of symbolic production . . . The uniqueness of bourgeois society consists not in the fact that the economic system escapes symbolic determination, but that the economic symbolism is structurally determining."

To demonstrate this point, Sahlins offered an account of "what Americans do produce in satisfying basic 'needs' for food and clothing." The "needs" are in quotation marks because they are culturally constructed, and it turns out that what Americans produce to satisfy these culturally specific needs are not useful things, but symbols. America is a consumer culture, in which relationships appear clothed in manufactured objects. These are the American totems, but they do not simply represent positions in society (blue jeans as a uniform for workers, or for the young). New commodities are constantly spewed out, and these elicit new identities. Food, drink, dresses, automobiles make statements; one is defined by what one eats, wears, drives. Marx had argued that we lend a false identity to commodities, fetishizing them and forgetting that they are the product of labor, the residue of social relations. Sahlins insisted that, on the contrary, social relations are produced by commodities, which operate as symbols; capitalists manufacture images of identities that have yet to be brought into being.

In short, bourgeois society—shopping in the mall—was dominated by conspicuous consumption. Tribal society lived at home, following family values. To quote a characteristic Sahlins aphorism: "money is to the West what kinship is to the Rest." But money and kinship worked their magic as symbolic discourses. It was a typical, defining error of Western social sciences to treat the symbols as facts of nature, and to assume that strategies of action were pragmatic and rational responses to objective constraints. Neoclassical economics, utilitarianism, even Marxism did not deliver analytical accounts of our Western (capitalist, bourgeois) societies. Rather, they were native ideologies, sophisticated restatements of our self-image. There was little to choose between them. "Historical materialism is truly a self-awareness of bourgeois society—yet an awareness, it would seem, within the terms of that society." Utilitarianism is not a genuine alternative to Marxism, but expresses "the way the Western economy, indeed the whole society, is experienced: the way it is lived by the participating subject, thought by the economist." In a similar vein, Sahlins dismissed sociobiology as an expression of the ideology of the market.

The great divide between primitive and civilized societies was therefore not caused by different modes of production. Rather, the fundamental contrast between the two types of society resided in the characteristic orientation of their symbolic systems. The "differences in institutional design . . . correspond to different modes of symbolic production, contrasting both in objective medium and in dynamic capacity." "In bourgeois society, material production is the dominant locus of symbolic production; in primitive society it is the set of social (kinship) relations." But because they differed in "dynamic capacity," these symbolic differences yielded very different types of social order. There remained a great divide in human history, which separated two kinds of society.

Recasting the argument in this idealist form, Sahlins therefore retrieved the classical dichotomy between two stages in social evolution, represented by primitive and civilized societies, or rather between what he termed tribal and Western or (using the Marxist idiom) "bourgeois" society. And because he retained this bipolar model he was able, like many of his predecessors, to oppose an idealized stone age world to the troubled civilization of his own society. The tribal world was represented by !Kung Bushmen, or by Fijian villagers, or by the Zulu in the time of Shaka. The epitome of modern, or Western, or bourgeois society was the contemporary United States itself, and the essence of American civilization was the culture of consumption. Sahlins was not much interested in the differences between, for example, the United States and France, and there was no place in this bipolar world for the Soviet Union and China, or the dynamic economies of the Pacific rim.

―――――――――

But what did drive cultural evolution, if not material forces? Committed now to discover purely cultural processes of evolutionary change, Sahlins turned back to his initial theoretical problem, the transformation of egalitarian tribal societies into chiefdoms and states.

In his early writings, Sahlins had revived the classic idea that chiefdoms had everywhere issued inevitably from the loose order of the tribe. Chiefdoms had then eventually developed uniformly into states. The driving force throughout was technological change. This classic model—associated with Morgan, Marx, and Engels—had been challenged by Boas and Lowie, who dismissed generalizations about the evolution of the state and insisted that local histories did not conform to a universal pattern. Structural changes might be seeded in any one of a variety of customs and institutions, and historical transformations were in any case more likely to result from culture contact or conquest than from endogenous development. Sahlins spurned this pussyfooting about with multiple causes and a plotless history. He remained convinced that there had been a worldwide movement from tribes to chiefdoms and states. However, he now needed to find a fresh explanation for this process, one that would locate the crucial changes in the realm of ideas.

This was clearly no small task, certainly for a structuralist. Edmund Leach had ruminated that a schema of categories of thought could not, by its very nature, model change, since it necessarily locked concepts to one another in a stable system. He suggested that for similar reasons tribal societies, with their static ideologies, could not contemplate change. Lévi-Strauss floated the notion that some societies were, in a sense, static, and so perhaps especially fitted for a structural analysis. There was a difference in kind between "cold" tribal societies, whose history was repetitive, and the "hot" societies, which were in a state of constant flux. So-called primitive societies tried to annul history, to recast events as mere repetitions of an established, cyclical pattern: "their ideal would be to remain in the state in which the gods or the ancestors created them at the origin of time," Lévi-Strauss remarked.

> Of course, this is an illusion, and they no more escape history than other societies. But this history, which they mistrust and dislike, is something they undergo. The hot societies—such as our own—have a radically different attitude toward history. Not only do we recognize the existence of history, we make a cult of it . . . We internalize our history and make it an element of our moral conscience.

Sahlins advanced essentially the same argument. "Cold" societies interpreted the accidents of events as recurrent, predictable incidents in a fixed, cyclical pattern. Nothing could happen for the first time. In contrast, the West welcomes change and conceives of history on the model of rapidly changing fashions, operating "an open, expanding code, responsive by continuous permutation to events it has itself staged." Change and stability are features of codes, not of events.

These ideas, sketched out in *Culture and Practical Reason,* provided the starting point for Sahlins's next project. The objective was to provide a cultural account of the movement from chieftaincy to state, and in the process to show how structuralists could explain history. The demonstration was to take the form of a structural history of Polynesian chiefdoms and states. Lévi-Strauss himself had observed: "Some Polynesian mythologies are at the critical point where diachrony irrevocably prevails over synchrony, making it impossible to interpret the human order as a fixed projection of the natural order by which it is engendered." In Polynesia, he suggested, one might therefore be able to see how such systems "succeed in eliminating history or, when that is impossible, integrating it." Sahlins was now determined to discover, in the mythology of the Polynesians, the key not only to their historiography, but to their history itself.

For Lévi-Strauss, a mythology was a mode of philosophizing. Myths are vehicles for cosmological discourse, a series of essays on nature and the human condition, governed by universal rules of logic, or mythologic. They are to be treated synchronically, not interrogated for clues to the origins of peoples and institutions, in the manner of the Victorian anthropologists. However, there was another, less speculative tradition in which myths were treated together with other sorts of narratives as a source of historical knowledge concerning the past of contemporary communities, or the diffusion of knowledge and practices. Boas had tried to reconstruct the microhistories of the peoples of the Northwest coast in this way. His approach was abandoned by the functionalists and structuralists, but in the 1960s there was a revival in the study of the past of colonized peoples, who had been thought to lack history since they had no written documents. Scholars began to link oral traditions with the evidence from archaeology and philology, and with the reports of early European observers, returning to something like the historical project of Boas. The times demanded it, after all. European colonies in Africa and

Oceania were gaining political independence, and they required the dignity of a history. In the 1970s, Sahlins himself had experienced "a burst of enthusiasm over the discovery that peoples of the Pacific I had studied indeed had a history."

Yet it was reasonable to question the extent to which the often fabulous stories transmitted in oral traditions referred to historical events. Lévi-Strauss and the British structuralist Edmund Leach took the view that it was impossible to distill history from myth, and they strongly suspected that all but the most refined scholarly histories were in fact myths. (Lévi-Strauss suggested that the French revolution functioned as a myth for Sartre, and for the French left in general.) Jan Vansina, who pioneered the new oral history in Africa, argued to the contrary that the traditions preserved by families or courts were the products of collective memory, and referred to events that had once been witnessed. He opposed these historical stories to myths of origin, which were inspired by cosmological speculations rather than by real happenings. Sahlins suggested that in Hawaii, and in Polynesia more generally, myths shaded into history, as stories about the remote age of creation and heroic ancestors led on to accounts of bygone chiefs. "A more mythic formulation of earlier epochs gives way to epic tales, even as continuity is maintained from the supernatural heroes of the remote past to recent chiefs through a series of local permutations."

Although they differed on the historical value of myths, anthropologists were generally agreed that myths and epics could teach us a great deal about the people who told them. The function of myths, as Malinowski had said, was to justify the present, to legitimize current practice. Ethnographers were particularly interested in rituals that enacted a myth, driving home its message with all the resources of music, dance, and dramatic performance. To these already conventional theses Sahlins added a rider: people set new events in storylines already established in their mythology. Myths of origin reappeared lightly transformed as historical epics, and then as the news of the day. "The final form of cosmic myth is current event." This suggested another proposition, which was more radical in its implications. Myths, in a sense, foretold what was to come—or, as Sahlins put it, Polynesians "think of the future as behind them." Consequently, myths could also offer guidelines for action, serving as prototypes on which people could model their own actions. Ordinary folk might behave as though they were themselves mythological characters.

Myth came to occupy the place in Sahlins's theory that culture, or more particularly religion, held in the theory of Geertz. Geertz defined culture as a symbolic system that provided both an account of the world and a set of rules for acting in it. Religion did the same work, but with even more efficacy, describing a cosmos and prescribing a morality. Religion was a heightened expression of culture, culture in its Sunday best. What Sahlins suggested, in effect, was that a mythology was the condensed essence of a religious cosmology, and that it performed the same two functions as religion or culture more generally. Myths explained change and also helped to effect it, offering at once an account of the past and a guide to action in the future. "Mythical incidents constitute archetypal situations. The experiences of celebrated mythical protagonists are re-experienced by the living in analogous circumstances. More, the living *become* mythical heroes."

Sahlins termed the reenactment of myths in contemporary circumstances "mythopraxis", and suggested that it came particularly easily to people in societies such as those of Polynesia where the characters of mythology were linked genealogically to the living. Chiefs were descended from the gods, and also related to their own people; and they identified themselves with their mythological ancestors and emulated their deeds. In Hawaii, "the royal heroes prove to be the true successors of the gods by duplicating the divine exploits on the plane of earth . . . Politics appears as the continuation of cosmogonic war by other means." In sum, myths were philosophical discourses, as Lévi-Strauss had shown, but they also offered a philosophy of history. They consecrated current arrangements, as Malinowski insisted, but they also provided scripts that could be followed in the future.

Sahlins claimed that the conventional opposition between structure and event could now be shown up as an illusion. From the native point of view, each event was a concrete example of an ideological structure. Nevertheless, a residue had to be admitted. Mythopraxis, or what Sahlins also called stereotypical reproduction (borrowing a phrase from his friend Maurice Godelier), could never perfectly replicate the prototypical, mythical structure. A structure had somehow to leave room for the tactical moves of individuals, and for the unpredictable incursions of outsiders, or the eruption of natural forces. This mix of structure and event Sahlins called "the structure of the conjuncture," a rather confusing mélange of terms from Lévi-Strauss, Braudel, and, indeed, Marx, but the central thesis was clear enough. Myths provided a model for understanding events. They also gave people guidelines for dealing with new situations. But some events had the power to subvert the framework of meaning that men and women tried to impose on them. Mythopraxis could not absorb every shock presented to it; it could not freeze history. In the most extreme cases, there would have to be changes in the symbolic order itself. "The great challenge to an historical anthropology," he concluded, "is not merely to know how events are ordered by culture, but how, in that process, the culture is reordered. How does the reproduction of a structure become its transformation?"

Sahlins worked up several case studies of mythopraxis in Polynesia in the early period of European contact, envisaging an eventual three-volume work, to be entitled *The Dying God, Or the History of the Sandwich Islands as Culture*. The particular case study to which he devoted the closest attention—and which provoked the greatest interest—concerned the visit of Captain Cook to Hawaii in 1778–1779, Cook's death there, and the revolutionary changes that followed.

The history of the first European contact with Hawaii had been the subject of scholarly interest from the moment news reached England of Cook's dramatic end. Several contemporary eyewitness accounts were published, and soon historians could draw upon the rich documentation of the voyage. From an early stage, attempts had also been made to recover the Hawaiian understanding of the events, but in the 1960s there was a new wave of post-colonial historiography that aimed to present the point of view of the natives, often neglected or played down in the conventional histories of the European expansion. Native initiatives were given pride of place in the new studies, and were treated sympathetically. Some authors even took sides against the colonialists and forced the locals, retrospectively, into camps of brave resistance fighters versus selfish and shortsighted collaborators. (At times it almost seemed as if the Vietnam war was being fought by proxy between colonial historians.) Sahlins was equally concerned to recover the native experience, but his message was less political and (though he would fiercely resist the description) rather postmodernist. In his view, there was no master narrative of colonialism. Each party was doing its best to follow its culturally specific script. The tragedy—like the death of Cook—followed from their unscripted convergence. This was not a clash between world-historical forces, but between two narratives.

Sahlins's reading of the death of Cook hinges on the claim that the Hawaiians had identified Cook as their god Lono. This was a well-established idea, though the available sources were open to conflicting interpretations, and at least one respected Polynesian scholar, Sir Peter Buck, had rejected it completely. However, most historians agreed that Cook was, in some sense, treated as an incarnation of Lono. According to a modern account that summarizes the state of scholarship on the issue shortly before Sahlins took up the case, the identification of Cook as Lono

> was a logical idea, for [Cook] came each time during the makahiki season, and Lono . . . was the makahiki god. There

was among the Hawaiians a tradition about Lono having gone away to Kahiki, and it was now supposed that he had returned. The sails of the foreign ships resembled the kapa banner attached to the image of Lono; and the way in which Cook's squadron sailed leisurely along the coasts of the various islands was more than a little suggestive of the progress of the god around the island during the makahiki festival.

Cook had touched the Hawaiian islands during the annual makahiki festival in 1778. When he landed in January 1779, at Kealakekua Bay, he was well on the way to being generally accepted as Lono.

> As soon as he went on shore, accompanied by some of his officers, he was taken in hand by priests and made the central figure of an elaborate ceremony in the heiau of Hikiau, by which the priests meant to acknowledge him as the incarnation of Lono; up to the last day of his life he was treated by the natives with a respect amounting to adoration. Whether Cook realized the religious significance of all this is uncertain.

After a period at anchor, taking in supplies from the hospitable islanders, and refitting, Cook set sail. However, his mast broke and he was obliged to return. Now "the old relations were resumed, although the Hawaiians were curious as to why the foreigners had returned." Thefts became more common. Blacksmiths' tools were taken, which led to a scuffle in which a chief named Palea was struck with an oar. Then came the more serious loss of a cutter. Cook followed his accustomed policy, and tried to take the king hostage until the stolen property was handed back. But the Hawaiians became suspicious. "Lono, if indeed this was Lono, had never before come to visit the chief in this fashion—armed, supported by an escort of soldiers, and with a concerted and apparently hostile movement of armed boats from the two ships." A crowd gathered, and some of the sailors panicked. Cook himself fired his gun twice. In the confusion, he was knocked to the ground and killed. The body was taken off by the Hawaiians and "treated like that of a high chief." The British regrouped and inflicted sharp reprisals. Eventually, after a week, peace was made. Some of Cook's bones—evidently his "hind parts"—were returned to the ships. These were buried at sea, and the English departed.

The version of the story that I have summarized here represents the informed scholarly consensus at the time of Sahlins's intervention. Its author, Ralph S. Kuykendall, was professor of history at the University of Hawaii, and his book on pre-colonial times was the first volume of what was in effect an official history of the islands, synthesizing contemporary scholarship. What Sahlins did was to follow through the logic of this generally accepted identification between Cook and Lono. As he read the evidence (and this remains a more controversial issue), when Cook first visited the Hawaiian islands of Kauai and Niihau, early in 1778, during the Makahiki season sacred to Lono, the English sailors were taken to be gods. However, the Hawaiians were quickly disabused of this idea, in particular because the sailors were so willing to sleep with the Hawaiian women and to share their meals with them. Cook alone escaped from this general disillusionment, and when he sailed to the islands of Maui and Hawaii the following year he was personally identified as Lono. The sails of his ship recalled the banner associated with Lono, and he landed close to the major temple of Lono; but the decisive factor was that he led his men to Hawaii around the time that Lono was due to make his annual visitation, inaugurating the Makahiki ceremonies. Then, prompted by the Lono priests, but perhaps not fully grasping what was happening, Cook conducted himself very much as though he were, indeed, the *akua* Lono.

The Makahiki, the Hawaiian New Year festival, began with the appearance of the Pleiades at twilight. This marked the season when the weather and the tides changed, and the first fruits were harvested. Lono was a god of peace and of fertility, and he was associated with the autochthonous people. The rest of the year was governed by the god Ku, who was associated with the ruling chiefs, with warfare, and with human sacrifice. When Lono arrived from Kahiki (perhaps Tahiti), or rather when the Lono priests brought out the image of Lono, the temple rituals for Ku were suspended, and the cult of Lono replaced them, accompanied by new tabus, including a tabu on warfare. Lono made a circuit of the island, traveling clockwise around it for twenty-three days, attended by priests, welcomed by the people with sacrifices, his passing celebrated with saturnalia. At the end of the Makahiki he was met by the king, and they engaged in mock combat. A few days later Lono suffered a ritual death and sailed away once more, in a special canoe loaded with food, not to return for another year.

Cook appeared off Maui in late November, 1778, and then sailed clockwise around Hawaii island before coming ashore at Kealakekua Bay on January 17, 1779. Sahlins argued that "it proves possible to collate the transactions of the Cook voyage, according to European calendar dates, with the ritual activities of the Makahiki as set forth in extant ethnographic descriptions by Hawaiian lunar dates." Cook's actions at that time strongly reinforced the Hawaiian surmise that he was Lono. "The correlation between the ritual movements of the Makahiki image Lono and the historical movements of Captain Cook in 1778–79 was not perfect, but it was sufficiently remarkable." Cook began his journey around Hawaii on the date when the Ku temples were closed, and tracked, at sea, the customary course that Lono took around the island by land, even if he took slightly longer over it than Lono did. He then anchored near the site of the temple where Lono's own circuit traditionally began and ended. "Upon landing, Cook was immediately escorted to the great temple of Hikiau, where he allowed himself to be led by priests through an elaborate set of rites, characterized in both British and Hawaiian accounts as 'adoration' or 'worship.'" To cap it all, Cook departed more or less when the Makahiki was due to come to an end. "On 2 February, King [one of Cook's officers] writes that the chiefs were now beginning to ask when the British would be leaving—and were relieved to learn their departure was imminent. Cook, however, did promise to come back next year! Everything was indeed proceeding historically right on ritual schedule."

Sahlins argues that the unfortunate sequel also followed a mythological script. Lono and Ku were rivals, and Lono's coming was in a sense an invasion, a challenge to the king. All of the Hawaiian dynasties had been founded by invading chiefs. Lono's challenge to the king was ritually overcome at the climactic event of the Makahiki when the two engaged in mock combat, after which the defeated Lono sailed away. In this case, however, the sequence was disrupted. The accident to the mast of the *Resolution* obliged Cook to turn back to Kealakekua Bay, where he arrived on February 11.

> Cook was now *hors* [out of] *catégorie*. Lono had come and bestowed his riches in iron, already largely in the hands of ranking chiefs—who had thus successfully weathered his passage and regained the land. Then he departed, presumably to return again a year later with the Pleiades. The abrupt reappearance of the ships was a contradiction to all that had gone before.

The obvious conclusion was that Lono was now bent on conquest.

Many Hawaiians responded to his return with a series of thefts. Cook was at last driven to his final resort in such situations, which was to take the leading man hostage. "One might say that he invoked his own native political rituals: the famous colonial disposition to 'find the chief.'" The king, initially willing, was persuaded to refuse to accompany Cook on board his ship. The crowd turned on Cook and his men, and Cook was felled by a blow with an iron dagger. (Sahlins even offers a solution to the murder mystery by identifying the ritual assassin, a close relative and constant companion of the king, a man named Nuha.) At this stage, the Hawaiians apparently felt that ritual equilibrium had been restored. Cook's body was taken off and treated like that of a dead chief, which meant either an ancestor or a rival who had been defeated in war. (Sahlins suggests that he was "historically sacrificed as a rival, to be ideologically recuperated at a later time as an ancestor.") To the surprise of the officers, the people then became friendly once more, and asked, with some urgency, whether Cook would return the following year.

"The incidents of Cook's life and death at Hawaii were in many respects historical metaphors of a mythical reality." And yet no myth is unambiguous. The myth of Lono, and other Hawaiian beliefs, were open to alternative readings by the Hawaiians themselves. "We need not suppose that all Hawaiians were convinced that Captain Cook was Lono," Sahlins comments, "or, more precisely, that his being Lono meant the same to everyone." The various Hawaiian factions each represented Cook and his party in different ways. For the Lono priests, Cook was always the *akua* Lono, but to the king he was potentially a threat, a rival, since new kings came to Hawaii from abroad and conquered their predecessors. To the women, the sailors were divine and generous lovers, for whom tabus were lifted. For the commoner men, they were the source of iron tools and trading opportunities. This trade soon aroused the jealousy of the chiefs, who tried to monopolize it, thus fostering new tensions between themselves and the common people. As Sahlins summed it up:

> Captain Cook appears as an ancestral god to Hawaiian priests, more like a divine warrior to the chiefs, and evidently something else and less to ordinary men and women. Acting from different perspectives, and with different social powers of objectifying their respective interpretations, people come to different conclusions and societies work out different consensuses.

But rival interpretations were not allowed free reign. There was a struggle to impose an authoritative reading of Cook/Lono. Sahlins suggests that

> the Hawaiian powers-that-be had the unique capacity to publicly objectify their own interpretation. They could bring structure to bear on matters of opinion, and by rendering to Cook the tributes of Lono, they also practically engaged the people in this religion of which they were the legitimate prophets.

However, the elite was itself divided. The priests around the main temple, Hikiau, adored Cook as an incarnation of the divine Lono; yet if they were correct then Cook was a less welcome revenant to the king and the warrior chiefs, who would have to confront him at the end of the Makahiki, this time, perhaps, in a real fight rather than a ritual encounter. The Lono priests remained friendly following Cook's unexpected return, and even after Cook was vanquished by the king's champion they tried to keep on good terms with Cook's men.

"Cook was a tradition for Hawaiians before he was a fact." But Cook's residence in Hawaii precipitated social conflicts and set in train revolutionary changes, and these had to be accounted for. Repeating the *mot* like a refrain, Sahlins insisted that the more things remain the same, the more they change. Mythopraxis does not necessarily recapitulate the past: it can precipitate a revolution.

The defeat of Cook gave the king and the chiefs the opportunity to incorporate his ritual power, or *mana*. From this point, the Hawaiian elite identified with England. Soon the king was modeling himself on King George. His ministers began calling themselves Billy Pitt, George Washington, and Charley Fox, and dressing up in a version of European aristocratic style. This precipitated a change in the relationship between chiefs and commoners. "The Hawaiian chief for whom 'King George' of England is the model of celestial *mana* is no longer the same chief, nor in the same relation to his people."

In a similar way, the Hawaiians initially interpreted the exchanges they engaged in with Cook's party in traditional terms, but these soon had to be rethought as they began to effect changes in conventional relationships. A pragmatic view would suggest that this trade flourished because each party understood what the other wanted, and profited from the exchange. It was a rational expression of a universal logic of reciprocity (about which Sahlins had written so extensively in his *Stone Age Economics*). The British sailors assumed that their dealings with the Hawaiians would follow a pattern that had been established during their visits to other Pacific islands. They wanted food, firewood, and sex, and they carried trade goods to exchange for these services. A system of reciprocal exchanges was soon established, although sometimes it had to be maintained by force. According to Robert Borofsky and Alan Howard, during the early contact period in the Pacific there was typically a cycle of trade, then theft and punishment, succeeded once more by a period of trade and generally peaceful relations, which would then again be followed by often violent provocations. The chiefs were willing, in general, to assist the sailors to control thefts, since this strengthened their hand with the Europeans, but the thefts were also challenges, requiring the Europeans to demonstrate any claims they might have to high status by proving their efficacy, particularly against challenges orchestrated by the chiefs themselves. In such situations, both parties were accustomed to use violence to establish their positions. Yet despite the occasional thefts, and the reactions that were provoked by retaliation, the British found that the Hawaiians, like the other Pacific islanders, were willing to engage in trade. If anything, they showed exceptional eagerness and generosity.

But these exchanges appeared to the Hawaiians in a different light. Sahlins points out that there were various traditional modalities of exchange. Sacrifice was appropriate for gods; chiefs were expected to make generous gifts to their inferiors, who, however, had to make tribute payments to them; and barter was practiced between equals. As Sahlins interprets the first contacts made by the British with Hawaiians, in 1778, the sailors were at first treated as gods, who required sacrifices. The women offered themselves in a way that was particularly appropriate in the Makahiki season, a time of fertility rituals. But the sailors repaid the services provided to them, recasting the transaction as a form of barter, and so they lost their godly status. "When sacrifice turned into trade, the *haole* 'foreigners' turned into men. The foreigners were secularized." From the first, the Hawaiian men were eager to trade goods (including women) for tools and weapons. As barter became general, men and women came into competition for the resources of the sailors. The chiefs then quickly moved in to cream off the most desirable goods, not hesitating to employ unaccustomed force against their own people in the process. The competition soon strained relationships between men and women, and, even more, between commoners and chiefs.

There was also the complication that trade relations were regulated by tabus. At times during the Makahiki, the sea itself was tabu. The British sailors persuaded many Hawaiians to break these tabus in order to trade with them. Other tabus were then transgressed, the women leading the way by eating with the male sailors, and consuming forbidden foods. The transgression of tabus represented a theoretical problem for Sahlins, for tabu was the sacred *habitus* of Polynesian life. "Constituting the social nature of persons and groups, tabu is itself the principle of these distinctions. For the same reason, tabu is never a simple reflection upon practice: it is *in* the order of practice, as the organization of it."

How then could practice escape from the rule of tabu, and with what consequences? The violations of tabu were motivated by what Sahlins himself called "the pragmatics of trade," but the effect was to upset the established relationships between the categories of men and women, commoners and chiefs, Hawaiians and foreigners. The upshot was a structural transformation: a reordering of the old categories. When sacrifice gave way to trade, the foreigners were transformed from gods into men. Other categories were also implicated. Traditionally, Hawaiian women were to their men as commoners were to chiefs, and as the secular was to the tabu. Therefore when women broke tabus by feasting with the sailors, the relationships between commoners and chiefs were also put at risk. "Hence it is not simply that values of given relationships—as between men and women, chiefs and common people—were revised. The relationship between such relationships was revised. Structure is revised."

The notion of structural transformation is based on the supposition that the relationship between two or more states of a structure is systematic. A change in one part of the structure must precipitate matching changes in other parts. So if, in this case, women have become more equal to men, one would expect commoners to become more equal to chiefs. In fact, the reverse appeared to happen, yet Sahlins argues that this, too, was a logical consequence of the initial disturbance of the old system of relationships.

> For everything that sharpens the distinction between chiefs and commoners, or weakens the distinction between men and women, undermines the equivalence of these oppositions . . . The class distinction between chiefs and the underlying population was this way foregrounded. It became more pertinent and consequential for social action than the tabu distinctions by gender that had before cut across it.

He also suggests that Europeans were to Hawaiians as chiefs were to commoners. That is why the Hawaiian chiefs adopted English names and modes of dress: they were structurally appropriate. Whatever happened, apparently, was structurally determined.

In the matter of trade, and in the drama of Lono/Cook, Sahlins's argument is, in short, that people enacted their interpretations of the past. Performance changed the script, but the new scripts were transformations of the old, like a performance of *Julius Caesar* in modern dress. One difficulty with this thesis, as a moment of reflection must show, is that such "transformations" can be constructed rather easily by the observer if there are only two states between which a "transformation" occurs. How much must change, and how unpredictably, before a change is no longer a "transformation"? Another difficulty is with the motivation of change. Sahlins sometimes invokes what he calls "interests," and admits that different factions could try to impose interpretations of a myth that fitted their material or political goals. He insists that these "interests" are themselves culturally constituted. Nevertheless, the possibility must then arise that rather than following a set cultural script, Hawaiian factions manipulated myths to legitimate their pragmatic policies. Finally, there is the difficulty that the myths may be interpreted in a variety of ways. They may also be more or less salient for different groups in a society. Sahlins cites, and accepts, early nineteenth-century statements to the effect that Hawaiian commoners were largely ignorant of the state religion, and that they had to be forced to comply with tabus. It is not evident, then, that they were intellectual prisoners of the cult of Lono, or that their actions would have been motivated to any great extent by mythological beliefs. These difficulties became very evident as Sahlins attempted to explain the cultural revolution of 1819, when the Hawaiian royals entirely abrogated the tabu system.

This is the most famous episode in early Hawaiian history after the death of Cook, and it has been the subject of a great deal of speculation on the part of historians and anthropologists. To summarize briefly: in May 1819 King Kamehameha I died. He had united the Hawaiian islands under a single ruler for the first time. Despite some resistance, he was succeeded by his son Liholiho, who became King Kamehameha II. Around the young king were four powerful figures: the favorite wife of his father, the queen mother, the prime minister, and the high priest. Together they decided to abolish the tabu system. Their particular target was the tabus that prohibited women from eating with men and from eating certain foods that were reserved for men. These particular tabus were central to the Hawaiians, and symbolized the whole system of restrictions. Infractions had typically been punished by death. In November a great feast was held at the court, in the course of which the tabus were ceremonially broken. Orders then went out to destroy idols, to profane temples, and to break tabus. This was a top-down revolution, in which the high priest was a leading figure. However, there was opposition, led by a cousin of the king who was next in line of succession to the priesthood. The conservatives were defeated, largely because the king's party had superiority in guns. By the time the first missionaries arrived in 1820, the changes had been generally accepted.

Many conflicting explanations have been offered for this remarkable event. Kroeber suggested that the abolition of tabus was an instance of what he called "cultural fatigue," a sentiment similar to that felt by the French after their defeat in 1940, or by the Americans after the 1929 stock market crash. "Once an attitude of the kind develops sufficient strength, novelty as such may come to seem a virtue and a boon." However, this did not explain why the Hawaiians suddenly began to suffer from cultural anomie. According to Robert Redfield, the Hawaiians were a changeable lot in any case, always ready to embrace novelties, and they were simply inspired to change by the example of the English sailors. Yet the tabu-breaking practices of the English would not necessarily have counted for very much. Foreigners were excluded from the tabu system, and Hawaiians called on natives of other islands to perform tabued acts, such as barbering. An alternative hypothesis suggested that this was a revolt of the women, on whom the burdens of tabu fell with especial weight, but the aristocratic women were in danger of losing more than they gained by abolishing part of the system on which their privileges rested. Moreover, this explanation would not account for the leading role played by the high priest in imposing the changes. In fact, none of these theories explained why the priest and the rest of the king's party were impelled to take such a political risk, opposed as they were by a strong conservative faction.

Sahlins deals with this episode—so crucial to his thesis—in a way that seems once again to recognize the pragmatic calculations of the actors, but only to discount them. There were, he argues, two main parties in the royal circle: the party of the king's affines, who had been given the duty of dealing with the Europeans, and who became the party of cultural revolution; and the party of the king's collateral kin, who had control of the ruler's gods and the tabu system, and who were the conservatives. The king balanced his relatives by marriage, who could not challenge for the succession, against his close kin, who were potential rivals. When Kamehameha I died, in May 1819, the pro-European party of his affines came to power. The conservatives tried to rally support in the name of the gods. The new rulers now had to counter the ideological claims of their opponents, and they did so by revoking tabus—itself "a ritual act," Sahlins notes, "as tabu-removal always is in Polynesia." And in 1824 the rulers imposed a new ritual code, strict Calvinism, on the island.

The story is clearly open to a Machiavellian interpretation, in which considerations of *realpolitik* determine action, and ritual and religion are manipulated to serve power. Sahlins raises this possibility himself, but he suddenly shifts gears and argues that "a structure of the long run" is unfolding beyond the control of the actors.

> Thus the set of inversions that, by *mauvaise foi,* nevertheless kept faith with the old system. Originally foreign, the King now appears as the native Hawaiian. The one who customarily placed the tabus at his accession, he would now throw them off. Kaahumanu's people, by category wife-givers and deposed native chiefs, seize power by virtue of their access to foreign resources. And the woman reestablishes the tabu order. Thus king and affines, men and women, foreign and indigenous, tabu and *noa* all exchanged their places.

And so once again the changes may be represented as transformations of a structure. Even the cultural revolution is to be understood as a conservative act. Machiavellian maneuvers are rewritten as mythopraxis.

Sahlins's account of the death of Cook was soon challenged by a Princeton-based anthropologist, Gananath Obeyesekere, provoking a ferocious response from Sahlins, and setting off a debate among historians and anthropologists that was soon to attract the interest of the intellectual press.

At one level, the argument was about what had happened long ago on a tropical beach in the South Seas, when the inhabitants of Hawaii made their fateful first contact with English sailors. Sahlins believed that the Hawaiians had interpreted the arrival of Cook in mythical terms, as a visitation of their god Lono, and acted accordingly. Obeyesekere argued that the Hawaiians were angered by the violence of Cook and his party, and by their desecration of sacred sites, and responded as rational people anywhere would react to an invasion of thugs and hooligans. Each cited sailors' diaries, Hawaiian texts, and commentaries by missionaries, and each offered his own views on such technical questions as the working of the Hawaiian lunar calendar.

But both protagonists insisted that much larger issues were implicated in the interpretation of that remote tragedy. Finding, again, that only French could supply the *mot juste,* Sahlins wrote that "such a confrontation of cultures affords a privileged occasion for seeing very common types of historical change *en clair*" (he may mean *clearly,* or may intend a more specialized meaning, implying a message sent, for once, not in code). For Obeyesekere, the debate raised fundamental issues about anthropological practice. Clifford Geertz agreed, writing that the arguments of Sahlins and Obeyesekere "push into view some of the most central and most divisive issues in anthropological study . . . What does 'knowing' about 'others' properly consist in? Is it possible? Is it good?" Obeyesekere himself seemed to be suggesting that only the native can know the native. This propelled the debate into the very heart of contemporary cultural controversies. The philosopher Ian Hacking acknowledged that the dispute "is germane to the American culture wars," but he insisted that it was "vastly more interesting," for it revived the classic issue between universalists and relativists, the question whether human beings are all guided by a similar rational calculus.

Yet a less elevated reading of the debate is in order. In the end, it all comes down to disagreements about the facts of the matter. As Robert Borofsky puts it, "Whether Obeyesekere's or Sahlins's analysis makes more sense to us is not the central issue. What we need to ask is which analysis accords better with Hawaiian and British understandings in 1778–79 as they have come down to us today." It might be added that the theoretical differences between the two authors are less salient than they seem to believe. Obeyesekere reports that he was driven to review the original texts because he was profoundly disturbed by a talk that Sahlins gave on Captain Cook in 1987 at Princeton. (As a matter of fact, it was in 1983, Sahlins has pointed out.) But his objection was not to Sahlins's theory of mythopraxis: "I am not unsympathetic to that theory: it is the illustrative example that provoked my ire." In fact, Obeyesekere advances a notion of "myth models" that is reminiscent of Sahlins's "mythopraxis." He writes, for example, that myths offer at once "in Geertz's felicitous phrase, models of and for reality. They are constructed out of real-life experiences and then, in turn, influence consciously or unconsciously both art (narrative) and lived existence." This is not to say that the two men have identical views on myth and mythopraxis, and while Sahlins writes particularly of the mythopraxis of the Hawaiians, Obeyesekere is more concerned with the "myth models" of the sailors. But it is not on the question of myth models that he differs substantially from Sahlins.

Nor is Hacking altogether justified in making Obeyesekere into the standard bearer for an Enlightenment universalism, while Sahlins is made to speak for the relativism of the Counter-Enlightenment. Admittedly, the polemical excitement drives each man to caricature his opponent's views. According to Obeyesekere, Sahlins treats natives as unreflecting slaves of custom. He himself insists on a generalized pragmatic competence, which he says is much the same as what Geertz termed "common sense" and Weber "practical rationality." People everywhere reflect on experience and look after themselves as best they can, and the native "can make all sorts of subtle discriminations in his field of beliefs." Yet just as Obeyesekere is sympathetic to the idea of mythopraxis, so Sahlins allows a space for what he calls "empirical reason." Sahlins in turn represents Obeyesekere as a vulgar Utilitarian, but Obeyesekere's point is not that everyone in the world is strictly rational and self-serving at all times. He is a Freudian, after all, and would be more likely to argue that we all tend to be rational and irrational in much the same way.

What Obeyesekere offers is an alternative way to make sense of Cook's Hawaiian adventure, which depends on a different reading of the behavior of the parties. In Sahlins's story, Cook—a man of the Enlightenment—confronts myth-driven Hawaiians. Obeyesekere insists that it is the sailors who are enacting myths, in their case myths of racial superiority, including the preposterous notion that they appear to the natives as gods. Sahlins has fallen for "the Western idea of the redoubtable European who is a god to savage people." This may have been a common Western illusion, as Obeyesekere suggests, yet several commentators have pointed out that it was only in Hawaii that Cook's men believed that they were actually accorded a god-like status. However, Obeyesekere is persuaded that the British sailors were prisoners of an Enlightenment myth model in which rational Europeans triumph over superstitious natives. Their historians, up to and including Marshall Sahlins today, had bought into this myth model. The story of Captain Cook is "a myth of conquest, imperialism, and civilization." But the Hawaiians were not driven by myths, at least not in this case. Infuriated by the sailors' provocative behavior, the Hawaiians had perfectly reasonably decided to drive them away.

Obeyesekere believes that he is less susceptible than Sahlins to Orientalist mumbo-jumbo, since he is a Sri Lankan. His gut sympathies are with the colonized rather than the colonizer. His colonial origins, and his experience of the tragic violence that is tearing his own country apart, give him a sympathetic insight into the reactions of the Hawaiians to the brutal and sacrilegious behavior of Cook and his party. This is the real flashpoint of the debate, but an outsider may hesitate to accept this self-representation of a Princeton professor as a spokesman for the Third World. It is at least equally implausible to suggest that Sahlins, who claims to be the eighth lineal descendant of the Ba'al Shem Tov, is a closet imperialist. But the identity issue is a red herring, however diverting. If one had the necessary biographical information, one might be able to trace the pathways by which each man came to believe his theory, but their arguments and interpretations would still have to be assessed without bothering about their origins. And it is their intepretation of the facts that is really at issue.

The key empirical argument has to do with whether Cook was taken by the Hawaiians for their god (or *akua*) Lono. More precisely, what did it mean that Cook was called Lono, and at what stage was he deified? Obeyesekere argues that Cook was welcomed as a chief, and as a potential ally in the wars in which the king was engaged. The rituals he underwent were those that mark the installation of a chief. Since chiefs are given the names of gods, he was called Lono. He was killed for the very secular reason that he threatened leading men after the theft of his cutter. After his death he was deified, because it was as a god that he could now serve the purposes of the King. Nor was this a departure from tradition—chiefs were often posthumously deified.

A judgment on these empirical differences must hinge on a reading of the sources: the diaries and notes of Cook and his officers, and those of later mariners; the Hawaiian texts that were collected in the nineteenth century; and ethnographic accounts of Hawaii in the nineteenth and twentieth centuries. Ultimately the specialists will have to make up their minds about these matters, but there is ample room for alternative readings of the texts. Moreover, each type of source presents its own particular difficulties. Obeyesekere tellingly cites an observation of one of the ship's journalists, the surgeon's mate Samwell: "It must be remembered, that there is not much dependence to be placed upon these Constructions that we put upon Signs and Words which we understand but very little of, and at best can only give a probable Guess at their Meaning." Although, as Sahlins points out, some of Cook's men had achieved a degree of fluency in Tahitian, and could identify Hawaiian cognates of Tahitian words, they were hardly in a position to grasp the nuances involved in distinguishing sacred chiefs from gods in human form.

The Hawaiian texts have different limitations. They date from forty-five years after Cook's death, well into the Christian period. Indeed, the first and most important set of Hawaiian texts was collected at the instance of a missionary by young men who were training at a seminary. One of the leading figures in this first cadre of Hawaiian historians was David Malo, born around 1793. His attitude to Hawaiian tradition was, characteristically for these young converts, "one of complete alienation, not to say intolerance." Obeyesekere is no doubt too quick to dismiss their work as no more than Christian apologetics, as "a mythic charter for the new vision of Hawai'i of the evangelical missionaries." Yet Sahlins, for his part, is too ready to suggest that the Christian element can be easily separated from authentically Hawaiian reminiscences. Nor is Christian influence the only problem presented by these sources. Little is known about the informants consulted by the first Hawaiian historians, but if the Makahiki rites had changed radically after Cook's death—as Sahlins himself argues—then even the least corrupt reminiscences collected in the 1820s may not have accurately recalled the rites and practices of Cook's own day. Furthermore, the Lono cult was in the hands of a dedicated priesthood, but by the time the texts were collected, indeed as early as Vancouver's visit to Hawaii in 1793, the Lono priests had been dislodged from their temple site. "Everything indicates that the Lono priests of Cook's time were soon after consigned to the dust bin of history," Sahlins writes, "leaving only their names in the British chronicles and a few genealogical traces in Hawaiian archives." This suggests that the one authoritative source on the Lono cult had disappeared at least thirty years before the first Hawaiian texts were systematically collected.

Given such problems with the sources, any conclusions about Hawaiian mythopraxis in the late eighteenth century must be tentative at best. Caution is further indicated if one admits, with Valerio Valeri, that the Hawaiians had complex and subtle ideas about gods and their incarnations. It was difficult at the best of times to resolve these into a simple judgment that someone or something is or is not a god. Commenting on the Sahlins-Obeyesekere debate, Valeri writes that there is "no necessary contradiction between the view that Cook was Lono the chief and the view that he was Lono the god." Problems arise only when we introduce foreign notions of "divinity" into the discussion. According to Herb Kawainui Kane, the Polynesian languages do not have "equivalents for such Western religious terms as 'divine,' 'god,' 'adoration,' 'holy,' 'sacrifice,' 'supernatural' and 'religion.'" Finally, as Sahlins emphasizes, not for the first time, there were conflicting Hawaiian interpretations of the myth of Lono, and "it need not be supposed that all Hawaiians were equally convinced that Cook was Lono, or, more precisely, that his being 'Lono' meant the same to everyone."

The most salient differences between Sahlins and Obeyesekere have to do with the question of when Cook was deified. This is an empirical matter, of great interest to students of Polynesian history, but I cannot see that large questions about human rationality depend on its resolution. Is it more rational to make the dead Cook into an *akua* than to deify the living Cook? Even if Sahlins is correct in his reading of these fragmentary texts (and he draws on an impressive command of the corpus of Polynesian mythology), he admits that there was a great deal of ideological conflict, informed by political interests, guided by what he himself calls "empirical reason." At times Sahlins prudently contents himself with a cautious formulation of his central thesis: "Cook was a living manifestation of the god: not your customary Makahiki image—and no less himself for it. It is thus testimony to Hawaiian empirical reason, as well as the flexibility of this indigenous rationality, that they remade Cook into the perceptual form of their own concept." Such a formulation may well accommodate Obeyesekere's insistence that the Hawaiians were guided by a rationality perhaps very like what Sahlins calls "empirical reason," and that they probably debated alternative interpretations of the meaning of events. For his part, Obeyesekere recognizes the power of myths and rituals in these historical processes. Indeed, he makes the shrewd point that the English sailors, whom Sahlins generally represented as rational operators, appealed to quasi-mythological beliefs about natives.

In the end, a sober judgment might be that the sources are not adequate to resolve the Sahlins-Obeyesekere debate. Given these problems, it is quite astonishing that neither man concedes a single point to the other. Geertz comments that Obeyesekere's strategy is to "beat-the-snake-with-whatever-stick-is-handy," but Sahlins also swings wildly at his opponent. Taken together, problems with the sources and the overwrought tone of both protagonists make it difficult to distinguish the particular empirical points at issue from the big theoretical questions, and to establish which matters of fact are critical to the theoretical debate.

There is another, equally fundamental, difficulty. It is hard to pin down precisely what Sahlins's theory involves. At times he argues robustly for an extreme form of cultural determinism. At other times, his formulations are less daring, occasionally even banal. He often seems to be arguing that the Hawaiians were driven to reenact the myth of Lono, and that when events diverged from the script, an ordered structural transformation resulted. In other passages by Sahlins, however, the course of history appears to be inflected by myth but shaped at the same time by political interests that can be read in terms of another sort of structure, an organization of factions and status groups that compete for advantage. In his recent two-volume history of a Hawaiian valley, written in collaboration with an archaeologist, Patrick Kirch, Sahlins describes his project in modest terms. His aim is to show "how Hawaii's entrance into this world history, through a series of local mediations, was realized in the cultural forms of Anahula history."

Sahlins is also ambiguous about the specificity of Hawaiian mythology. "Different cultures, different historicities," he writes at one point (but though this may ring clearly enough, one wonders whether the term *historicity* is introduced to provide room for maneuver, in case anyone rashly assumes that it means "history," or "historiography"). Yet at other times he insists that the myth of Lono is a variant of a pan-Polynesian story, or even a version of a Frazerian myth of the dying king, one that, he suggests, may underpin divine kingship everywhere. He is also still convinced that all monarchical states evolved from tribal chiefdoms. This raises the possibility that mythological reflection is no more than the local interpretation of a universal process that is beyond the grasp of the actors.

Matters are not improved by the flights of neo-Hegelian abstraction in which Sahlins indulges when he launches himself into theoretical mode. Nor does it help that he periodically reverts to Marxist idioms in making his anti-Marxist points. For all these reasons, it is never quite clear what the theory is that has to be proved. Sahlins can accordingly protect himself against his critics by objecting that they impose a strong reading of his theory upon him, while he is really only concerned to establish the milder proposition that people do think about what happens to them, and that they are limited by their own knowledge. His critics can be dismissed as fundamentalist Marxists or narrow Utilitarians, vulgar materialists all.

Replying to Jonathan Friedman's charge that he is a cultural determinist, Sahlins asks, "Does Friedman really think I am Leslie White reincarnated as Lévi-Strauss?" I cannot answer for Friedman, but I must admit that reading Sahlins sometimes drives me to precisely this conclusion. I agree with Friedman that Sahlins collapses social processes into cultural processes, and I sympathize with his summary comment on Sahlins's theory (strong version):

> If we take mythopraxis to mean the actualization of the cosmology in human life, so that "social structure is the humanized form of cosmic order" [quoting *Islands of History*, p. 58], a relation between the script and the performance, then I think it is safe to say that the concept is *identical* to simple cultural determinism . . . The problem can be stated simply: Are there any societies whose members act out their origin myths? It is commonly assumed that ritual action is an organization of action by means of a mythical scheme. But there is more to social life than ritual. Mythopraxis would appear to be ritual writ large, as the entirety of social activity. In other words, mythopoetical societies are literally texts in action.

Sahlins defends himself in characteristic fashion. He restates his thesis in weak terms, and then claims that Friedman has misrepresented him, chastising his critic as a vulgar Marxist. However, the thrust of Friedman's argument is that Sahlins reduces social relations and economic processes to cultural codes, and this cannot be dismissed as a crude or malicious misrepresentation. Friedman is a knowledgeable critic, and he, and Obeyesekere, and I myself, differing as we do on so much else, nevertheless all read Sahlins with some care, and we all understand him to be making a strong culturalist argument—at least, for part of the time, when the mood takes him. It must be admitted that a weaker thesis can also be recovered from Sahlins's writings: people try to make sense of events, and can do so only within the limits of their knowledge. This is true enough, if hardly surprising. Yet Sahlins usually comes across as a crusading cultural determinist, and he is inclined to assume that anyone who disagrees with him must therefore be a vulgar Marxist, or an unreconstructed Utilitarian.

Sahlins has written that his aim "is to explode the concept of history by the anthropological experience of culture." He believes that he has, at last, liberated history from its failure to grasp culture, structuralism from its failure to cope with history, and social theory in general from its false dichotomies between idea and act, culture and social structure, structure and event. These claims cannot be conceded, not yet. A resolutely idealist conception of culture will not be adequate to achieve this great intellectual revolution. No worthwhile theory of change can exclude objective economic interests and material forces, the social relations that constrain choices, the organization of power, and the capacity of the people with guns to impose new ways of thinking and acting on those without them. It is equally the case that no historian can afford to ignore the ideas that motivate and inform actions. The sensible if unexciting conclusion is surely that one does not have to accept either extreme position. Culture does not provide scripts for everything, but not all ideas are afterthoughts.

The early Sahlins aspired to put American anthropology to rights by introducing a new theoretical inspiration, drawn from Marx. The mature Sahlins tried to repair the deficiencies of the Marxist model by drawing on Lévi-Strauss. To put it another way, for the first half of his career Sahlins accepted the arguments against cultural determinism. In Paris, he accepted, and developed, the arguments against dialectical materialism. Perhaps he was right on both these counts. In any case, he is best understood as a protagonist in the central, great argument that has dominated American anthropology, divided as it always has been between evolutionary materialists and cultural relativists. He took Marx and Lévi-Strauss and made them into the key spokesmen for the two sides in this specialized American debate. They certainly enlivened it, even if they both lost something in translation.

It is a curious irony that Sahlins's account of Hawaiian mytho-praxis is now fashionable among Parisian anthropologists. They may be nostalgic for the great days when French structuralism and Marxism were at the center of every anthropological discussion, and so they welcome the revival of these theories in the hands of a leading American anthropologist. They would do well to remember what Lévi-Strauss has amply demonstrated, that although myths can travel long distances, they are transformed in the process.

Chapter 6

B R A V E

N E W

W O R L D

On or about December 1910 human character changed.

Virginia Woolf

The generation of American anthropologists who came to maturity (and were granted tenure) in the 1980s had passed through graduate school during "the sixties," a decade of protest politics and carnival that really got going on campus with the Free Speech Movement at Berkeley in 1964, and came to an end with the American retreat from Saigon in 1974. To be sure, not everyone was caught up in the excitement of the time, and it would be absurd to lump all the students of the sixties together as dissidents, revolutionaries, anarchists, or millenarians. Yet they did seem to be very different from the immediate postwar cohort, whom David Riesman had depicted as "outer-directed" conformists, precociously grown-up and resigned to their future as organization men.

No doubt there were various reasons for the shift of mood and style that swept the young along. The campus was itself changing, as universities expanded, the "multiversity" was born, and the student body became more diverse. Yet the discontents were not merely parochial. There was a potent sense that the metamorphosis of the universities coincided with a turning point in the affairs of the nation, even of the world. Imperialism was fighting its last-ditch battles. Its passing would hasten the final crisis of capitalism. After all, Nkrumah—or was it Lenin?—had remarked that imperialism was the last stage of capitalism. According to World System Theory, the essential theme of modern history was the expansion of capitalism to all corners of the world, with colonialism as its carrier. The Latin American dependency school argued that imperialism had become an essential prop of the capitalist system, providing the multinational companies with a remote proletariat that could be exploited without restraint. As the European empires finally collapsed, the United States began to intervene, in the Congo, in Indonesia, and above all in Indochina, but "American imperialism" was also doomed to fail. Perhaps imperialism and capitalism were now facing extinction, locked together in a final, desperate embrace.

This global crisis could not be ignored in the ivory towers. Students were being drafted to fight capitalist/colonial wars in the paddy-fields of Southeast Asia. Back on campus, scientists and engineers served the military-industrial complex. The social sciences were the instruments of Wall Street and the Pentagon. Anthropology had been the handmaiden of colonialism. Edward Said's *Orientalism*, published in 1978, argued that all the "colonial sciences" have a common structure: they dichotomize the peoples of the world into two parties, ourselves and others, we and they. The archetypal others, the natives of exotic places, are then represented as an undifferentiated group, marked out by their difference from ourselves, a difference that is always to their disadvantage—they are irrational and superstitious, stubbornly conservative, driven by emotion, sexually uncontrolled, prone to violence, and so on. These differences then motivate, or justify, colonialism. Orientalism is "a kind of Western projection onto and will to govern over the Orient." These sordid connections between academe and imperialism were exposed in

EXPERIMENTS

countless campus teach-ins, which took the place of more staid lecture courses. The long march through the institutions then began. Soon, business meetings of the American Anthropological Association were rocked by debates on the collusion of anthropologists in counter-insurgency projects in Chile and Thailand.

It has been said that nobody who lived through the sixties can remember them. Certainly it is difficult to summon up the atmosphere of those years without lapsing into caricature. In any case, my interest is more specific. I am concerned with the young anthropologists who were graduate students in the sixties. How was it for them? According to Sherry Ortner, a leading figure in the new generation:

> The anthropology of the 1970s was much more obviously and transparently tied to real-world events than that of the preceding period . . . radical social movements emerged on a vast scale. First came the counterculture, then the antiwar movement, and then, just a bit later, the women's movement: these movements not only affected the academic world, they originated in good part within it. *Everything* that was part of the existing order was questioned and criticized.

Renato Rosaldo, another central figure in the cohort, recalls that

> Marxist and other discussion groups sprang up. Questions of political consciousness and ideology came to the foreground. How people make their own histories and the interplay of domination and resistance seemed more compelling than textbook discussions of system maintenance and equilibrium theory. Doing committed anthropology made more sense than trying to maintain the fiction of the analyst as a detached, impartial observer. What once appeared to be archaic questions of human emancipation now began to sound an urgent note.

Those heady days marked this generation for life. Ortner notes that "we are still in the process of playing out many of the changes set in motion in the sixties."

Ortner recalls that radical young critics began by exposing the guilty liaison between anthropology and colonialism, but they "quickly moved to the deeper question of the nature of our theoretical frameworks, and especially the degree to which they embody and carry forward the assumptions of bourgeois Western culture." Rosaldo notes that the real fireworks began when students recognized that the imperial project operated within the United States itself. The New Left, he explains, stimulated "internally imperialized groups" to organize "around forms of oppression based on gender, sexual preference, and race." This project of emancipation required new theories, and the most cherished ideas of anthropology were discarded as wrong-headed and even mischievous. The notion of culture itself was called into question. As Rosaldo sums it up, the "received notion of culture as unchanging and homogeneous was not only mistaken but irrelevant (to use a key word of the time)."

What, then, was the engaged new anthropology to be about, what methods would it employ, what theories would motivate its projects? In 1984 Sherry Ortner published an influential essay entitled "Theory in Anthropology since the Sixties," which traced the intellectual course of recent American anthropology. The generation that entered the field after World War II had flirted with British functionalism and French structuralism, but they reverted to more traditional concerns, which had to do with "culture" rather than "society." They had also divided between the grand old parties of anthropology, the evolutionists and the relativists, rebranded in the 1960s as "cultural ecology" and "symbolic anthropology." The evolutionists, the party of science, wrote about cultural adaptations to biological needs and environmental pressures. For the humanist party, culture was not a machine for living but a form of life, a source of meanings rather than proteins, driven by ideas and not by genes. Culture was to be interpreted, not explained away. But, according to Ortner, even the militants in the two camps had a sneaking feeling that neither paradigm was adequate. Each was "unable to handle what the other side did (the symbolic anthropologists in renouncing all claims to 'explanation,' the cultural ecologists in losing sight of the frames of meaning within which human action takes place)." Moreover, "both were also weak in what neither of them did, which was much of any systematic sociology," the field that the European functionalists had worked with their primitive implements.

By the 1970s the established paradigms in cultural anthropology were vulnerable, their exponents poorly equipped to withstand a Marxist critique that accused them of ignoring history and conflict, and, perhaps unwittingly, serving imperialism. The Marxism that became fashionable among American social scientists was fastidiously distinguished from a "vulgar Marxism" of class conflict and technological determinism. Yet however abstract its language, and however idealist its tone, this diffuse, cultural Marxism still offered a medium that could link the scholar with the political activist. "It was in many ways the perfect vehicle for academics who had been trained in an earlier era," Ortner remarks, "but who, in the seventies, were feeling the pull of critical thought and action that was exploding all around them." But by the 1980s, the initial radical impetus had dissipated. Marxism was no longer *de rigueur,* though it could still add a certain street-credibility to the critical vocabulary. Writing in 1984, Ortner described a field in the grip of a sort of nervous exhaustion. "Now there appears to be an apathy of spirit," she wrote. "We no longer call each other names. We are no longer sure of how the sides are to be drawn up, and of where we would place ourselves if we could identify the sides."

Ortner herself prophesied a turn toward a sociology of action, but one that would draw on Bourdieu rather than Parsons. As it turned out, however, the new anthropology that emerged was in many ways very like the old. Its starting point was the interpretive ethnography of Clifford Geertz. Rosaldo noted that in the 1970s, Geertz was preaching the blurring of disciplinary boundaries, the "refiguration of social thought," and he rather fancifully suggested that there was a connection between Geertz's advocacy of interpretive ethnography and the New Left's adoption of a rainbow coalition of minority causes. As Rosaldo saw it, the "reorientation of anthropology was itself part of a series of much broader social movements and intellectual reformulations." Be that as it may, Geertz's writings had formed the new generation of anthropologists, just as much as their flirtations with the New Left. Those who elected to follow an academic career had prudently written conventional interpretive ethnographies. But Geertz's advocacy of literary theory did offer an opening toward a more radical reorientation. Providentially enough, exciting new literary theories now appeared, as "deconstruction" swept through the departments of literature. It is therefore not altogether surprising that the next turn in American anthropology was toward an extreme relativism and culturalism, the program of Geertz, but stripped of all reservations.

This new trend announced itself in 1986, with a book—at once manifesto and conference proceedings—entitled *Writing Culture*. Its eleven contributors were anthropologists and literary theorists, all roughly of the same generation, forty-somethings, a cohort of friends, several of whom had been graduate students in the Department of Social Relations at Harvard in the early 1970s, just as the Parsonian synthesis finally began to disintegrate into its component parts. In unexpected defiance of the *Zeitgeist*, they were, with one exception, all men. (It was quickly noted that the photograph that serves as the frontispiece, showing one of the contributors in the field, writing away, was taken by his wife. Just like old times, some feminists remarked.)

It is tempting to call this group a school, and the term "postmodernist anthropology" was much bandied about by friends and enemies. There were some indications of institutionalization. Closed seminars were organized, and a special section of the American Anthropological Association was created, to which, it was initially proposed, members would be admitted by invitation only. The new grouping launched a journal, *Cultural Anthropology*, edited from 1986 to 1991 by one of the editors of *Writing Culture*, George Marcus, who was particularly active in orchestrating something like a common enterprise. Citations had a friendly bias toward other members of the circle. (Fashionable French writers were, however, also generously acknowledged.) Clifford Geertz was recognized as the father of the enterprise, though Oedipal rivalries were freely expressed, and he was often reproached for having retreated at the very borders of the promised land.

Despite differences of emphasis, the contributors to *Writing Culture* focused on common themes, and took for granted certain fundamental premises, though not all of them were made explicit. The overriding concern, the very "task" of the Writing Culture seminar, according to George Marcus, "was to introduce a literary consciousness to ethnographic practice by showing various ways in which ethnographies can be read and written." Geertz had asked, rhetorically, "What does the ethnographer do?" and answered: "he writes." The contributors to *Writing Culture* zeroed in on this act of writing. The classical ethnographer had represented himself as an authoritative scientific observer, who crossed cultural barriers while retaining a heroic detachment, and who reported the facts in objective language. This image could now be exposed as an illusion. Drawing on the resources of modern critical theory, the rhetorical tricks of authorship ("authorizing") could be revealed. Like any author, the ethnographers were writing "fictions." Nor were these innocent fictions. An ethnographer spoke not only for himself (or, for that matter, herself). Caught up as they were in the colonial projects of the great powers, the classical ethnographers were all concerned to impose an order on the actual chaos of voices, perspectives, and situations that they confronted in the field—to inscribe one point of view on history. In this way, they served the interests of a political class that wished to impose an alien order on colonial subjects abroad, or on minorities at home.

It must be said that the readings of ethnographies on which the critique was based were, in general, very thin. Some call a halt as soon as an ignoble political motive has been identified. Others are content to reveal that an ethnography borrows, here and there, some cliché from travel writing. It is also noteworthy that a handful of classic monographs are reviewed again and again—Evans-Pritchard's

The Nuer being the favorite. Historical settings, particular colonial situations, and even academic debates are only very lightly sketched, or neglected altogether. Clifford Geertz's *Works and Lives: The Anthropologist as Author* (1988) is the most sophisticated of these exercises, but even he makes only perfunctory attempts to contextualize the monographs he discusses, or to follow up the influence an ethnography might have had on scholars, administrators, or their subjects.

In any case, the logic of the critique implied that there must be a better way to write ethnographies. Since there were no privileged perspectives, no neutral voice-over was to be tolerated. The writer of the new kind of ethnography was instructed to appear in person, as an actor—not a director, nor a camera, much less a recording angel. Ethnographers were urged to experiment, to play with genres and models, to speak ironically, revealing and even undermining their own assumptions. The ethnography should represent a variety of discordant voices, never coming to rest, and never (a favorite term of abuse) "essentializing" a people or a way of life by insisting on a static representation of what, for example, "the Balinese" think, or believe, or feel, or do—let alone what "Balinese culture" amounts to. Some insisted that there was a further duty, the white man's new burden, which was to give a privileged hearing to the muted voices of the downtrodden, to speak for the oppressed. (Perhaps not all voices were equal, after all.)

The contributors to *Writing Culture* were not only preaching methodological renewal. They believed that a new historical era was beginning, and that the very object of ethnography was being transformed. Other cultures were no longer insulated from our own. The West (or perhaps capitalism) had spread its tentacles into every last crevice of the world. Yet the citizens of the post-colonial states did not simply succumb to Westernization. The natives are answering back. They reject our representations of them, and refuse to sit still any longer before the ethnographer's camera. They are engaged in their own syncretic cultural projects. Consequently, there are no longer conservative, bounded cultures to be described by observers in that timeless tense, the ethnographic present. Every cultural site heaves with movement. History is being made by contending cultural projects, and culture is now a cosmopolitan bazaar in which people rummage about for the wherewithal with which to fashion fresh identities. "Culture is contested, temporal, and emergent," James Clifford announced.

A great historical divide has opened up between our times and the past, but conventional anthropology had nothing to say about the cosmic revolution that was in progress. In his introduction to *Writing Culture*, James Clifford invoked this momentous historical transformation in the idiom of millenarian prophecy:

> A conceptual shift, "tectonic" in its implications, has taken place. We ground things, now, on a moving earth. There is no longer any place of overview (mountaintop) from which to map human ways of life, no Archimedian point from which to represent the world. Mountains are in constant motion. So are islands: for one cannot occupy, unambiguously, a bounded cultural world from which to journey out and analyze other cultures. Human ways of life increasingly influence, dominate, parody, translate, and subvert one another. Cultural analysis is always enmeshed in global movements of difference and power . . . a "world system" now links the planet's societies in a common historical process.

The inescapable conclusion was that the old anthropology had been rendered obsolete.

These were the common themes of the new movement, but perhaps it will not do, even in a preliminary way, to essentialize the contributions to *Writing Culture* in such gross terms. There were variations in emphasis and tone among the authors. They drew with different degrees of commitment on a range of critical perspectives, including literary theory, the "subaltern" critiques of colonial science, Marxism, and World System Theory—and it need hardly be said that none of these currents of thought represents a single, monolithic body of dogma. Moreover, paths diverged in the years that followed. One can make a case, then, for paying attention to the more extensive texts written in the following years by central figures in the *Writing Culture* team.

In 1988 James Clifford, co-editor of *Writing Culture*, published *The Predicament of Culture*, a linked series of essays that had originally appeared between 1979 and 1986. Clifford is affiliated with the interdisciplinary History of Consciousness Program at the University of California, Santa Cruz, and is not himself an anthropologist but rather (in his own words) a "historian and critic of anthropology." At once literary theorist and intellectual historian, he reads the ethnographic texts of the twentieth century between the lines, and finds that what they reveal is not the nature of other cultures, as they pretend, but rather what he calls the predicament of culture. Clifford circles around this concept from various starting points, but the central proposition seems to boil down to this: the world has changed. The West encompassed the little worlds of the Rest, and was in turn exposed to the jostling presence of immigrants. Culture, and therefore identity, are in flux; they are not stable and given but fluid and more or less consciously constructed. They cannot any longer be taken for granted. "Ultimately my topic is a pervasive condition of off-centeredness in a world of distinct meaning systems, a state of being in culture while looking at culture, a form of personal and collective self-fashioning. This predicament—not limited to scholars, writers, artists, or intellectuals—responds to the twentieth century's unprecedented overlay of traditions."

Yet cultural differences persist in this changing world, and might even be sharpened. "Distinct ways of life once destined to merge into 'the modern world' reasserted their difference, in novel ways." A cosmic cultural war is in progress, but the West is not guaranteed victory on its own terms. "It is too early to say whether these processes of change will result in global homogenization or in a new order of diversity." Clifford writes (in the impersonal voice he prefers, somewhat strangely given his insistence that the author should be onstage at all times) that his book "does not see the world as populated by endangered authenticities . . . Rather, it makes space for specific paths through modernity."

The three terms of Clifford's argument, inextricably inter-twined, are "culture," "identity," and their inscription in "ethnography." Culture and identity are in flux. In consequence, ethnography is in crisis, and its theoretical basis must be reconstituted. First, the problematic notion of culture must be historicized. The modern concept of culture appeared as a liberal response to older ideologies. It was pluralist and relativist, innovations that (following Stocking) Clifford attributes to Matthew Arnold rather than to Tylor, though he is inclined to push the claims of Nietzsche as the hidden father—genitor if not pater—of the relativist conception of culture. Somewhat mysteriously, given this paternity, Clifford suggests that the modern idea of culture was also democratic, at least in the sense that culture came to be regarded not as a privileged possession of the elite, but as something that was enjoyed by all, high and low, in every society. However, insidious assumptions lingered on from the old paradigm, notably the dogma that a culture was an organic whole. This romantic notion of cultural integrity could not survive the fragmentation of the modern world.

The artists were apparently the first to sense the changes that were in progress. Hyper-alert to the *Zeitgeist,* they found themselves in a world that had lost its familiar shape. The Surrealists, returning from the trenches after World War I, "began with a reality deeply in question." Across the Atlantic, at the same time, a young doctor and poet, William Carlos Williams, mused uneasily about his servant, "an ambiguous person of questionable origin," who had nevertheless penetrated what Clifford describes as Williams's "bourgeois domestic space" in a New Jersey suburb of New York City. The anthropologists belatedly recognized these transformations (variously characterized by Clifford as post–World War I, post-colonial, and postmodern). The fiction of cultural wholes was at last abandoned. Ethnographers learned that cultural boundaries are uncertain and subject to negotiation, and that all cultural fabrications are contested from within. Yet Clifford believes that although we must abandon the presumption that a culture is an enduring whole, its values shared by all, we must hang on to the concept of culture itself. "Culture is a deeply compromised idea I cannot yet do without."

The reason that we still need the notion of culture is a moral one, or a political one. The concept of culture provides us with the only way we know to speak about the differences between the peoples of the world, differences that persist in defiance of the processes of homogenization. And cultural difference has a moral and political value. We should nurture it, making a political commitment to the power of culture to resist Westernization (or modernization, or globalization, or, simply, misrepresentation). This is something of a leap of faith, and Clifford muses that his book (once more apparently an autonomous being, with a mind of its own) may have a utopian bias, and that its "persistent hope for the reinvention of difference risks downplaying the destructive, homogenizing effects of global economic and cultural centralization."

As the illusion—once perhaps the reality—of fixed, coherent cultures dissolved, so did the assurance that identities were fixed by birth, rooted in a settled status system. Again, Clifford tries to situate this change in history, this time somewhat earlier, "around 1900." But whenever precisely the rupture occurred, in modern (or postmodern, or post-colonial) times, both the native and the ethnographer then faced a struggle to make themselves up, to find an identity in the chaos of the changing, converging world. In the course of Clifford's book, Native Americans, Melanesian villagers, and the poet's Hispanic servant in New Jersey all appear in the same role, lumped together as displaced persons, fumbling for identities as they confront the threatening West. Even if we stay in the metropolis we are (like William Carlos Williams) unsettled by their gaze, no longer quite at home. Travelers and migrants—and ethnographers—are, of course, completely at sea. Joseph Conrad and Bronislaw Malinowski, two footloose Polish intellectuals, are depicted by Clifford as paradigmatic intellectual refugees traveling in exotic parts in a doomed attempt to find themselves.

Since cultures are in flux, and identity is a matter of catch-as-catch-can, it is hardly to be wondered at that ethnography is in crisis. Itself a cultural invention, ethnography is "a hybrid activity" that "appears as writing, as collecting, as modernist collage, as imperial power, as subversive critique." The dominant academic mode of ethnographic ordering is, however, a written text that fashions the objects of analysis, and that persuades the reader. Its unstated agenda is to enact "a specific strategy of authority. This strategy has classically involved an unquestioned claim to appear as the purveyor of truth in the text." But the insights conveyed by the ethnographers are at best contextual: "the truths of cultural description are meaningful to specific interpretive communities in limiting historical circumstances." The process of composition rather than the collection of data—the form of the ethnography, not the content—is of special interest. One should therefore read an ethnography in order to expose the ways in which a particular perspective is imposed, and a claim to authority established.

Clifford's rather condensed history of twentieth-century ethnography suggested a progression, or at least a growing sophistication. Initially, the roles of ethnographer and anthropologist were distinct. A professional scientist—a Tylor, or a Frazer, or a Mauss—directed the collecting work of amateurs in the field, and selected data to illustrate his own theoretical schemas. The professionalization of ethnographic fieldwork, pioneered by Malinowski, brought the expert into the field. The ethnographer now claimed the double authority of the scientist, who knows what to look for and how to look for it. But these were hollow boasts, for the Malinowskian method of participant observation was inescapably subjective. The ethnographer's authority rested on his individual experience, but, acting in bad faith, he revealed little or nothing of the nature of that experience to the reader. Clifford Geertz introduced a more sophisticated hermeneutical approach based on the "interpretation" of "texts." He made visible the creative, poetic "processes by which 'cultural' objects are invented and treated as meaningful." It became apparent that an ethnographer constructs data in a dialogue with informants, who are themselves interpreters. But Geertz did not go far enough, according to Clifford. The native authors of these texts remained anonymous, undifferentiated figures—"the Balinese." And Geertz did not reveal himself; he took no risks with his identity. If an ethnography is fabricated by exchanges between the ethnographer and native informants, the text should describe the mechanisms of this process, the maneuvers and the artifices, acknowledging that the natives may be fabricating texts and editing them as furiously as the ethnographer. Like Bakhtin's ideal novel, avant-garde ethnography should represent a multivocal conversation, and it must be especially attentive to subversive reinventions of culture and identity. "Paradigms of experience and interpretation," Clifford concluded, "are yielding to discursive paradigms of dialogue and polyphony."

The subtitle of Clifford's book is "Twentieth-Century Ethnography, Literature, and Art," and he treats ethnography as a literary genre. He makes this easier for himself by excluding the positivist tradition of ethnography, and the project of cross-cultural comparison that it was designed to serve.* Ethnographies interest Clifford as forms of writing, not as representations of something that may (or may not) exist out there in the world, whether it is written about or

*There is a striking footnote, on p. 22 of *The Predicament of Culture*, in which Clifford qualifies the body of ethnography that he will address (as ever, in the passive voice, as though bowing to necessity): "It is assumed . . . in the antipositivist tradition of Wilhelm Dilthey, that ethnography is a process of interpretation, not of explanation. Modes of authority based on natural-scientific epistemologies are not discussed. In its focus on participant observation as an intersubjective process at the heart of twentieth-century ethnography, this discussion scants a number of contributing sources of authority: for example the weight of accumulated 'archival' knowledge about particular groups, of a cross-cultural comparative perspective, and of statistical survey work." (Footnotes are a particular focus of deconstructionist analysis, so it is with particular pleasure that I dedicate this footnote to a footnote.)

not. He accordingly shows no interest in what anthropologists believe they have found out, and he does not inquire how well their reports have stood up. For example, in writing about Malinowski, the founding father of modern ethnographic research, Clifford focuses on Malinowski's problems of identity and self-representation, and on the "poetics" of *Argonauts of the Western Pacific,* written by Malinowski in 1922. This work inspired Marcel Mauss to write his *Essay on the Gift* in 1924, a classic of generalizing sociology still regularly invoked with great respect by anthropologists of every school, but Clifford is oblivious to this sort of intellectual development: ethnographies are related only to highly selective biographies of the authorial imagination.

Whereas Clifford is a critic of ethnographic writing, Renato Rosaldo is an accomplished ethnographer, and he has more interest in the kind of knowledge that may be won in the field. In his *Culture and Truth,* published in 1989, he also rejects appeals to scientific authority, but he urges instead the integrity of experience. The Ilongot, among whom he worked as an ethnographer, had explained to him why they used to go in for headhunting: it was the only way of coping with the rage that followed bereavement. Rosaldo recorded this cultural explanation in his notebooks, of course, but he then tried to discover a more satisfactory sociological explanation for headhunting. It was not until he experienced the tragic loss of his wife, who died in an accident while they were engaged in fieldwork in the Philippines, that he came to appreciate what bereavement and anger meant to an Ilongot headhunter, and was led to accept their account of what motivated their headhunting.

The moral of this story ("Grief and a Headhunter's Rage") is that insight follows from personal experience. You can only understand the experience of others if you have suffered in a similar fashion. Good ethnography must be based on empathy. If an ethnographer describes mourning, he should be obliged to explain whether he himself has known loss. And feelings matter. Rosaldo criticizes one of the founding fathers of British social anthropology, A. R. Radcliffe-

Brown, for his classic analysis of ceremonial weeping in the Andaman Islands. According to Radcliffe-Brown, the Andamanese weep on prescribed occasions during life-crisis rituals. He interprets weeping as a symbolic act, a convention. Rosaldo objects that such an analysis ignores and devalues the emotions of the Andamanese as they cope with tragic events.

If knowledge about other people is won by way of your own experience of your own emotions, then appeals to science are to be resisted. There is no warrant for the special authority of any particular cultural perspective. The claim to be objective is a move in a battle for authority, an ideological ploy. "Such terms as *objectivity, neutrality* and *impartiality* refer to subject positions once endowed with great institutional authority," Rosaldo writes, "but they are arguably neither more nor less valid than those of more engaged, yet equally perceptive, knowledgeable social actors." And there was a further reason for abandoning the old sciences. The world had changed: it had become post-colonial. "Analytical postures developed during the colonial era can no longer be sustained . . . Despite the intensification of North American imperialism, the 'Third World' has imploded into the metropolis." In a world in which all cultures were hybrids, all cultural boundaries punctured and contested, traditional conceptions of culture no longer made sense. "All of us inhabit an interdependent late-twentieth-century world marked by borrowing and lending across porous national and cultural boundaries that are saturated with inequality, power, and domination."

Rosaldo's arguments about history, science, and culture are similar to those presented more elaborately by Clifford. When it comes to identity, however, Rosaldo strikes off on a different path. For Clifford, identity has become decentered and fractured. It is fabricated from whatever props happen to be at hand, not given but a matter of agonized choice, at best an imaginative act of resistance to power. Clifford's postmodern hero is incapacitated by uncertainty when it comes to knowing, judging, choosing. He is the WASP who has lost his way. Rosaldo's own case is very different. His father was a foreign professor of Spanish in the United States, and he regards himself as a Chicano. This provides him with not only an identity but a community, and also with a firm basis for making political and theoretical choices. "For me as a Chicano, questions of culture emerge not only from my discipline, but also from a more personal politics of identity and community." As a Chicano, Rosaldo is also in sympathy with oppressed peoples of the world, and his duty is clear: to promote "social criticism made from socially subordinate positions, where one can work more toward mobilizing resistance than persuading the powerful." This criticism is to be motivated by the "headhunter's grief and rage," or rather by intellectual variants of these primal emotions, which "range from Fanon's uncompromising rage through Frake's modulated anger to Marx's and Hurston's more oblique modes, where it becomes . . . a weapon for use in social conflict." His problems of identity resolved, Rosaldo can be subjective without succumbing to a paralyzing relativism. His experience provides him with an authentic guide to the anger that (real, oppressed) people feel. Identity, politics, and theory form a seamless web.

The argument of George Marcus and Michael Fischer's *Anthropology as Cultural Critique* (published in 1986) begins with the observation that the revolutionary moment of the sixties has passed. The world is changing once again, and fresh perspectives are required to represent the new realities. Today, the burning issues are methodological. "At its broadest level, the contemporary debate is about how an emergent postmodern world is to be represented as an object for social thought in its various contemporary disciplinary manifestations." For anthropologists, the most pressing question is how to write about other peoples, and Marcus and Fischer identify two models of ethnography that have emerged from recent debates. "Ethnographies of experience" speak to the inner life of the fieldworker that conventional interpretive ethnographies left out. Like Rosaldo, their authors grapple with emotions and with the psychodynamics of the self. But even the most sensitive and reflexive interpretivists may neglect issues of power and economic exploitation, and pass over the insidious spread of global capitalism. The alternative genre, "political-economy ethnographies," depict on a small canvas the specific ways in which the juggernaut of capitalism has "affected, and even shaped, the cultures of ethnographic subjects almost anywhere in the world."

On the face of it, these two approaches would seem to be irreconcilable. The project of the political-economy school is to provide a universal grand narrative. In stark contrast, Marcus and Fischer admit that "contemporary interpretive anthropology is nothing other than relativism, rearmed and strengthened for an era of intellectual ferment." Yet they believe that somehow the relativist and subjective "ethnography of experience" can be reconciled with a neo-Marxist sociology—though they do concede that an "interpretive anthropology fully accountable to its historical and political-economy implications . . . remains to be written." The opening to "political economy" provides them, however, with an alternative solution to the ethical and political problem of the postmodernist. They cannot, like Rosaldo, claim an identity with the oppressed, but they are free to turn their guns on the oppressors. The role of anthropology is to offer a "cultural critique" of the West, to expose the factitious and self-serving nature of its ruling ideologies as they appear in art, literature, scholarship, the media, and, of course, in ethnography.

Despite differences of emphasis, these authors all return to a few central themes. At the heart of their arguments there are three linked propositions, which are not easily reconciled with each other, and all of which are vulnerable to criticism in their own terms. The first is that there has been a world-historical shift in the terms of cultural trade. Second, it is no longer possible (if it ever was) to construct objective accounts of other ways of life. The third proposition is that there is a moral obligation to celebrate cultural difference, and to stand up for those who are resisting Westernization.

Although these writers agree that a world-historical transition is in progress, the actual dating is somewhat uncertain. Virginia Woolf famously fixed on 1910. Clifford proposes various pivotal dates, including 1900, 1918, and 1950, while his colleagues seem to think that the 1960s were the critical years. Precisely what changed is also left vague, but there is no doubt that something very large is happening. "Ours is definitively a postcolonial epoch," Rosaldo asserts. "American society, if not . . . Western societies globally," according to Marcus and Fischer, "seem to be in a state of profound transition." The crucial measure of change is the shift from secure cultural identities to a state of cultural flux. The precipitating events are apparently the end of colonialism and the globalization of culture.

There are many objections to be made against this history, even if it is presented in a poetic, allusive style that makes it hard to pin down. One objection that springs to mind is that this is not how it appears to the natives, at least in the West. Where are the great events that dominated our consciousness over the past generation? World War II is passed over, and with it the Holocaust. The Cold War is ignored, and with it Stalinism, Mao's Cultural Revolution, and the nuclear stand-off. For almost half a century after World War II, Americans contrasted their own society to that of the Soviet Union. In Western Europe, the relevant Other in the last generation was Eastern Europe, or perhaps the United States itself. The Orient appeared in the guise of OPEC, or as a consortium of protectionist "tigers" that manufactured cars and electronic goods, burying British Motors and even threatening Detroit.

And yet whatever its eccentricities, the postmodernist account of history (or at least this anthropological version) is not as new as it may seem. It is essentially a cultural history of a familiar, modernist sort. Its theme is the spread of science, technology, and utilitarian values at the expense of the little traditions, the embattled nations of the periphery. It is evolutionist, but its theme may be modernization, westernization, imperialism, or capitalism. Traditionally, this view of history was contested between two parties: the Enlightenment party, which welcomes the progress of universal values at the expense of local customs and superstitions, and the Romantic party, which stands for resistance to this imperial civilization. Clifford, Marcus, and company are, of course, of the Romantic persuasion, although they constitute a postmodern faction. They do not value the integrity of ancient traditions, and they side with minorities rather than with nations. Nevertheless, as Ernest Gellner remarks, the whole confrontation between the postmodernists and their opponents

> might be seen as a kind of replay of the battle between classicism and romanticism, the former associated with the domination of Europe by a French court and its manners and standards, and the latter with the eventual reaction by other nations, affirming the values of their own folk cultures . . . In our time, moreover, it was not only the ex-colonial nations who attained liberation; it was also the period of the feminist movement, and of various other self-affirmation movements by minority or oppressed groups.

This version of the romantic view of history is linked to their second common theme: the romantics repudiate appeals to invariant scientific truths, or to common human values. Knowledge is culturally constructed, and culturally relative. There are no absolutes, no universals. Science itself should be treated as a cultural discourse, with an ideological purpose. Positivism is the dehumanizing ideology of a capitalist, imperialist, and patriarchal class. Its claims to objectivity and authority rest, however, on nothing more substantial than rhetoric. Invocations of science are disguised power plays, strategies for the imposition of one set of values on the whole world. Ernest Gellner offers a satirical summary:

> Colonialism went with positivism, decolonization with hermeneutics, and it eventually culminates in postmodernism. Positivism is a form of imperialism, or perhaps the other way round, or both. Lucidly presented and (putatively) independent facts were the tools and expression of colonial domination;

by contrast, subjectivism signifies intercultural equality and respect.

There is an obvious contradiction between this relativist epistemology and the claim to be able to pinpoint a cosmic cultural crisis. "If we note that the world has changed," Gellner points out, "we would seem to be in possession of some objective information about it after all." There is a further contradiction between the denial that objective knowledge can be achieved and the firm moral tone that these authors habitually employ. They may not know anything for sure, but they do know what they like. They are on the side of the peoples of the world who are resisting "Westernization," or "modernization," or "globalization." But on what basis can they take sides at all? What warrants their political affiliation? In the name of what principles can they call us to arms?

In characteristic romantic style, Clifford castigates Edward Said for what he calls a vapid humanism. Said insists on universal values, and is uneasy about identity politics. "Is the notion of a distinct culture (or race, or religion, or civilization) a useful one," he asks, "or does it always get involved in self-congratulation (when one discusses one's own) or hostility and aggression (when one discuses the 'other')?" He points out that appeals to cultural identity can be used to "mobilize passions atavistically," calling people to war. According to Clifford, Said insists so much on common human values that he is left with no language for writing decently about difference. However, Clifford himself has an equivalent difficulty with the specification of what people have in common. "To stress . . . the paradoxical nature of ethnographic knowledge," he admits, "does mean questioning any stable or essential grounds of human similarity." Said is, in the end, a cosmopolitan, demanding a common human response to human dilemmas. Clifford opts for difference, and hopes that the consequences will be benign. He is prepared to question "any stable or essential grounds of human similarity," to emphasize differences at the expense of what he derides as cosmopolitanism (a term of abuse that has its own sinister pedigree in modern totalitarian discourses). But Clifford is left with no good reason for siding with the victims of globalization.

There is a related difficulty, which might be described as the problem of legitimacy. Who can speak for the Other? The European Left traditionally accorded special authority to leaders with a working-class background. In the tradition of romantic nationalism, only the native can speak for the native. If the quarrel is rather between imperialists and their victims, and if only identity can give authority to speak, then the floor must surely be given to people who can claim to share the origins of the victims. These assumptions are obviously problematic, and not only because there are natives and natives, factions and competing spokesmen—including, often, those old opponents, the modernizer and the traditionalist. There may, surely, be a difference between speaking about, and speaking for; between claiming to represent someone else in a political context, and offering a representation of their beliefs or actions.

This manichean opposition between natives and colonialists, oppressed and oppressors, may also impose a factitious uniformity on all the post-colonial peoples, essentializing them, dragooning them into playing the role of a stereotyped victim in a Western passion play. And the role they are offered certainly has its drawbacks. To begin with, despite the hopes of Gandhi, resistance to science and technology is by no means universal in the post-colonial world. On the contrary, Lévi-Strauss pointed out a generation ago that the rulers of the New States were clamoring for *more* Western technology. Nor is the emphasis on cultural difference necessarily welcomed in post-colonial societies. In many places, historical experiences have bred skepticism, even hostility, to the celebration of cultural difference, which was often exploited in a politics of divide and rule. In South Africa the language of cultural identity, the ideology of cultural destiny, supported a hideous tyranny. Immigrants to the West might also be troubled by the exhortation to cherish and build upon their differences, when they would, perhaps, enjoy the opportunity to become unhyphenated citizens.

What is the prophet of difference to say to those who resist imperialism, but preach a universal humanism? Edward Said, for example, uneasy about appeals to difference and identity, speaks out against the presumption that "only women can understand feminine experience, only Jews can understand Jewish suffering, only formerly colonial subjects can understand colonial experience." Lila Abu-Lughod, who identifies herself as a feminist and a "halfie" (half-American, half-Arab), resists the emphasis on cultural difference in similar terms, arguing that the assertion of difference carries with it an assertion of hierarchy, and "always entails the violence of repressing or ignoring other forms of difference." (Gender, for example, may have a cross-cultural salience.) She concludes that "perhaps anthropologists should consider strategies for writing against culture," and she urges them to bring out "similarities in all our lives."

Leaving aside its logical problems, the postmodernist movement has had a paralyzing effect on the discipline of anthropology. It denies the possibility of a cross-cultural, comparative anthropology. It promises a breakthrough in ethnography, and there have been some imaginative and successful postmodernist ethnographies, but its main effect has been to make young ethnographers so nervous that they can hardly be persuaded to go into the field at all. They feel themselves to be "harassed," Clifford Geertz remarks, "by grave inner uncertainties, amounting almost to a sort of epistemological hypochondria, concerning how one can know that anything one says about other forms of life is as a matter of fact so."

Why, then, was this intellectual movement so successful? One possibility, much canvassed, is that postmodernism is an ideology of consumer choice, but this hardly squares with the reflex hostility of postmodernists to the American Dream. Others have located its appeal more specifically within the universities. Joel Kahn suggests that "what is perhaps most striking about all this debate on culture and difference is how little it appears to relate to the world outside the academy, and how much it appears to focus on issues like curriculum, student selection, hiring practices, promotion, tenure and so on, that are of general concern largely to academics." The ignoble suggestion has also been made that the postmodernist program served a useful purpose in academic battles for promotion and academic power. "These proclamations must be seen as political moves within the academic community," according to Paul Rabinow (in an occasionally subversive contribution to *Writing Culture*). The audience for which Clifford and the rest are writing is close to home; it is "the academy in the 1980s. Hence, though not exactly false, situating the crisis of representation within the context of the rupture of decolonization is . . . basically beside the point." As Ernest Gellner sums up this argument, "Sturm und Drang und Tenure might well be their slogan."

No doubt these considerations are relevant, but they might apply to any academic novelty. They do nothing to explain why this particular movement took hold in anthropology. It is better to begin by recalling Geertz's success in reorienting cultural anthropology in the United States as a discipline within the humanities. When the wind changed in the departments of philosophy and literature, then obviously the anthropologists were inclined to trim their sails accordingly. If culture is a text, then interpretations of culture depend on what the accredited experts say a text really is. Geertz hoped that anthropology would reform the humanities, but the effect of his program was to subordinate the theoretical concerns of cultural anthropology to those of the mainstream disciplines in the humanities. All shared the same subject matter, all were in the same game: the interpretation of culture. And the canonical form of culture was literature and art.

But American postmodernism was also sustained by a social movement in which "difference" (ethnic identity, gender, sexual orientation, even disabilities) became the basis for a claim to collective rights. There was a common logic to all these claims: it was not accidents of biology but cultural identities that made for difference, and cultural identity had to be asserted and respected. The ruling orthodoxy of the society was no more than one cultural position, which had become hegemonic. Western Civilization was simply the preferred culture of a particular white male elite. Whereas in Europe postmodernism was a lament for the end of Marxism, in the United States it became a source of ideological support for identity politics, a movement that established its nerve centers in the arts faculties of American universities.

Chapter 7

CULTURE,

DIFFERENCE,

IDENTITY

The most extraordinary feature of [the Basotho Chief's] intellectual character is his talent for generalization. While Mr. Casalis is reading to him any portion of ancient or of modern history, which he sometimes does at his request, his mind is always occupied with the philosophy of the subject, and striking his thigh with his right hand, and throwing himself back on the sofa of the Missionary, like a man who has found a new principle, or new proofs he had been hunting after in support of one which he wishes to be more firmly established, he will sometimes express himself with feelings bordering on ecstasy. "Casalis," he will explain, "I see men have been the same in all ages. Greeks and Romans, Frenchmen, Englishmen, and Basutoos have all one common nature."

A missionary's report on the Basotho Chief, Moshoeshoe, written in 1843

These days, anthropologists get remarkably nervous when they discuss culture—which is surprising, on the face of it, since the anthropology of culture is something of a success story. While other venerable concepts have mostly faded out of the social science discourse, even a postmodernist can talk unselfconsciously about culture (in quotes if necessary, but still . . . Compare the fate of personality, social structure, class, or, most recently, gender). Indeed, culture is now more fashionable than ever. Other disciplines have taken it up, and a new specialty, cultural studies, is devoted entirely to it.

Until very recently, there was also a high level of consensus on the subject. Even today a list of hypotheses about culture could be drawn up which most anthropologists would happily check off (at least if they were permitted to note their personal reservations in the margin). First of all, culture is not a matter of race. It is learned, not carried in our genes. (This point will immediately be conceded, although there is now more interest in some circles about what precisely the genes are up to.) Second, this common human culture has advanced. We are talking here of the very long term, and progress has no doubt been uneven and liable to setbacks, but irreversible technical advances have been logged at an accelerating tempo. Technical progress can be measured, and its effects traced in the spread and growth of the human population, as well as in the development of increasingly large-scale and complex social systems. (This point may be more grudgingly conceded, and only with the qualification that what some might welcome as a new dawn may be a catastrophe for others.)

Third, there is general agreement about what culture involves in the sense in which most American cultural anthropologists have used the term, writing about Kwakiutl culture, or even American culture, rather than a global civilization. Culture is here essentially a matter of ideas and values, a collective cast of mind. The ideas and values, the cosmology, morality, and aesthetics, are expressed in symbols, and so—if the medium is the message—culture could be described as a symbolic system. American anthropologists also tend to emphasize that these symbols, ideas, and values appear in an almost infinitely variable range of forms. At one level, this is an empirical proposition (different folks, different strokes). However, a thoroughgoing philosophical relativism is often adduced from the observation that not only customs but also values are culturally variable. It seems to follow that there are no generally valid standards by which cultural principles and practices can be judged. (To make this argument stick, it helps to downplay what people have in common, aside, of course, from the capacity to develop very different cultures.)

It is this conception of culture which has become common currency, and not only in America. The anthropologists naturally welcomed the popularization of their ideas, which, they believed, could only foster greater tolerance, but they still expected to be acknowledged as the academic experts on the subject. However, although everyone is now talking about culture, they do not look to the anthropologists for guidance. This can be hard to take. "Anthropologists have been doing a lot of complaining that they are being ignored by the new academic specializations in 'culture,' such as cultural studies, and by both academic and extra-academic manifestations of 'multiculturalism,'" writes the anthropologist Terence Turner. "Most of us have been sitting around like so many disconsolate intellectual wallflowers, waiting to be asked to impart our higher wisdom, and more than a little resentful that the invitations never come."

This is a rather dated cultural image. I can't see my colleagues as wallflowers at a dance, although they do sometimes make one think of the owners of an old-fashioned delicatessen operating in the shadow of a mall. But Turner has put his finger on the reason for the anthropologists' loss of market share. The debate about culture has become political again. "*Multiculturalism,* unlike anthropology," Turner points out, "is primarily a movement for change." Something similar has happened before, more than once, in the intellectual history of culture theory, for the subject has always led a double life. Secluded for the most part in libraries and lecture halls, it keeps an ear cocked for the cries from the barricades, and sometimes loses itself in dreams of war or revolution. Talcott Parsons, Clyde Kluckhohn, and Alfred Kroeber tried to foster an objective science of culture in the 1950s, and in the next generation Clifford Geertz pressed the claims for a detached, cerebral hermeneutics of culture. But the scholarly Dr. Jekyll drank his potion once again, and the subversive Mr. Hyde took to the streets. In the 1990s, culture theory in America could hardly be distinguished from cultural politics. Inevitably, the anthropologists were sidelined. To a politicized generation, essays about cock-fights in Bali seemed quaint, far from the action.

In response, some American anthropologists have urged their colleagues to enter the political arena, to bring the insights of anthropology to bear in public debate. After all, the great writers on culture, from Herder through Nietzsche to Adorno, Gramsci, Elias, and Williams, never doubted that culture was a political question. In anthropology, Boas, Malinowski, Mead, and Lévi-Strauss did not hesitate to address large political issues. Even the skeptical anthropologist may find that the current politicized discourse on culture provokes uneasy reflections on the implications of anthropological theory.

———————

A potent challenge is presented by the new academic discipline of "cultural studies." "Culture" in cultural studies includes the fine arts, literature, and scholarship, the stuff of the curriculum in the humanities, but it also takes in the black arts of the media, and the vaguely demarcated sphere of popular culture (a mix of what used to be called folklore and proletarian art, plus sports). These forms of culture are valued very differently. Roughly speaking, official high culture is suspect, and mass-produced culture condemned as ersatz, if not irremediably corrupt (though a certain camp pleasure in soap operas may be allowed), but popular culture is treated sympathetically.

The radical academic does not regard high culture as a common good, to be conserved and passed on. Elite "culture" is rather to be understood as a form of conspicuous consumption, a mark of status. It buttresses the oppressive power of the ruling class, and its fetishization disempowers and silences the majority. In multicultural America, courses in Western Civilization are said to alienate students from other backgrounds. But the critical intellectual is troubled even more by the cultural power wielded by the mass media. Instruments of capital, the media market not only soft drinks but also false aspirations. Reviewing an influential anthology on cultural studies, Stefan

Collini remarks on the almost paranoid misgivings that gnaw away at critics of cultural production:

> The suspicion is that most forms of cultural activity are essentially a disguise for the fact that Somebody is Trying to Screw Somebody Else . . . hardly a page of this fat volume goes by without our being told that somebody who possesses some kind of power . . . is trying to 'dominate,' 'suppress,' 'occlude,' 'mystify,' 'exploit,' 'marginalise' . . . someone else, and in response it is the duty of those engaged in Cultural Studies to 'subvert,' 'unmask,' 'contest,' 'de-legitimize,' 'intervene,' 'struggle against.'

The best hope for such resistance is represented by popular culture, and it accordingly became the initial focus of cultural studies. As cultural studies developed in British universities in the 1960s, inspired by Raymond Williams, rooted in the British New Left, popular culture was the hot topic. Not that popular culture was necessarily regarded as benign, as Stuart Hall, a pioneering figure in the field, recalls—there was always a risk that it would be co-opted in the service of the powerful. "It is partly where hegemony arises, and where it is secured." On the other hand, to the extent that popular culture can be controlled by the people themselves, "it is one of the places where socialism might be constituted."

Whether celebrating popular culture or doing its bit to combat hegemony, cultural studies has always been at once an academic pursuit and a political movement. Cultural and political criticism merge in the study of film, television, and sports, and the oppressive message of the media is contested by the agitprop of class, race, and gender activists. The title page of the international journal *Cultural Studies* declares that it is "dedicated to the notion that the study of cultural processes, and especially of popular culture, is important, complex, and both theoretically and politically rewarding." In Europe, at least, it is taken for granted that the practitioners of cultural studies are on the left. "All the basic assumptions of cultural studies are Marxist," John Storey writes. Marxism has been less influential in the United States, but cultural studies in America is characterized by the traditional radical reluctance to separate theory from practice. The cultural specialist may conveniently engage in both without leaving her office, which is probably in a university, in a department of literature or education. Urgent political issues are close at hand, having to do with the recruitment of students and faculty and the definition of the canon.

A case can be made that anthropology should be folded into cultural studies, if it indeed has a civic duty to unmask the enemy (capitalism, Western hegemony, patriarchy). This was the broad thrust of Marcus and Fischer's *Anthropology as Cultural Critique*, and in an essay published in 1992 George Marcus specifically urged that cultural anthropology should be recast as a branch of cultural studies. Many anthropology students have responded eagerly to this call, finding it morally less troubling, and perhaps generally easier, to study television programs in a familiar living room rather than to venture into the territory of the Other.

At the very least, anthropologists are urged to take on board the central propositions of cultural studies: that culture serves power, and that it is (and should be) contested. There is clearly something in this. Even if culture is not quite the same thing as ideology, there is surely a place for the critical account of the merchants of culture. Nevertheless, many anthropologists will feel cheated by the cultural studies program. The obvious objection is that, when culture is restricted to the arts, the media, and the educational system, it deals with only some aspects of what anthropologists mean by culture, and then from a very particular perspective. A few institutions are singled out as the cultural producers. The main concern is then who is paying for them, and what interests they serve. Moreover, the traditional cultural charity of the anthropologist has no place in these exercises. Every cultural product is judged, not on aesthetic grounds but by applying the simple test of the radical. It is either oppressive or liberating. This activist engagement also feeds an unfortunate tendency to endorse certain kinds of censorship (much derided by its opponents as political correctness).

Finally, the model for the operation of culture is based on an understanding of what is happening in modern Western consumer society. When they look abroad, which they do not do very often, what the cultural studies writers see is a process of Americanization (called globalization). The rest of the world is apparently condemned to repeat the cultural drama that had its premiere in the metropolis. Subject to the same media, the whole world will enact the same struggles. Alas, the traditional ethnographer, getting to know what life is like in some village, has little to say about all this. Monographs on village affairs therefore remain on the shelves, while publishers compete for accounts of how Indonesian urbanites read Mexican soaps.

If American anthropologists anxiously contemplate cultural studies as a threat to their academic monopology, many regard multiculturalism rather as an opportunity. Yet the latter may represent a more subversive challenge, since it is a political translation of some core ideas about culture to which anthropologists might subscribe, in more nuanced form. It therefore raises troubling questions about the implications of their own theories.

It must be conceded at once that multiculturalism is not a coherent social movement. Some sympathizers would disdain the label. Among those who describe themselves as multiculturalists, one could distinguish between schools, factions, tendencies. Terence Turner, for instance, opposes a *difference* multiculturalism (to be deplored) to a *critical* multiculturalism, which he finds admirable. Difference multiculturalism is inward-looking, self-regarding, pumped up with pride about the importance of a particular culture and its claims to superiority. Critical multiculturalism, in contrast, is outward-looking, organized to challenge the cultural prejudices of the dominant social class, intent on uncovering the vulnerable underbelly of the hegemonic discourse. This critical multiculturalism is, in fact, heavily influenced by cultural studies, and critical cultural studies in

America has adopted much of the multicultural agenda. (This tendency has become apparent in Britain as well. The master's program in cultural studies at the University of Leeds deals with "issues in the politics of representation, sexuality and gender, race and ideas of difference.") So closely have the two movements coalesced that Lawrence Grossberg, editor of the influential journal *Cultural Studies*, remarks on "a noticeable tendency to equate cultural studies with the theory and politics of identity and difference."

Yet in spite of the real distinctions that may be drawn between its various modalities, all forms of multiculturalism share some common premises. And although its academic theorists cite European philosophers, and despite the fact that its influence has spread across the Atlantic, particularly to Britain, the underlying assumptions of multiculturalism are distinctively American. Based in the humanities departments of the universities, multiculturalism is the latest and most American critique of establishment ideology. It echoes earlier discourses of dissent that were once fashionable on campus, calling for the cultural empowerment of the weak and their emancipation.

The common purpose is to replace the ideology of the American melting pot with what is in effect an ideology of anti-assimilation. The multiculturalist rejects the view that the immigrant should assimilate to the American mainstream, and even denies that there is a mainstream, that all proper Americans share the same ideals and aspirations. On the contrary, the America of the multiculturalists is culturally fragmented. They do not regard this as a problem in itself. The trouble is not that differences exist, but that they are treated with disdain, as deviations from the norm. A hegemonic culture (white, Anglo, middle-class, male, hetero) imposes its rules on everyone else. The rest of the population is stigmatized for being different. Their differences define them: they are not white, not Anglo, not middle-class, not male, not heterosexual.

From one point of view, the dominant group simply imposes its own ideal characteristics as the defining norm, and labels anyone who is different as a deviant. An alternative perspective suggests that these minorities are authentically different groups from the point of view of their own members. They are what they are because each group has its own culture. The ruling group oppresses them by denying equality—or equivalence—to the values and symbols of their cultures. It refuses to acknowledge their difference, or devalues it. The multiculturalist translates these propositions into a political program, affirming the right to be different and the value of difference. Each cultural constituency must be granted both a good measure of self-determination and an equal voice in collective affairs.

Multiculturalism is distantly related to certain Counter-Enlightenment discourses about ethnic identity. Not surprisingly, its hereditary enemy, the Enlightenment vision of a common human civilization, carried by a vanguard nation, also persists in America. Indeed, it flourishes. Its premise is that the nation can be strong and united only if there is cultural consensus. The multiculturalist critique concerns American conservatives, because the celebration of difference undermines common values and threatens national coherence. Moreover, conservatives agree that culture is transmitted through education and the media, and they worry that the multiculturalists are entrenched in positions of power in many schools and universities, in the newspapers, and in TV stations, where they are strategically placed to foster difference. To the extent that they are successful, the multiculturalists will endanger America's leadership in world affairs. This would be a catastrophe, since America has taken on the burden of the universal civilization (sometimes disobligingly described by their opponents as the white man's burden). Restating the neo-Enlightenment project, Samuel Huntington asserts that America must be united if it is to rally the forces of Western Civilization in the coming struggle against barbarism.

The protagonist in the multicultural struggle is not the worker, or the citizen, but the cultural actor. Politics are dictated by cultural identity, and they are about the control of culture. The notion of identity is central to this discourse, but although often taken for granted it is not easy to pin down. On the face of it, the term *identity* is an oxymoron when used in relation to an individual, since how can an individual not correspond to—be identical to—himself or herself? In psychology, identity may refer to the continuity of a personality over time: one is identical (more or less) to what one used to be. More commonly, however, the notion of identity is connected rather to the idea that the self has certain essential properties and some contingent ones. There is a real me, which may not correspond to the person I appear to be. I might choose, or be forced, to disguise elements of my true self, which remain hidden from the world. I may not be able to find my own voice, or to recognize myself in the representations that surround me.

This modern cluster of ideas carries a moral charge that may be Protestant in inspiration. In the Protestant tradition there is an idea that a still voice speaks inside one, the voice of conscience, to which one must listen, shutting out the noise of the world. It is God's way of talking to us. The Romantic doctrine was that this inner voice represents a person's true nature. There is then a moral obligation to dig deep into oneself, in order to discover who one really is. According to Charles Taylor, this notion of the true self "arises along with an ideal, that of being true to myself and my own particular way of being . . . If I am not, I miss the point of my life; I miss what being human is for *me*."

But identity is not only a private matter. It must be lived out in the world, in a dialogue with others. According to the constructionist, it is in this dialogue that an identity is fabricated. But that is not the way in which identity is experienced. From a subjective point of view, identity is discovered within oneself, and it implies identity with others. The inner self finds its home in the world by participating in the identity of a collectivity (for example, a nation, ethnic minority, social class, political or religious movement). This identification is often expressed in exalted, mystical terms. The real me (my soul, some would say—though not, of course, many sociologists) is joined to the spiritual life of a community. As Georg Simmel put it at the turn of the century, expressing himself in the language of high idealism: "Cultivation comes about only if the contents absorbed out of the suprapersonal realm seem, as through a secret harmony, to unfold only that in the soul which exists within it as its own instinctual tendency and as the inner prefiguration of its subjective perfection." To put it somewhat more prosaically, the idea is that identity is realized by participation in a culture. "The concepts of identity-building and of culture," Zygmunt Bauman notes, "were and could only be born together."

Cultural identity goes hand in hand with cultural politics. A person can only be free in the appropriate cultural arena, where his or her values are respected. Every nation must therefore be independent. In a multicultural society, cultural difference must be respected, even fostered. Cultural survival is the bottom line of this politics. All this is, of course, part of a certain liberal European tradition, but it inevitably raises a problem for another liberal political tradition, dominant in America, that is based on the principle that all citizens are equal—and the same—before the law. Charles Taylor has attempted to find some basis for reconciling these two liberal traditions, but it is an intractable task. This is not only because cultural politics actually demands positive discrimination, though there is that problem; but it also requires conformity. Once a cultural identity has been established, the pressure is on to live it, even if that means sacrificing one's individuality.

Commenting on Taylor's argument, K. Anthony Appiah objects that he plays down the cost of defining identity in cultural terms. An individual may not be willing to accept a stereotypical role, or to follow a party line. Yet in coming out as a gay man, or making common cause with other African-Americans, a person may find that he is expected to conform to strict expectations about the way he conducts himself. "Demanding respect for people as blacks and as gays requires that there are some scripts that go with being an African-American or having same-sex desires. There will be proper ways of being black and gay, there will be expectations to be met, demands will be made. It is at this point that someone who takes autonomy seriously will ask whether we have not replaced one kind of tyranny with another." In short, Appiah rejects the politics of recognition precisely because it conflicts with liberal individualism, as indeed it must.

It could be argued that this dilemma appears only in modern Western societies that place a high value on individualism. But it is a real issue in such societies nevertheless. America in particular has traditionally emphasized the right to individual self-fulfillment. At the same time, for the immigrant, or the member of a minority group, collective identities matter. Erik Erikson noted in an autobiographical essay that when he started to use the terms "identity" and "identity crisis" in the 1930s and 1940s, "they seemed naturally grounded in the experience of emigration, immigration, and Americanization."

Weighing these two values, collective identities against personal identities, the sacrifice of individuality in the interest of cultural solidarity may seem an unattractive prospect, even repugnant. There may also be a strategic reason to emphasize individual rights in dealing with the wider society. In practice, members of minority groups are more likely to be troubled by racial or religious or legal discrimination than by a more subtle denial of cultural recognition. Rather than claiming a right to be different, it might seem more sensible in such a situation to insist on the right to equal and similar treatment. Where America is concerned, Michael Walzer opts in the end for the culture-blind liberalism of equal rights "in part, at least, because I think that immigrants to societies like this have already made the same choice . . . the communities they have created here are different from those they knew before precisely in this sense, that they are adapted to, shaped significantly by, the liberal idea of individual rights."

Debates about culture and identity in the United States were once inspired by concerns about immigration. In the 1950s and 1960s, the issue was race rather than immigration, and in particular the place of African-Americans in the society. Uncomfortable questions were raised about the realities of civil rights in America, and the willingness of the majority to assimilate minorities. It was suggested that perhaps African-Americans should establish themselves as a separate nation. But the cultural politics of the 1980s and 1990s have been more concerned with categories of people that are, on the face of it, very different from immigrant groups, or native Americans, or black Americans: groups defined by gender, for instance, or by sexual orientation, or by disability, or by religious beliefs.

There have been attempts to suggest that all these minorities, old and new, are in a similar situation, though being black in America may appear to be a very different matter from being a Jew, or Spanish-speaking, or a lesbian. In any case, an obvious distinctive characteristic of these self-defined minorities is that they only recently attained visibility, although it is sometimes argued that a category such as "gays," for example, or "Black Muslims," existed before they were recognized, even by their members. A second distinctive feature of the new cultural politics is that identity appears to be a matter of choice, although the underlying belief seems to be that just as the collectivity has an authentic identity that will emerge in time, so the individual has a necessary identity with a particular cultural collectivity, even if it remains to be discovered, perhaps after a period of denial. So although the popular American notion of cultural identity has been stretched beyond ethnic groups to other kinds of minorities, it remains doubly essentialist: one has an essential identity, and this derives from the essential character of the collectivity to which one belongs. Membership in a group may be established only after a protracted process of self-examination, but one cannot escape one's identity. It is fixed by something even more essential: by one's very nature.

Contemporary anthropologists are uneasy about the essentialism implicit in this popular culture theory. The sophisticated scholars whom Terence Turner calls critical multiculturalists (to distinguish them from essentializing naifs) shy away from the conclusion that identity is primordial, inherited, even biologically given. Their discourse on identity is pitched against biological determinism and every kind of essentialism. They are anti-racist, anti-sexist, anti-ageist. They insist moreover that both culture and identity are made up, invented, unstable discursive fabrications. Every culture is fragmented, internally contested, its boundaries porous. The pursuit of identity is a desperate existential struggle to put together a life-style that can be sustained for at least a brief moment.

And yet they are committed to the value of difference, and cannot do without something like the ideas of culture and identity. So James Clifford, for instance, describes himself as "straining for a concept that can preserve culture's differentiating functions while conceiving of collective identity as a hybrid, often discontinuous inventive process." Roger Keesing complains, however, that "in practice, American post-modernist anthropologists, with their roots in the interpretive/cultural constructionist tradition, often rhetorically invoke radical alterity," and assume that different identities are rooted in a preexisting cultural difference. He cites in evidence passages from Marcus and Fischer's *Anthropology as Cultural Critique,* where the authors "talk about 'the most intimate experiences of personhood . . . distinctive of particular cultures' and of 'Moroccan masculinity' as only 'superficially similar to masculinity in other cultures.' 'What [they ask] if persons in certain other cultures act from different conceptions of the individual?' "

Contemporary American anthropologists repudiate the popular ideas that differences are natural, and that cultural identity must be grounded in a primordial, biological identity, but a rhetoric that places great emphasis on difference and identity is not best placed to counter these views. On the contrary, the insistence that radical differences can be observed between peoples serves to sustain them. This is immediately evident from a review of the arguments that are made about about a wide range of sensitive topics, for example, those who claim that cultural treasures should be returned to native lands, or those who object to the idea of a white scholar being the director of an African-American studies program. For how can one know whether a person's cultural identity is authentic? Only if it is further assumed that identity is fixed by descent.

In the United States, this sort of logic is commonly taken for granted in popular discourse. It is hardly surprising, then, that culture often comes to serve as a politically correct euphemism for race. Walter Benn Michaels has demonstrated how inseparably these two concepts are bound together even in some very sophisticated discourses. American writers who invoke cultural identity and cultural difference do not necessarily abandon the idea of race in favor of culture. Rather they tend to assume that "it is only when we know which race we are that we can tell which culture is ours."

There is nothing new about this, nor can it be easily waved away as the vulgarization of a more subtle and acceptable idea. Although Michaels pays particular attention to literary sources, he shows that an essentialist argument along these lines was made by the anthropologists Edward Sapir and Melville Herskovits. When Sapir described an American Indian as having "slipped out of the warm embrace of a culture into the cold air of a fragmentary existence," he was making the assumption that one is born to a culture, even if one does not have it. Michaels comments that:

> if the Indian's culture were simply identical to his behavior and in no way related to his race, then he could never slip out of its warm embrace. In order for a culture to be lost, then, it must be separable from one's actual behavior, and in order for it to be separable from one's actual behavior, it must be anchorable in race. Sapir's critique of race by culture is actually the continuation of race through culture.

The case of Herskovits is rather different. He began as a traditional Boasian, for whom culture was something acquired, changeable, made up of borrowings. Racial memory was a myth. Ancestral African customs did not persist in North America. African-American culture soon became unambiguously American. Any differences that might be remarked in Harlem simply reflected carryovers from rural life in the South. But in *The Myth of the Negro Past* (1941) Herskovits made a very different argument. He now insisted that black Americans in some sense possessed African culture, even if they had apparently lost it. "The things the African Negro used to do count as the American Negro's past," Michaels comments, "only because both the African and the American are 'the Negro.' " Of course, Herskovits's motives were anything but racist. Yet as Michaels remarks, his "antiracist culturalism" seems to require "a commitment to racial identity."

"The modern concept of culture is not . . . a critique of racism," Michaels concludes, "it is a form of racism. And, in fact, as skepticism about the biology of race has increased, it has become—at least among intellectuals—the dominant form of racism." The same argument applies to identity: "what's wrong with cultural identity is that, without recourse to the racial identity that (in its current manifestations) it repudiates, it makes no sense." The anti-racist celebrates Chicano identity and stands up for the particular rights of the Chicano, but these rights are available only to a person who was born to be a Chicano. Although Michaels does not make the point, a similar argument could be developed with reference to some feminist discourses. While insisting that "gender" (culturally constructed) does not derive directly from the biology of "sex," appeals to gender solidarity proceed in practice from the assumption that identity depends on biology. Perhaps that is also why some gay activists are ready to believe that there must be a gene for homosexuality.

One alternative to this slide into essentialism is to make identity into a cultural construct./Culture then invests a person with an identity. But this is to make culture (or discourse) into the only power in the land, and one that is apparently without any independent justification. It just is, or rather, it just makes itself up./Stuart Hall points out, moreover, that once this move has been made the analyst is left with no way of explaining why a particular person ends up with a specific identity. The difficulties are multiplied if the claim is made that both culture and identity are freely invented, that each person makes up his or her own identity, choosing between allegiances, beliefs, and values. Identity—James Clifford's "hybrid, often discontinuous inventive process"—is then a matter of life-style, chosen on a whim, or, on a more gloomy reading, dictated by fashion.

This is a popular move in recent cultural studies texts. David Chaney, for example, urges us to think about life-styles as "interpretive frameworks" that "facilitate creative adaptation," "a particular exemplification of an aesthetics of representation." But however much emphasis may be put on creative, imaginative acts, the analysis soon tends to reintroduce conventional notions of culture and community. (You may choose to be a vegan, but you have to shop in the same supermarket as everyone else, and follow the recipes of the vegan cookbook, and explain yourself to your mother.) Chaney himself immediately concedes that "culture is always the bridge between individuals and their collective identities." A life-style is then just a way of clothing (or feeding) an identity. Chaney makes the rather vague claim that life-styles "provide an appropriately ambiguous, for postmodern society, mediation between individuality and community," but it is hard to see what this tortuous formula adds to the conventional idea of identity.

Another problematic aspect of multiculturism is the cult of difference, which seems at times to be the one undisputed value. For James Clifford, culture represents "the continuing ability of groups to make a real difference." It is for that reason that we must preserve "the concept's differential and relativist functions" and avoid "the positing of cosmopolitan essences and human common denominators."

There are many objections to be made to this position. Lévi-Strauss, for example, suggested that most people insist on their uniqueness and their difference from others, and tend to regard the customs of the others as monstrous and scandalous, and their bearers as not fully human. The Spaniards sent out commissions just after the discovery of America to ascertain whether or not the natives had souls, while the natives themselves were busily drowning white prisoners in order to check whether their corpses were subject to putrefaction. This faith in difference and superiority may be a useful illusion, but it remains an illusion nevertheless. A barbarian "is first of all the man who believes in barbarism." Lévi-Strauss urged anthropologists to demonstrate that the differences between peoples are not to be measured on a single scale, for values are culturally variable, and at the same time to affirm that human differences are inscribed upon a common foundation. The measure of human uniformity is our common ability to learn, to borrow, to assimilate. The great historical breakthroughs have been made in different parts of the world. Every culture is multicultural: "All cultures are the result of a mishmash, borrowings, mixtures that have occurred, though at different rates, ever since the beginning of time." In a sense, it is what we share that produces the differences between us, which in turn depend on our interrelationships. "Diversity is less a function of the isolation of groups than of the relationships which unite them."

Another kind of objection to the cult of difference, one that must be most troubling to its advocates, is that this is not how things appear, in general, to people who have to make their way among foreigners. Despite what is taken to be the inescapable reality of alterity, and the force of cultural determinism, the fact is that immigrants, refugees, and traders seem in general to manage very well, given the chance, in their new homes—not forgetting their origins, but ever adaptable. They know what they are doing, they instruct greenhorns in tactics, and they write home to convey their experiences. (Their practical successes should persuade ethnographers stumped by the Catch-22 of cultural determinism that it is possible for them to learn another way of life just as well as many immigrants do, and to write back about it just as effectively.) As Gerd Baumann has shown so well, immigrants (like ethnographers) can also learn to manipulate dominant discourses about culture with great fluency, if it suits them. Success depends upon learning a language, asserting common interests, and grasping similarities, and at the same time learning to recognize where significant differences lie and what they mean, if only in order to minimize them, or to cope with them.

In short, contrary to what the theory predicts, the experience of crossing over from one cultural context to another does not necessarily heighten the sense of difference. Reviewing modern culture theory in a generally sympathetic fashion, the late Roger Keesing was moved to insist that his own experiences in the field did not impress on him the radical nature of otherness. "I recently spent some weeks immersed in conversation with a brilliant young Kwaio (Solomon Islands) man who still practices his ancestral religion and lives in a world where magic, ritual, and conversations with the dead are the stuff of everyday life," he wrote.

> Maenaa'adi's cultural alterity is perhaps as radical as any in the world of the early 1990s (although he too lives in the collages of our time, riding buses and checking the time on his watch when he comes to town). He takes for granted that if his shadow were cast on a fissure where a leprosy victim's body has been thrown, he would die of leprosy. He takes for granted that every night his shade encounters the shades of his ancestors, who give him messages of impending events. He recites magical spells a dozen times a day, with complete faith that they should work. Obviously, I am not claiming that Maenaa'adi's world of experience and mine are minor variants of one another: There is more to it than that. Yet I see no reason, in all the texts, to infer that the pragmatic way in which he finds his way in the world is qualitatively different from the way in which I find my way through mine; or that his culturally constructed senses of individuation and agency (or personhood or causality or whatever) are strikingly different from mine.

This is the last testament of an outstanding ethnographer, who devoted a lifetime to his study of the Kwaio. It should not come as a surprise. Good ethnographers, like successful immigrants, are often struck by the continuities between the most exotic field setting and their own home towns. At some point they may stop worrying that cross-cultural understanding is beyond their grasp, and begin to worry rather whether by some malign chance they have landed in a society hardly worth describing, since it is so disconcertingly familiar and prosaic.

Modern theories about culture recycle earlier ones, and lend themselves to similar political purposes. Each also confronts well-worn objections that are posed by its rivals. Formulated in ambiguous and weak terms, the theories all say something that is now rather obvious, hardly remarkable, even if the diffuse light they shed may sometimes be helpful. They retain the power to shock, even to interest, only if they are stated in very strong terms—but then their claims seem to be over the top, not to be reconciled with what we know from our own experience. At full strength, moreover, we may suspect that they are not good for the health.

These theories also have fundamental weaknesses in common. Complex notions like culture, or discourse, inhibit an analysis of the relationships among the variables they pack together. Even in sophisticated modern formulations, culture—or discourse—tends to be represented as a single system, though one shot through with arguments and inconsistencies. However, to understand culture, we must first deconstruct it. Religious beliefs, rituals, knowledge, moral values, the arts, rhetorical genres, and so on should be separated out from each other rather than bound together into a single bundle labeled culture, or collective consciousness, or superstructure, or discourse. Separating out these elements, one is led on to explore the changing configurations in which language, knowledge, techniques, political ideologies, rituals, commodities, and so on are related to each other.

It may be objected that the abstraction of a system of cultural processes is a purely methodological requirement. The cultural sphere may properly be treated as though it were an autonomous whole, if only for purposes of analysis. But the problems return, in more acute form, when this methodological strategy is turned (usually implicitly) into a presumption that culture can be explained in its own terms, a move that must disable further analysis. I have tried to show that the major ethnographic case studies of Geertz, Schneider, and Sahlins can be treated as critical experiments in cultural determinism. They fail when they overreach themselves and presume that culture rules, and that other factors can be excluded from the study of cultural processes and social behavior.

A well-established strategy is to treat culture in a preliminary way as if it were a single system (a subsystem, in Parsonian terms). It is then fitted together with an analysis of social or biological processes. Leaving aside the problematic images of systems and subsystems, this is still to treat culture as a whole, which is related as a whole to something else. However, if the elements of a culture are disaggregated, it is usually not difficult to show that the parts are separately tied to specific administrative arrangements, economic pressures, biological constraints, and so forth. "A 'culture,'" Eric Wolf concluded, "is thus better seen as a series of processes that construct, reconstruct, and dismantle cultural materials, in response to identifiable determinants."

For Roy D'Andrade, a central feature of modern cognitive anthropology has been precisely

> the breaking up of culture into parts . . . cognitively formed units—features, prototypes, schemas, propositions, theories, etc. This makes possible a *particulate* theory of culture; that is, a theory about the "pieces" of culture, their composition and relations to other things.

D'Andrade's conception of culture is psychological—it is "in the mind"—but a similar point could be made if culture is conceived of rather as a public discourse, comparable to a language. It would still make sense to break it up into parts, and then to see whether elements in the complex mix of culture may have their own specific (though not fixed) "relations to other things." Perhaps kinship and the division of labor by sex have something to do after all with the biology of reproduction; or, as Foucault insisted, knowledge is to be understood in relation to power; or, as Bourdieu writes, the arts should be analyzed with reference to funding, and to the prestige they lend to the connoisseur; and cultural identity may make sense only when it is placed in the context of a particular electoral system.

In short, it is a poor strategy to separate out a cultural sphere, and to treat it in its own terms. Parsons attempted a synthesis among culture theory, social theory, and psychology. He failed, however grandly, but unless we separate out the various processes that are lumped together under the heading of culture, and then look beyond the field of culture to other processes, we will not get far in understanding any of it. For the same sort of reason, cultural identity can never provide an adequate guide for living. We all have multiple identities, and even if I accept that I have a primary cultural identity, I may not want to conform to it. Besides, it would not be very practical. I operate in the market, live through my body, struggle in the grip of others. If I am to regard myself only as a cultural being, I allow myself little room to maneuver, or to question the world in which I find myself. Finally, there is a moral objection to culture theory. It tends to draw attention away from what we have in common instead of encouraging us to communicate across national, ethnic, and religious boundaries, and to venture between them.

NOTES

I have made suggestions for further reading in places where it seemed useful to direct the reader to general background sources in addition to the sources referred to in the notes. The notes themselves refer to quotations in the text, in which case they appear in quotation marks, or they provide references for statements made in the text, in which case the statement is repeated, and the sources given in the following lines. I have occasionally included further comments or quotations that expand on the text.

Some works that provide thoughtful alternatives to the perspective on culture theory developed in this book include Michael Carrithers, *Why Humans Have Cultures: Explaining Anthropology and Social Diversity* (Oxford: Oxford University Press, 1992); Morris Freilich et al. (eds.), *The Relevance of Culture* (New York: Bergen & Garvey, 1989); Bennett M. Berger, *An Essay on Culture: Symbolic Structure and Social Structure* (Berkeley: University of California Press, 1995); and Margaret Archer, *Culture and Agency* (Cambridge: Cambridge University Press, 1996).

Preface

ix "is, indeed, the sole and exclusive subject-matter": Robert H. Lowie, *Culture and Ethnology* (New York: McMurtrie, 1917), p. 5.

ix "culture concept of the anthropologists": Stuart Chase, *The Proper Study of Mankind* (New York: Harper, 1948), p. 59.

x "the idea of culture": A. L. Kroeber and Clyde Kluckhohn, *Culture: A Critical Review of Concepts and Definitions* (Cambridge, Mass.: Papers of the Peabody Museum, Harvard University, vol. 47, no. 1, 1952), p. 3.

xiii The Afrikaner nationalists were suspicious of the "civilizing mission" . . . For a review of Afrikaner ethnology, and of Eiselen's career, see Robert Gordon, "Apartheid's Anthropologists: The Genealogy of Afrikaner Anthropology," *American Ethnologist*, 13(3) (1988): 535–553, and for a more general account of South African anthropology see W. D. Hammond-Tooke, *Imperfect Interpreters: South Africa's Anthropologists 1920–1990* (Johannesburg: Witwatersrand University Press, 1997).

xiv "We do not observe a 'culture' ": A. R. Radcliffe-Brown, "On Social Structure," *Journal of the Royal Anthropological Institute*, 70 (1940): 1–12.

xiv "For what is happening in South Africa": ibid.

Introduction: Culture Wars

1 "I don't know how many times": Raymond Williams, *Politics and Letters* (London: New Left Books, 1979), p. 174.

1 "We tried to sell 'semiotics' ": Larissa MacFarquahar, "This Semiotician Went to Market," *Lingua Franca*, September/October 1994, p. 62.

2 "Somebody sees sociology": Jessica Marshall, "Shelf Life," *Lingua Franca*, March/April 1995, p. 27.

2 " 'Culture'—the word itself": Marshall Sahlins, "Goodbye to *Tristes Tropes*: Ethnography in the Context of Modern World History," *Journal of Modern History*, 65 (1993): 3–4.

2 "question what the terms *culture* and *community*": Gerd Baumann, *Contesting Culture: Discourses of Identity in Multi-Ethnic London* (Cambridge: Cambridge University Press, 1996), p. 145.

2 "We consider the main threat": *International Herald Tribune*, September 21, 1996, p. 5.

3 "Reciprocity would mean changing laws": Quoted by Ian Buruma, *The Missionary and the Libertine: Love and War in East and West* (London: Faber, 1996) p. 235.

3 Samuel P. Huntington, "The Clash of Civilizations?" *Foreign Affairs*, Summer 1993, p. 22.

3 "major differences in political and economic development": Samuel P. Huntington, *The Clash of Civilizations and the Remaking of World Order* (New York: Simon and Schuster, 1996), p. 29. The following quotations are from pages 20 and 28. Note that the original essay

asked a question ("The clash of civilizations?"). Now the question has, apparently, been answered, in the affirmative.

3 "The multiculturalists notwithstanding": Roger Kimball, "Tenured Radicals," *New Criterion,* January 1991, p. 13.

4 "the greater clash": Huntington, *The Clash of Civilizations,* p. 321.

4 "So culture as a theme": Fred Inglis, *Cultural Studies* (Oxford: Blackwell, 1993), p. 109.

4 Within the élite, Pierre Bourdieu has argued, the value of high culture . . . Pierre Bourdieu, *Distinction: A Social Critique of the Judgement of Taste* (London: Routledge, 1984).

5 "naively identify his own particular culture": Louis Dumont, *German Ideology: From France to Germany and Back* (Chicago: University of Chicago Press, 1994), p. 3.

6 "I have seen Frenchmen, Italians, Russians": Joseph de Maistre, *Considerations on France* (Cambridge: Cambridge University Press, 1994; French publication, 1797), p. 53.

7 "Man isn't at all one": Henry James, letter to William Dean Howells, May 1, 1890.

8 "the most spiritual": F. Nietzsche, *Jenseits von Gut und Böse* (1886; Munich: Goldmann, 1980), 254, p. 145.

8 "a truly barbarous country": Baudelaire, cited by Jean Starobinski, *Blessings in Disguise: Or, The Morality of Evil* (Cambridge, Mass.: Harvard University Press, 1993), p. 54.

9 "the best that has been known and said": Matthew Arnold, *Literature and Dogma* (London: McMillan, preface to 1873 edition).

9 "As civilisation advances": Thomas Babington Macaulay, "Milton." First published 1825; collected in *Critical and Historical Essays,* 1843; reissued by Everyman's Library (London: Dent, 1907), p. 153.

11 "romantic rebellion": Richard A. Shweder, "Anthropology's Romantic Rebellion Against the Enlightenment," in *Culture Theory: Essays on Mind, Self, and Emotion,* ed. Richard A. Shweder and Robert A. LeVine (Cambridge: Cambridge University Press, 1984).

12 "one can think of the ideas of culture": Christopher Herbert, *Culture and Anomie: Ethnographic Imagination in the Nineteenth Century* (Chicago: University of Chicago Press, 1991), p. 29.

13 "are Germanised": Quoted by Erwin H. Ackerknecht, *Rudolf Virchow: Doctor, Statesman, Anthropologist* (Madison: University of Wisconsin Press, 1953), pp. 215–216.

14 In the 1980s, Michael Moffatt . . . Michael Moffatt, *Coming of Age in New Jersey: College and American Culture* (New Brunswick, N.J.: Rutgers University Press, 1989).

15 Alfred Kroeber at Berkeley and Clyde Kluckhohn at Harvard . . . A. L. Kroeber and Clyde Kluckhohn, *Culture: A Critical Review of Concepts and Definitions* (Cambridge, Mass.: Papers of the Peabody Museum, Harvard University, vol. 47, no. 1, 1952).

16 "has come to be so completely associated": Roy Wagner, *The Invention of Culture* (Chicago: University of Chicago Press, 1975), p. 1.

16 "a modern anthropologist": Herbert, *Culture and Anomie*, p. 20.

17 "For centuries the humanities and the social sciences": Claude Lévi-Strauss, *Structural Anthropology* (New York: Basic Books, 1963), pp. 70 and 71. I have slightly altered the translation of the second quotation.

19 "(re)construct an essentialized culture concept": Robert Brightman, "Forget Culture: Replacement, Transcendence, Relexification," *Cultural Anthropology*, 10(4) (1995): 510.

1. Culture and Civilization: French, German, and English Intellectuals, 1930–1958

FURTHER READING

Philippe Bénéton, *Histoire de mots: Culture et civilisation* (Paris: Presses de la Fondation Nationale des Sciences Politiques, 1975); Louis Dumont, *German Ideology: From France to Germany and Back* (Chicago: University of Chicago Press, 1994). A fascinating study, at a tangent to the theme of this chapter, is Wolf Lepenies, *Between Literature and Science: The Rise of Sociology* (Cambridge: Cambridge University Press, 1992). Background materials on Febvre, Elias, and Williams are given in the notes below.

23 "Civilisation nâit à son heure": Lucien Febvre, "Civilisation," in *Civilisation: Le mot et l'idée*, presented by Lucien Febvre, Émile Tonnelat, Marcel Mauss, Alfredo Niceforo, and Louis Weber, 1930 (Paris: Centre International de Synthèse, La Renaissance du Livre), p. 16. A translation is published in Peter Burke (ed.), *A New Kind of History: From the Writings of Febvre* (London: Routledge and Kegan Paul, 1973). Burke also provides a brief account of Febvre's career in the introduction to the volume.

23 "To reconstruct the history": ibid. (Burke's translation, here slightly amended), p. 219.

24 "But for a long time now": ibid., p. 220.

27 In a companion paper . . . the sociologist Marcel Mauss . . . Marcel Mauss, "Les civilisations," in Febvre's volume, *Civilisation: Le mot et l'idée*, pp. 105 and 106.

27 "penetrates all forms of music": ibid., pp. 105–106.

28 In 1954 the linguist Emile Benveniste ... This essay has been published in translation in Emile Benveniste, *Problems in General Linguistics* (Coral Gables, Fla.: University of Miami Press, 1971), p. 291.

28 "Emancipation, or what is the same thing": Jean Starobinski, "The Word *Civilization*," in *Blessings in Disguise; or, The Morality of Evil* (Cambridge, Mass.: Harvard University Press, 1993; first published in French, 1989), p. 3.

28 "The two words were destined": ibid., p. 4.

28 "describe both the fundamental process": ibid., p. 5.

29 "The critique thus took two forms": ibid., p. 8.

29 "new blood ... pagan blood": quoted ibid., p. 25.

29 Norbert Elias, a German-Jewish exile writing in London ... See Stephen Mennell, *Norbert Elias: Civilisation and the Human Self-Image* (Oxford: Blackwell, 1989), and Norbert Elias, *Reflections on a Life* (Oxford: Polity Press, 1994).

29 "at the same time carriers of German cultural life": Elias, *Reflections on a Life*, pp. 18 and 19.

30 "expresses the self-consciousness of the West": Norbert Elias, *The Civilizing Process: The Development of Manners. Changes in the Code of Conduct and Feeling in Early Modern Times* (New York: Urizen Books, 1978; first German edition, Basel, 1939), pp. 3–4.

30 "refers essentially to intellectual, artistic, and religious facts": ibid., p. 4.

31 "the middle-class counterweight to the court": ibid., p. 24.

33 Elias remarked that at the time ... he was more influenced by Freud ... Mennell, *Norbert Elias*, p. 111.

33 "Human civilisation, by which I mean": Sigmund Freud, *The Future of an Illusion* (Standard Edition, London: Hogarth Press, 1961; first published in German in 1927), pp. 5–6.

33 "every civilisation must be built": Sigmund Freud, *Civilisation and Its Discontents* (Standard Edition, London: Hogarth Press, 1961; first published in German in 1930), p. 7. The following quotations are from the same page.

34 "the bloodless intellect": Oswald Spengler, *The Hour of Decision* (New York: Kropf, 1934), p. 88.

34 "contending national spirits": Ernst Troeltsch, cited by Fritz K. Ringer, *The Decline of the German Mandarins: The German Academic Community, 1890–1933* (Cambridge, Mass.: Harvard University Press, 1969), p. 101.

35 "the endowment of a finite segment": cited by Ralph Schroeder, *Max Weber and the Sociology of Culture* (London: Sage, 1992), p. 6.

35 "that beliefs and values": this is Ralph Schroeder's formulation, ibid., p. 8.

36 "That is to say, they were interested": Woodruff D. Smith, *Politics and the Sciences of Culture in Germany, 1840–1920* (New York: Oxford University Press, 1991), p. 3.

36 "a doubt of the validity": T. S. Eliot, *The Idea of a Christian Society* (London: Faber and Faber, 1939), p. 64.

37 "I mean first of all": These lectures were published as an appendix to *Notes Towards the Definition of Culture* (London: Faber and Faber, 1948). The citation is from p. 120.

37 "the culture of the individual": Eliot, *Notes Towards the Definition of Culture*, p. 21.

37 "possesses a function": ibid., p. 37.

37 "What is important is a structure of society": ibid., p. 48.

37 "Derby Day, Henley Regatta, Cowes": ibid., p. 31. Eliot was probably following Robert Lowie's earlier exemplary list of the traits that make up American culture. Lowie had remarked that electric lights are part of this culture, so is enthusiasm for baseball, "so are moving pictures, *thés dansants,* Thanksgiving Day masquerades, bar-rooms, Ziegfeld Midnight Follies, evening schools, the Hearst papers, woman suffrage clubs, the single-tax movement, Riker drug stores, touring-sedans, and Tammany Hall" (Robert Lowie, *Culture and Ethnology* [1917], p. 7).

38 "We may go further": ibid., p. 28; "bishops are a part": ibid., p. 32.

38 "any religion": ibid., p. 34.

38 "Culture may even be described": ibid., p. 26.

38 "We can also learn to respect every other culture": ibid., p. 65.

39 "Ultimately, antagonistic religions": ibid., p. 62.

39 Raymond Williams (1921–1988): See Fred Inglis, *Raymond Williams* (London: Routledge, 1995).

39 "a moralist": E. P. Thompson, *Making History: Writings on History and Culture* (New York: The Free Press, 1994), p. 244.

40 "the discovery that the idea of culture": Raymond Williams, *Culture and Society* (first published, London: Chatto and Windus, 1958; revised edition, New York: Columbia University Press, 1983), p. vii. This argument was repeated in Raymond Williams, *Keywords* (Oxford: Oxford University Press, 1976).

40–44 The citations from Shelley, Coleridge, Arnold, Eliot, Leavis, and others on these pages were those selected by Williams to illustrate his argument in *Culture and Society.*

41 "largely self-regarding feelings of class": Williams, *Culture and Society*, rev. ed., p. 117.

42 (essays that had been edited by Leavis): *Mill on Bentham and Coleridge*, ed. and introduced by F. R. Leavis (Cambridge: Cambridge University Press, 1950).

42 "the pivotal figure": ibid., p. 161.

42 "We can say of Eliot": ibid., p. 227.

43 "has been most marked": This and the following quotation from ibid., pp. 232–233.

43 "got him to read the sociologists": Inglis, *Raymond Williams*, p. 130.

44 epitomized by Middletown . . . Robert Lynd and Helen Lynd, *Middletown: A Study in Contemporary Culture* (New York: Harcourt Brace, 1929).

44 "*Middletown* is a frightening book": Williams, *Culture and Society*, p. 260.

45 "couldn't read German": Inglis, *Raymond Williams*, p. 145.

45 "At the beginning": Introduction to the second edition of *Culture and Society*, 1983, pp. x–xi.

2. The Social Science Account: Talcott Parsons and the American Anthropologists

FURTHER READING

Martin Martell, "Talcott Parsons," in *International Encyclopedia of the Social Sciences*, vol. 18, Biographical Supplement, 1979, pp. 609–630; Bruce C. Wearne, *The Theory and Scholarship of Talcott Parsons to 1951* (Cambridge: Cambridge University Press, 1989); Michael Schmid, "The Concept of Culture and Its Place Within a Theory of Social Action: A Critique of Talcott Parsons's Theory of Culture," in Richard Munch and Neil J. Smelser (eds.), *Theory of Culture* (Berkeley: University of California Press, 1992); James Peacock, "The Third Stream: Weber, Parsons and Geertz," *Journal of the Anthropological Society of Oxford*, 7 (1981): 122–129.

For the anthropologists the literature is voluminous, but in addition to the sources cited below see George W. Stocking, Jr., *Race, Culture and Evolution: Essays in the History of Anthropology* (New York: Free Press, 1968), and Han Vermeuelen and Arturo Roldan (eds.), *Fieldwork and Footnotes: Studies in the History of European Anthropology* (London: Routledge, 1995).

47 "We suggest that it is useful to define the concept *culture:*" A. L. Kroeber and Talcott Parsons, "The Concept of Culture and of Social System," *American Sociological Review*, 23 (1958): 583.

48 "Against mechanism": Talcott Parsons, *The Structure of Social Action: A Study in Social Theory with Special Reference to a Group of Recent European Writers* (New York: Free Press, 1937), p. 485.

49 "the reciprocal interaction": ibid., p. 11.

49 "the central fact": ibid., p. 19.

49 "the fact that the phenomena": ibid., p. 480.

50 "Pareto's development": ibid., p. 460.

50 "ends and norms are no longer merely individual": ibid., p. 464.

50 "explicitly stating that society exists only": ibid., p. 442.

50 "In this breakdown": ibid., p. 470.

50 "In fact Durkheim": ibid., p. 445.

51 "a hiatus which still persists": ibid., p. 474.

51 "A corollary of human freedom": ibid., p. 477.

51 "a complex of meanings": ibid., pp. 482–483.

52 "a remarkable point-for-point convergence": ibid., p. 717.

52 "It is convenient": Talcott Parsons, *The Social System* (New York: Free Press, 1951), p. 4.

53 "Cultural objects are symbolic elements": ibid., p. 4.

53 "A cultural system does not 'function' ": ibid., p. 17.

53 "what, according to the current trend": ibid., p. 553.

54 "In anthropological theory": ibid., p. 15.

54 "Only by some such definition": ibid., p. 554.

54 "Meeting in each other's homes": Talcott Parsons, "Clyde Kluckhohn and the Integration of the Social Sciences," in W. W. Taylor et al. (eds.), *Culture and Life: Essays in Memory of Clyde Kluckhohn* (Carbondale, Ill.: Southern Illinois University Press, 1973), p. 32.

55 "Why not English?": Clifford Geertz, *After the Fact* (Cambridge, Mass.: Harvard University Press, 1995), p. 100.

55 "social structure is part": Clyde Kluckhohn, note (pp. 26–27) in Talcott Parsons and Edward A. Shils (eds.), *Toward a General Theory of Action* (Cambridge, Mass.: Harvard University Press, 1951).

55 "an authentically independent level": Parsons, "Clyde Kluckhohn and the Integration of the Social Sciences," p. 55.

55 "in a sense far more restricted": A. L. Kroeber and Clyde Kluckhohn, *Culture: A Critical Review of Concepts and Definitions* (Cambridge, Mass.: Papers of the Peabody Museum, Harvard University, vol. 47, no. 1, 1952), p. 15.

55 "has moved in the anthropological direction": ibid., p. 135.

55 "Our incomplete satisfaction with Parsons": ibid., p. 136.

56 . . . an idea, they affirmed, with explanatory power: "If we are asked, 'How can a logical construct like culture explain anthing?' we could

reply that other logical concepts and abstractions like 'electromagnetic field' or 'gene'—which no one has ever seen—have been found serviceable in scientific understanding. Analytic abstractions summarize an order of relationship between natural phenomena, and relations are as real as things." Kroeber and Kluckhohn, *Culture*, p. 190.

56   "Culture, or Civilization": E. B. Tylor, *Primitive Culture* (London: John Murray, 1871), p. 1.

57   "Certainly there is as of 1951": Kroeber and Kluckhohn, *Culture*, p. 153.

57   "those properties of culture" and following quotations, ibid., pp. 171–173.

58   "Culture consists of patterns": ibid., p. 181.

58   "The resistance appears to be stylistic": ibid., p. 147.

59   "A generation or two later": ibid., p. 147.

59   "idea of culture was perhaps closer": George W. Stocking, Jr., *Race, Culture and Evolution: Essays in the History of Anthropology* (New York: Free Press, 1968), p. 73.

59   His anthropological thought "was part": ibid., p. 76.

59   "had contacts with German thought": ibid., p. 90.

60   "Prior to about 1900": ibid., p. 201.

60   "far from hindering": ibid., p. 202.

60   "a number of central elements": ibid., p. 230.

60   He has since conceded that this plural usage . . . See George W. Stocking, Jr., *Victorian Anthropology* (New York: The Free Press, 1987), especially pp. 302–304.

60   Kroeber and Kluckhohn . . . suggested that it was Ralph Linton and Margaret Mead: "Linton's and Mead's definitions appear to be the first to make an implicit distinction between 'culture' and 'a culture'. This point is simple but of great theoretical importance." Kroeber and Kluckhohn, *Culture*, p. 49.

61   "an integrated spiritual totality": ibid., p. 214.

61   "a cultural phenomenon is intelligible": Robert H. Lowie, *The History of Ethnological Theory* (New York: Holt, Rinehart and Winston, 1937), p. 145.

61   "Most English and American historians": Woodruff D. Smith, *Politics and the Sciences of Culture in Germany, 1840–1920* (New York: Oxford University Press, 1991), p. 241, note.

61   Woodruff Smith even suggests that it was through Boas . . . In fact, he concludes that "the greatest long-term impact of German neo-liberal anthropology was felt not in Germany but in the United States—in the work of Franz Boas"; ibid., p. 113.

62   "were gradually acquiring": Kroeber and Kluckhohn, *Culture*, p. 9.

62 "a thing *sui generis*": Robert H. Lowie, *Culture and Ethnology* (New York: McMurtrie, 1917), p. 66.

63 "We may liken the progress": ibid., p. 78.

63 "Cultures develop mainly": Robert Lowie, *Primitive Society* (New York: Harper, 1920), pp. 440–441. A number of American anthropologists argue that this passage does not mean what it seems to say, and that Lowie was not such a radical diffusionist as this suggests. In my view, Lowie could be counted on to say what he meant to say, and without ambiguity.

64 "the ethnologist and the culture-historian": Edward Sapir, "Culture, Genuine and Spurious," *American Journal of Sociology,* 29 (1924): 401–429. Reprinted in D. G. Mandelbaum (ed.), *Selected Writings of Edward Sapir* (Berkeley: University of California Press, 1949), p. 309.

64 "is the least easy to define": ibid., p. 310.

65 "a particular people its distinctive place": ibid., p. 311.

65 "nothing is spiritually meaningless": ibid., p. 317.

65 "spiritual hybrid": ibid., p. 318.

65 "the frequent vitality of cultures": ibid., p. 321.

66 "our spiritual selves go hungry": ibid., p. 323.

66 "must needs grow organically": ibid., p. 324.

66 "underlying the elements of civilization": ibid., p. 314.

67 "The life-history of the individual": Ruth Benedict, *Patterns of Culture* (Boston: Houghton Mifflin, 1934), pp. 2–3.

67 "A culture cannot be paranoid": Judith T. Irvine (ed.), *Edward Sapir: The Psychology of Culture* (Berlin: Mouton de Gruyter, 1994), p. 183. This is an edited reconstruction of Sapir's Yale lecture course on culture.

67 "felt that sufficient work": Margaret Mead, *Blackberry Winter* (New York: William Morrow, 1972), p. 126.

68 "nothing to do with anthropology": Robert Lowie (ed.), *Letters from Edward Sapir to Robert H. Lowie* (mimeo, Anthropology Department, University of California, Berkeley, 1965).

69 "a jurisdictional agreement": Howard S. Becker, "Culture: A Sociological View," *Yale Review,* 71 (1980): 517.

69 "It was a great satisfaction to me": Talcott Parsons, "Culture and Social System Revisited," in Louis Schneider and Charles M. Bonjean (eds.), *The Idea of Culture in the Social Sciences* (Cambridge: Cambridge University Press, 1973), p. 33.

69 "We suggest that it is useful": A. L. Kroeber and Talcott Parsons, "The Concept of Culture and of Social System," *American Sociological Review,* 23 (1958): 583.

70 "We therefore propose a truce": ibid., p. 585.

70 "I think it perhaps can be said": Parsons, "Culture and Social System Revisited," p. 33.

71 "a system of symbols and meanings": David M. Schneider, "Notes Toward a Theory of Culture," in K. Basso and H. Selby (eds.), *Meaning in Anthropology* (Albuquerque: University of New Mexico Press, 1976), p. 198.

71 "contrasts with norms": ibid., pp. 202–203.

71 "connection between a particular symbol": Parsons, *The Structure of Social Action*, p. 484.

72 "The fact of the matter": Edward Sapir, "The Status of Linguistics as a Science," 1929; reprinted in D. G. Mandelbaum (ed.), *Selected Writings of Edward Sapir* (Berkeley: University of California Press, 1949). Citation (in Mandelbaum edition) on p. 162.

72 " 'nature' and the 'facts of life' ": David M. Schneider, "Notes Toward a Theory of Culture," p. 204.

3. Clifford Geertz: Culture as Religion and as Grand Opera

FURTHER READING

Geertz's autobiographical reflections are to be found in Clifford Geertz, *After the Fact* (Cambridge, Mass.: Harvard University Press, 1995) and in an interview he gave to a colleague, Richard Handler, "An Interview with Clifford Geertz," *Current Anthropology*, 32(5) (1991): 603–613.

Jeffrey Alexander sets out a Parsonian critique of Geertz in lecture 17 of his *Twenty Lectures: Social Theory Since World War II* (New York: Columbia University Press, 1987). A useful book-length review of Geertz's oeuvre is Jan Willem Bakker, *Enough Profundities Already! A Reconstruction of Geertz's Interpretive Anthropology* (Utrecht: ISOR, 1988); pp. 119–141 review and assess the main anthropological criticisms of his work. See also J. W. Bakker et al. (eds.), *Antropologie Tussen Wetenschap en Kunst: Essays Over Clifford Geertz* (Amsterdam: VU Uitgeverij, 1987). For other critiques by anthropologists (by and large), see, inter alia, Talal Asad, "Anthropological Conceptions of Religion: Reflections on Geertz," *Man*, 18 (1983): 237–259; Aletta Biersack, "Local Knowledge and Local History: Geertz and Beyond," in Lynn Hunt (ed.), *The New Cultural History* (Berkeley: University of California Press, 1989); Roger Keesing, "Anthropology as Interpretive Quest," *Current Anthropology*, 28(1) (1987): 161–176; Vincent C. Pecora, "The Limits of Local Knowledge," in H. A. Veeser (ed.), *The New Historicism* (London: Routledge, 1989); William Roseberry, "Balinese Cockfights and the Seduction of Anthropology," *Social Research*, 49(4) (1982):

1013–28); Paul Shankman, "The Thick and the Thin: On the Interpretive Theoretical Program of Clifford Geertz," *Current Anthropology,* 25(3) (1984): 261–279); and Dan Sperber, *On Anthropological Knowledge* (Cambridge: Cambridge University Press, 1985). For a recent collective review of Geertz's ideas see a recent issue of the journal *Representations* (Summer 1997) that was devoted to essays on Geertz, in particular the introduction by Sherry B. Ortner and the essay by William H. Sewell, Jr., "Geertz, Cultural Systems, and History."

References to discussions of specific studies by Geertz can be found in the notes below.

75   "No matter how much one trains one's attention": Clifford Geertz, *After the Fact* (Cambridge, Mass.: Harvard University Press, 1995), p. 43.

76   "I grow uncomfortable": Clifford Geertz, *The Interpretation of Cultures* (New York: Basic Books, 1973), p. vii.

76   "Argument grows oblique": Clifford Geertz, *Local Knowledge: Further Essays in Interpretive Anthropology* (New York: Basic Books, 1983), p. 6.

76   "I went to Antioch College": Richard Handler, "An Interview with Clifford Geertz," *Current Anthropology,* 32(5) (1991): 603.

76   "Stumbling out of an undergraduate major": Geertz, *After the Fact,* p. 98.

77   "She didn't know us from Adam": Handler, "Interview," p. 603.

77   "In the summer after my first year": Geertz, *After the Fact,* pp. 102–103.

77   "was the very stamp": ibid., p. 103.

78   "In that sense it was a failed plan": Handler, "Interview," p. 606.

78   "which I suppose Clyde": ibid.

79   "at some intermission": Geertz, *After the Fact,* p. 117.

80   "There had been a time": John Updike, *The Afterlife and Other Stories* (New York: Knopf, 1994), pp. 66–67. Updike graduated from Harvard College in 1954, so he is referring to the period when Geertz was a graduate student in Social Relations. The passage continues: "She used to say she loved the way his hair was going thin even in college. She thought that was a sign of seriousness. It showed his brain was working to save mankind. All those soc-rel majors wanted to save the world."

81   "general ideological position": Geertz, *The Interpretation of Cultures,* p. 200, footnote.

81   "From Plato to Parsons": Alvin Gouldner, *The Coming Crisis of Western Sociology* (New York: Basic Books, 1970).

81 "an enormous increase in interest": Geertz, *The Interpretation of Cultures*, p. 29.

82 "the analogies are coming": Geertz, *Local Knowledge*, p. 22.

82 "the move toward meaning": Geertz, *After the Fact*, p. 115.

82 *"Man is the symbol-using animal"*: Kenneth Burke, *Language as Symbolic Action: Essays on Life, Literature and Method* (Berkeley: University of California Press, 1966), p. 3.

82 "the edifice of human knowledge": Susanne K. Langer, *Philosophy in a New Key*, 3rd ed. (Cambridge, Mass.: Harvard University Press, 1957), p. 21.

84 "to find in the contrast": David A. Apter, *Political Change: Collected Essays* (London: Cass, 1973), p. 160.

84 "just after a successful political revolution": Clifford Geertz, "Culture and Social Change: The Indonesian Case," *Man*, 19 (1984): 521.

85 Boeke was criticized . . . Among his critics was B. H. Higgins, who had directed the Java expedition that launched Geertz's career as an ethnographer. See B. H. Higgins, *Economic Development: Principles, Problems and Politics* (New York: Norton, 1959).

86 "frank individualism": Clifford Geertz, *Agricultural Involution: The Process of Ecological Change in Indonesia* (Berkeley: University of California Press, 1968), p. 123.

86 "progressive complication, and variety": Alexander A. Goldenweiser, "Loose Ends of a Theory on the Individual Pattern and Involution in Primitive Society," in Robert Lowie (ed.), *Essays in Anthropology Presented to Alfred Kroeber* (Berkeley: University of California Press, 1936).

86 "a richness of social surfaces": Geertz, *Agricultural Involution*, p. 103.

87 "I danced for rain": Geertz, "Culture and Social Change," p. 514. This essay is Geertz's own review of the debates stimulated by his book. For a sophisticated and balanced critical review see Joel Kahn, "Indonesia after the Demise of Involution," *Critique of Anthropology*, 5(1) (1985): 69–96. For a review that cites especially Indonesian and Dutch studies, see Koenjararingrat, *Anthropology in Indonesia* (The Hague: Nijhoff, 1975). An excellent critique of the ecological argument is presented by A. van Schaik, "Agrarische Involutie en Ecologische Processen," in J. W. Bakker et al. (eds.), *Antropologie Tussen Wetenschap en Kunst: Essays over Clifford Geertz* (Amsterdam: VU Uitgeverij, 1987).

87 "Indonesia is now": Clifford Geertz, *Peddlers and Princes: Social Change and Economic Modernization in Two Indonesian Towns* (Chicago: University of Chicago Press, 1963), p. 3.

87 "between 'East' and 'West' ": ibid., p. 7.

88 "the more traditional social loyalties": ibid., p. 16.

88 *"The function of the entrepreneur"*: ibid., p. 152.

88 As the Dutch sociologist W. F. Wertheim commented ... See W. F. Wertheim, "Peasants, Peddlers and Princes in Indonesia," *Pacific Affairs,* 37(3) (1964): 309–310.

89 "three main social-structural nuclei": Clifford Geertz, *The Religion of Java* (Glencoe, Ill.: Free Press, 1960), p. 5.

89 "the Javanese version": ibid., p. 11. On the *slametan* in village Java see Robert Hefner, *Hindu Javanese: Tenngar Tradition and Islam* (Princeton, N.J.: Princeton University Press, 1985), chap. 5.

89 "The *slametan* concentrates": Geertz, *Religion of Java,* p. 29.

89 "organized around rather different types of social structure": ibid., p. 234.

90 "the most truly nationalist": ibid., p. 381.

90 "The search for a viable form": Clifford Geertz, *The Social History of an Indonesian Town* (Cambridge, Mass.: MIT Press, 1965), pp. 4–5.

91 "From one perspective": ibid., p. 207.

91 To illustrate this mismatch between ritual and social change ... Geertz, "Ritual and Social Change: A Javanese Example" (first published 1957, collected in *The Interpretation of Cultures*).

92 "The investigation of Modjokuto's progressive malaise": *The Social History of an Indonesian Town,* p. 5.

92 "a collection of estates": ibid., p. 10.

92 According to Koentjaraningrat, the terms *santri* and *abangan* ... Koentjaraningrat, *Anthropology in Indonesia: A Bibliographical Review* (The Hague: KITLV, 1975), pp. 200–202.

93 Recent studies have also brought out the regional variation ... See, for example, Hefner, *Hindu Javanese,* beginning with the lengthy footnote on pp. 3–4.

93 "The terms *abangan* and *santri"*: Geertz, *Religion of Java,* pp. 111–112.

93 "This model is essentially": Geertz, *The Social History of an Indonesian Town,* p. 8.

94 "With each tremor": ibid., pp. 150–151.

94 "brought to open view": Geertz, "The Politics of Meaning" (first published 1972, collected in *The Interpretation of Cultures*), p. 322.

94 "that the native eclecticism": Geertz, *The Interpretation of Cultures,* p. 246.

95 "a great deal was going on in Asia": W. W. Rostow, "The Case for the War: How American Resistance in Vietnam Helped Southeast Asia to

Prosper in Independence," *Times Literary Supplement,* 1995, no. 4810, pp. 3–5.

95 "The Johnson Administration": Quoted by Vincent C. Pecora, "The Limits of Local Knowledge," in H. A. Veeser (ed.), *The New Historicism* (London: Routledge, 1989), p. 251. Pecora also cites evidence for clandestine American involvement in the coup.

95 Geertz's own account of an election in Modjokuto . . . *The Social History of an Indonesian Town,* pp. 153–208.

96 "If in 1971": Geertz, *After the Fact,* pp. 10–11.

96 "the structure of meaning": *The Interpretation of Cultures,* p. 312.

97 "this redefinition of culture": ibid., p. vii.

98 "cutting the culture concept to size": ibid., p. 4.

98 "The Parsonian theory of culture": ibid., p. 254.

98 "an ordered system of meaning and symbols": This and the following quotations are from *The Interpretation of Cultures,* on pp. 245, 89, and 52. For a detailed review of Geertz's conception of culture, with full references, see Kenneth Rice, *Geertz and Culture* (Ann Arbor: University of Michigan Press, 1980).

98 "Believing, with Max Weber": *The Interpretation of Cultures,* p. 5.

98 "To be human here": ibid., p. 83.

99 "to distinguish analytically": ibid., p. 144.

99 A more vexing issue had to do with the inescapable limits of "local knowledge" . . . These issues are explored especially in the essays collected in *Local Knowledge* (1983). For some recent reflections see Geertz's essay, "Local Knowledge and Its Limits: Some *Obiter Dicta,*" *The Yale Journal of Criticism,* 5(2) (1992): 129–135. For critical commentaries see Jack Goody, "Local Knowledge and Knowledge of Locality: The Desirability of Frames," *The Yale Journal of Criticism,* 5(2) (1992): 137–147, and Pecora, "The Limits of Local Knowledge."

100 "Culture is the fabric of meaning": *The Interpretation of Cultures,* p. 145.

100 "a cluster of sacred symbols": *The Interpretation of Cultures,* p. 129.

101 "essence of religious action": ibid., p. 112.

101 "the whole landscape presented to common sense": ibid., p. 122.

101 "the difficulty lies in the fact": ibid., p. 164.

102 "The new states are, today": ibid., p. 278.

102 "novel symbolic forms": ibid., p. 220.

102 Among the least well defined elements in Geertz's conceptual apparatus . . . Geertz's fullest discussion of "common sense" is to be found in his essay "Common Sense as a Cultural System," first published in 1975

and reprinted in *Local Knowledge*. For a critique see Jarich Oosten, "Het Gezond Verstand van Clifford Geertz," in J. W. Bakker et al. (eds.), *Antropologie Tussen Wetenschap en Kunst: Essays over Clifford Geertz.*

103 "Most of the time men": *The Interpretation of Cultures*, p. 107.

103 "They both incline toward Mecca": Geertz, *Islam Observed: Religious Development in Morocco and Indonesia* (New Haven: Yale University Press, 1968), p. 4.

103 "by symbolic forms and social arrangements": ibid., p. 99.

103 "coming unstuck": ibid., pp. 2–3.

103 "So too, I think": ibid., pp. 102–103.

103 "trans-commonsensical cultural perspective": ibid., pp. 103–104.

104 "a kind of all-embracing secular religiosity": ibid., p. 107.

104 "one of the characteristics of good ethnographic reporting": *The Religion of Java*, p. 7.

105 "explicating explications": *The Interpretation of Cultures*, p. 9.

105 "what we inscribe": ibid., p. 20.

105 "Doing ethnography": ibid., p. 10.

106 "inscription of action": ibid., p. 19.

106 "the human sciences may be said to be hermeneutical": Paul Ricoeur, "The Model of the Text: Meaningful Action Considered as a Text," *Social Research*, 38(3) (1971): 544.

106 The title of this essay . . . "Deep Play: Notes on the Balinese Cockfight" (first published 1972, reprinted in *The Interpretation of Cultures*), p. 434.

This essay has been extensively reviewed. See, inter alia, William Roseberry, "Balinese Cockfights and the Seduction of Anthropology," *Social Research*, 49(4) (1982): 1013–28; James Clifford, "On Ethnographic Authority," *Representations*, 1(2) (1983): 118–146; Vincent Crapanzano, "Hermes' Dilemma: The Making of Subversion in Ethnographic Description," in James Clifford and George Marcus (eds.), *Writing Culture: The Poetics and Politics of Ethnography* (Berkeley: University of California Press, 1986), pp. 51–76; Vincent Pecora, "The Limits of Local Knowledge," in H. A. Veeser (ed.), *The New Historicism* (London: Routledge, 1989).

106 "It is in large part": Geertz, *The Interpretation of Cultures*, p. 434.

107 "is fundamentally a dramatization": ibid., p. 437.

107 "What makes Balinese cockfighting deep": ibid., p. 436.

107 "What . . . the cockfight talks most forcibly about": ibid., p. 447.

108 "Its function, if you want to call it that": ibid., p. 448.

108 "it brings together themes": ibid., pp. 449–450.

108 "societies, like lives": ibid., p. 453.

108 "that if one looks at Bali": ibid., p. 452, note 43.

109　"Every people, the proverb has it": ibid., pp. 449–450.

109　"piled-up structures": ibid., p. 7.

109　an illustrative story, which occurred in Morocco in 1912 . . . The text of the story is to be found in *The Interpretation of Cultures*, pp. 7–9.

110　"extraordinarily thick": ibid., p. 9.

110　"three unlike frames of interpretation": ibid., p. 9.

111　"a social discourse . . . Cohen invoked the trade pact": ibid., p. 18.

112　"The culture of a people": ibid., p. 452.

113　"The ethnographer 'inscribes' social discourse": ibid., p. 19. More extensive reflections on the text analogy can be found in Geertz's essay "Blurred Genres: The Refiguration of Social Thought," in *Local Knowledge*. See especially pp. 30–35.

113　"Asking whether Pare": Geertz, *After the Fact*, p. 19.

114　"a work of political philosophy": Quentin Skinner, "The World as a Stage," *New York Review of Books*, April 16, 1981, p. 37.

114　"the numinous center of the world": Geertz, *Negara: The Theater State in Nineteenth-Century Bali* (Princeton, N.J.: Princeton University Press, 1980), p. 126.

115　"The state cult was not a cult of the state": ibid., p. 102.

115　"enacted, in the form of pageant": ibid., p. 120.

115　"The problem was that the negara changed": ibid., p. 132.

116　"culture came from the top down": ibid., p. 85.

116　"a society stretched taut": ibid., p. 128.

116　"The dramas of the theater state": ibid., p. 136.

116　In a recent study J. Stephen Lansing argues, contra Geertz . . . *Priests and Programmers: The Technologies of Power in the Engineered Landscape of Bali* (Princeton, N.J.: Princeton University Press, 1991).

116　"careful, detailed descriptions": Geertz, *Negara*, p. 215, note. For comments on the texts, see H. Schulte Nordholt, "Origin, Descent and Destruction. Text and Context in Balinese Representations of the Past," *Indonesia*, 5(4) (1992): 27–58.

116　"the concept of the theatre state": H. Schulte Nordholt, "Leadership and the Limits of Political Control: A Balinese 'Response' to Clifford Geertz," *Social Anthropology*, 1(3) (1993): 295.

117　"Money is the nerve": ibid., p. 303.

117　"With no real room or will": M. C. Ricklefs, *A History of Modern Indonesia* (Bloomington: Indiana University Press, 1981), pp. 120–121.

117　Authorities on comparable systems . . . are skeptical, and Stanley Tambiah specifically questions . . . S. J. Tambiah, *Culture, Thought, and Social Action* (Cambridge, Mass.: Harvard University Press, 1985). But cf. David Gellner, "Review Article: *Negara*," *South Asia Research*, 3(2) (1983): 135–140.

118 "literary studies have appropriated Geertz's insights": Pecora, "The Limits of Local Knowledge," pp. 248–249.

118 "both his starting point": Donald G. Walters, "Signs of the Times: Clifford Geertz and Historians," *Social Research*, 47 (1980): 539.

119 "virtually the patron saint": Introduction to John Ingham and Paul K. Conkin (eds.), *New Directions in American Intellectual History* (1979), pp. xvi–xvii.

119 "anthropology offers the historian": Robert Darnton, *The Kiss of Lamourette: Reflections in Cultural History* (New York: W. W. Norton, 1990), p. 216.

119 "Reading Geertz": Walters, "Signs of The Times: Clifford Geertz and the Historians." Cf. Aletta Biersack, "Local Knowledge, Local History: Geertz and Beyond," in Lynn Hunt (ed.), *The New Cultural History* (Berkeley: University of California Press, 1989), especially pp. 76–77. On the other hand, some historians are troubled by Geertz's lack of interest in chronology and change. See William Sewell, Jr., "Geertz, Cultural Systems, and History: From Synchrony to Transformation," *Representations*, 59 (Summer 1997).

119 Within anthropology, there are two broad critical responses to Geertz's intellectual trajectory . . . See the sources cited above under "Further Reading."

120 Notwithstanding his protestations to the contrary, the fact of the matter is that Geertz became an extreme idealist . . . Geertz has, however, vigorously defended himself against the charge that he is a relativist. See his distinguished lecture to the annual conference of the American Anthropological Association, "Anti Anti-Relativism," *American Anthropologist*, 86 (1984): 263–278.

121 "I am going to revel": *Local Knowledge*, p. 183.

4. David Schneider: Biology as Culture

FURTHER READING

David M. Schneider, *Schneider on Schneider: The Conversion of the Jews and Other Anthropological Stories*, as told to Richard Handler (Durham, N.C.: Duke University Press, 1995); Ira Bashkow, "The Dynamics of Rapport in a Colonial Situation: David Schneider's Fieldwork on the Islands of Yap," in George W. Stocking, Jr. (ed.), *Colonial Situations: Essays on the Contextualization of Ethnographic Knowledge* (Madison: University of Wisconsin Press, 1991), pp. 170–242.

122 "There are only cultural constructions of reality": David Schneider, "Notes Toward a Theory of Culture," in K. Basso and H. Selby

(eds.), *Meaning in Anthropology* (Albuquerque: University of New Mexico Press, 1976), p. 204.

123 "I never learned to read": *Schneider on Schneider,* p. 50.

123 "I gave everybody an 'A' ": ibid., p. 223.

123 "didn't like [Murdock]": ibid., p. 34.

124 "So I was not very tactful": ibid., p. 62.

124 "because I thought he was very clear": ibid., p. 77.

124 "Clyde had parties": ibid., p. 72.

125 "I told him that to the best of my knowledge": ibid., p. 70.

125 "in fact, my relationship to my father": ibid., p. 75.

126 "of the need of selling social science": See Bashkow, "The Dynamics of Rapport."

126 In due course, Schneider quarreled with his three associates... *Schneider on Schneider,* chap. 6.

127 "saying that the material": ibid., p. 22.

127 he later co-edited a collection of essays that elaborated Audrey Richard's general model of matrilineal kinship systems... David M. Schneider and Kathleen Gough (eds.), *Matrilineal Kinship* (Berkeley: University of California Press, 1961.)

127 However, he reacted in characteristically prickly fashion... *Schneider on Schneider,* chap. 7.

127 The first published volley... The conference was the decennial meeting of the Association of Social Anthropologists of Great Britain and the Commonwealth, held in Cambridge in 1963. Schneider's paper was "Some Muddles in the Models: Or, How the System Really Works," in Michael Banton (ed.), *The Relevance of Models for Social Anthropology* (London: Tavistock, 1965).

128 He now collaborated with... George Homans... George Homans and David Schneider, *Marriage, Authority and Final Causes: A Study of Unilateral Cross-Cousin Marriage* (Glencoe, Ill.: Free Press, 1955). This study was exhaustively criticized by Rodney Needham in *Structure and Sentiment* (Chicago: University of Chicago Press, 1962.) Schneider never formulated a defense, but he subsequently made a point of targeting Needham in his own polemics, and he later disassociated himself from the book, claiming that it was Homans's work.

128 "really screwed up": *Schneider on Schneider,* p. 30.

128 He had quarreled with a key informant... ibid., chap. 8.

129 Schneider was undergoing psychoanalysis... Bashkow, "The Dynamics of Rapport," p. 230. Bashkow suggests that this experience of psychoanalysis, with its emphasis on symbolism and subjective experience, may have moved Schneider toward a cultural approach that gave a central place to symbolism.

129 "I beat the culture drum": *Schneider on Schneider,* p. 203.

130 "So we all agreed": ibid., p. 174.

130 Schneider felt that he was being sidelined . . . ibid., p. 190.

131 "make biology and sexual intercourse go away": Schneider, "Kinship and Biology," in A. J. Coale et al. (eds.), *Aspects of the Analysis of Family Structure* (Princeton, N.J.: Princeton University Press, 1965), pp. 97–98.

132 "my interest in developing a theory of culture": Schneider, *American Kinship: A Cultural Account* (Chicago: University of Chicago Press, 1968; second edition, with new chapter, "Twelve Years After," 1980), p. 118.

132 "The book is about symbols": ibid., p. 18.

132 His study had initially been conceived in collaboration with Raymond Firth . . . *Schneider on Schneider,* p. 208. See Raymond Firth, Jane Hubert, and Anthony Forge, *Families and Their Relatives: Kinship in a Middle-class Sector of London: An Anthropological Study* (New York: Humanities Press, 1970). Firth describes the project on p. ix.

132 "these two are to be understood as *independent*": Schneider, *American Kinship,* p. 117.

132 "I have chosen to assume": ibid., p. 130.

133 "By symbol I mean": ibid., p. 1.

133 "Since it is perfectly possible": ibid., p. 7.

133 "a cultural unit": ibid., p. 4. The argument is elaborated in his essay "Kinship and Biology," pp. 97–98.

134 "The fact of nature": *American Kinship,* p. 37.

135 "Sexual intercourse between husband and wife": ibid., p. 50.

135 "is erotic, having the sexual act": ibid., p. 38.

135 "love is what American kinship is all about": ibid., p. 40.

135 "It is the symbol of love": ibid., p. 39.

135 "Sexual intercourse is love": ibid., p. 52.

135 "Love can be translated": ibid., p. 50.

136 Reviewing *American Kinship* . . . Anthony F. C. Wallace, review of *American Kinship: A Cultural Account* by David Schneider (*American Anthropologist,* 71 [1969]: 100–106). The quotation is from p. 102.

136 Parsons had himself formulated a rather similar definition . . . of romantic love . . . Talcott Parsons, *The Social System,* pp. 85–86, Table 1, pp. 108ff., Table 2c. "The love relationship is defined as diffuse and affective" (p. 389). Parsons added (p. 390) that "the erotic love relationship becomes a major nucleus of the kinship system with all that that implies. The erotic relationship itself is thus tied in with the acceptance of the parental roles and their responsibilities."

137   "In America, it is the order of law": Schneider, *American Kinship*, p. 109.

137   "The rule is very simple": ibid., p. 62.

138   "[Blood] not only means the red stuff": ibid., p. 111.

138   "marriage is simply the code for conduct": David M. Schneider and Calvert B. Cottrell, *The American Kin Universe: A Genealogical Study* (Chicago: The University of Chicago Studies in Anthropology, Series in Social, Cultural and Linguistic Anthropology, No. 3, Department of Anthropology, University of Chicago, 1975).

138   "Informants describe the family": Schneider, *American Kinship*, p. 34.

138   "the natural aspect being sexual love": Wallace, review of *American Kinship*, p. 102.

139   In a contemporaneous analysis of Yankee kinship terminology... Ward H. Goodenough, "Yankee Kinship Terminology: A Problem in Componential Analysis," in E. A. Hammel (ed.), *Formal Semantic Analysis*, Special Publication, *American Anthropologist*, 1965, vol. 67, no. 5, part 2, pp. 269–287.

139   For reasons that were not explained, Schneider decided to exclude step-relatives... See Scheider and Cottrell, *The American Kin Universe*, p. 30.

139   According to Goodenough, Yankees distinguished between two categories of relations by marriage. . . See "Yankee Kinship Terminology"; but cf. David Schneider, "American Kin Terms and Terms for Kinsmen: A Critique of Goodenough's Componential Analysis of Yankee Kinship Terminology," in E. A. Hammel (ed.), *Formal Semantic Analysis*, Special Publication, *American Anthropologist*, 1965, vol. 67, no. 5, part 2, pp. 288–308.

139   Schneider himself provided evidence that undermined his assertion... *American Kinship*, p. 81.

140   Harold Scheffler has argued that Schneider got himself into this absurd position... Harold W. Scheffler, "Sexism and Naturalism in the Study of Kinship," in Micaela di Leonardo (ed.), *Gender at the Crossroads of Knowledge: Feminist Anthropology in the Postmodern Era* (Berkeley: University of California Press, 1991), especially p. 368. See also Scheffler, "Remuddling Kinship: The State of the Art in Oceania," Faculty seminar presentation, University of the Witwatersrand, Johannesburg, August 11, 1995 (manuscript).

141   In a later essay, Schneider argued that it had perhaps been a mistake... "Kinship, Nationality and Religion in American Culture: Towards a Definition of Kinship," in Victor Turner (ed.), *Forms of Symbolic Action*, Proceedings of the 1969 Annual Spring Meeting of the American Ethnological Society, 1969, pp. 116–125.

141 "Western cultural constructs": Schneider, *A Critique of the Study of Kinship* (Ann Arbor: University of Michigan Press, 1984), p. 80.

141 "I read every single interview": *Schneider on Schneider*, p. 209.

142 This so enraged his wife ... Ibid., p. 211.

142 Another source of bias was the selection of interviewees ... For a full account of the study and the sample, see Schneider and Cottrell, *The American Kin Universe*.

142 This conclusion was soon challenged by other scholars ... Anthony Wallace made the point in his review of *American Kinship* in the *American Anthropologist*. It is interesting to compare Schneider's project with a contemporary sociological study of kinship in Champaign and Urbana, two hours' drive from Chicago. In his *Kinship and Class: A Midwestern Study,* published in 1971 (New York: Basic Books), Bernard Farber explained that a primary intention of the study was "to investigate differences in conceptions of kinship at various socioeconomic levels in an American community. These differences may then be considered as a reflection of the diverse roles which kinship must play in modern society" (p. 6).

It was also objected that Schneider's analysis might not fit specific minority groups. See, for example, Sylvia Yanagisako, *Transforming the Past: Tradition and Kinship among Japanese Americans* (Stanford: Stanford University Press, 1985).

142 Schneider was sufficiently moved by these criticisms ... See David M. Schneider and Raymond T. Smith, *Class Differences and Sex Roles in American Kinship and Family Structure* (Ann Arbor: University of Michigan Press, 1973).

142 Schneider now proposed a refined definition of culture ... "Notes Toward a Theory of Culture."

143 Schneider did not discuss the substantive account of the American family that Parsons offered ... See Talcott Parsons and Robert F. Bales, *Family, Socialization and Interaction Process* (London: Routledge, 1956), especially chap. 1; Parsons, "The Kinship System of the Contemporary United States," *American Anthropologist,* 45 (1943): 22–38; and Parsons, "The Normal American Family," in S. M. Farber (ed.), *Man and Civilization: The Family's Search for Survival* (New York: McGraw-Hill, 1965).

144 "a kind of natural experimental situation": Parsons, "The American Family: Its Relations to Personality and to Social Structure" (chap. 1 of Parsons and Bales, *Family, Socialization and Interaction Process*), p. 10.

144 "It makes particularly good sense": Schneider, *American Kinship*, p. viii.

144 For a Parsonian, society was a system . . . "But the familiar sociological fact that a given actor has a plurality of roles, calls our attention to the fact that the particular system which is isolated for analysis never stands alone but is always articulated with a plurality of other systems, specifically though not exclusively the systems in which the same actors have other roles, such as kinship units and occupational organizations in our own society." Parsons, "The Kinship System of the Contemporary United States," p. 389.

144 "A person as a cultural unit": Schneider, *American Kinship*, p. 59.

144 "each defined by reference": ibid., p. 60.

144 This notion of the person . . . ibid., note 62, where Schneider raises the question whether the notion of a person may be found in other cultures.

146 "appears to fit the data": Schneider, *A Critique of the Study of Kinship*, p. 19.

146 "I have spoken to many people": ibid., p. 198.

146 "a special custom": ibid., p. 201.

146 "kinship has been defined": ibid., p. 193.

147 "The ideas of kinship": ibid., p. 3.

147 "The implicit assumption": ibid., p. 126.

147 The philosopher-anthropologist Ernest Gellner . . . See Gellner, "Ideal Language and Kinship Structure" (1957), "The Concept of Kinship" (1960), and "Nature and Society in Social Anthropology" (1963). These papers are all collected in Ernest Gellner, *The Concept of Kinship* (Cambridge: Cambridge University Press, 1973).

147 "kinship systems have no 'reality' ": Edmund Leach, *Pul Eliya: A Village in Ceylon* (Cambridge: Cambridge University Press, 1961), p. 305.

148 "there is no such thing as kinship": Rodney Needham, "Remarks on the Analysis of Kinship and Marriage," in Rodney Needham (ed.), *Rethinking Kinship and Marriage* (London: Tavistock, 1971), p. 5.

148 "Robbed of its grounding in biology": Schneider, *A Critique of the Study of Kinship*, p. 112.

148 "What once seemed so indubitable": Hildred Geertz and Clifford Geertz, *Kinship in Bali* (Chicago: University of Chicago Press, 1975), p. 153.

148 "arising out of the experience": ibid., p. 169.

149 "The assumptions and presuppositions": Schneider, *A Critique of the Study of Kinship*, pp. 196–197.

149 Consequently, his initial description of a "double descent" system in Yap . . . Schneider, "Yap Kinship Terminology and Kin Groups," *American Anthropologist*, 55 (1953): 215–236; "Double Descent on Yap," *Journal of the Polynesian Society*, 71 (1962): 1–24.

150 Schneider had emphasized in his first paper on Yap kinship . . . Schneider, "Yap Kinship Terminology," quotations from pp. 216, 218, and 224.

150 "the fact that [in Yap]": Schneider, *A Critique of the Study of Kinship*, p. 232.

151 "In 1947–48 I was told by Yapese that coitus had no role in conception": There is some slippage between Schneider's summary of "the first description" and the facts described in his earlier published reports. In 1962, he had presented a more nuanced account of Yap beliefs: "Prior to the German administration of Yap, the ideology was that coitus had no bearing on conception. Conception was the reward arranged by happy ancestral ghosts, who intervened with a particular spirit to bestow pregnancy on a deserving woman. The bond between father and child, therefore, had no biological content. Even in 1947 this ideology had not been gravely altered. Despite the knowledge imparted by Germans, Japanese, and Americans, the official line on this matter had not been altered in any significant degree, partly because the Yaps themselves tended to take an attitude of indifference toward it. It was an interesting piece of information which might well be true, but it was irrelevant to any matters of significance on Yap and it was not integrated into the ideology of patrilineal relationships at the time I was there." Schneider, "Double Descent on Yap," pp. 5–6.

151 "There is no father-child relationship": Schneider, *A Critique of the Study of Kinship*, p. 81.

151 "Although the relationship between woman and child": ibid., p. 80.

152 Although he did not know it . . . See Bashkow, "The Dynamics of Rapport," pp. 202–203, 211–214.

152 "When kinship can be traced": Schneider, "Yap Kinship Terminology," p. 224.

153 "Are we aiming to understand": Schneider, *A Critique of the Study of Kinship*, pp. 74–75.

153 His own field materials were thin. . . See *Schneider on Schneider*, pp. 97–98.

154 "Although a woman was landless": David Labby, *The Demystification of Yap: Dialectics of Culture on a Micronesian Island* (Chicago: University of Chicago Press, 1976), p. 28.

154 "A woman was said to be a 'garden' ": ibid., p. 25.

154 "Because the father planted the seed": ibid., p. 26.

154 Yet Schneider insisted that according to true Yap belief . . . *A Critique of the Study of Kinship*, p. 73.

155 "the child eventually will discover": J. T. Kirkpatrick and C. R. Broder, "Adoption and Parenthood on Yap," in I. Brady (ed.), *Transactions in Kinship* (Honolulu: University Press of Hawaii, 1976), p. 209.

155 "The effect of adoption": Sherwood Lingenfelter, "Political Leadership and Culture Change in Yap" (doctoral dissertation, University of Pittsburgh, 1971), p. 60. Kirkpatrick and Broder, "Adoption and Parenthood on Yap," specifically endorse his observation.

155 "The importance of the belief": Schneider, "Double Descent on Yap," p. 7.

155 "Yapese cultural constructs": Labby, *The Demystification of Yap*, p. 10.

156 "A 'cultural analysis' ": ibid.

156 "This is ultimately *the* question": Schneider, *American Kinship*, p. 127.

156 Schneider, however, assumed that the Yap cultural system had been stable . . . See, for example, his concluding remarks in the essay "Yap Kinship Terminology," pp. 234–235.

157 "In the late 1940s, Yapese often told dollar-toting American visitors": Bashkow, "The Dynamics of Rapport," p. 198 (caption to photograph). The rest of the paragraph and the following paragraph draw on Bashkow. Lieutenant Carroll's views are reported on p. 203, note 3. According to Bashkow, Schneider also believed at first (perhaps following Murdock) that the Yap were moving from a matrilineal to a patrilineal system of kinship. On the Yap responses to infertility, see Bashkow, pp. 187–188 and 195–196.

157 Other ethnographers found . . . See Kirkpatrick and Broder, "Adoption and Parenthood on Yap," p. 203.

157 Schneider suggested that infertility . . . "Abortion and Depopulation on a Pacific Island," in Benjamin D. Paul (ed.), *Health, Culture and Community* (New York: Russell Sage Foundation, 1955), pp. 211–235.

157 As it turned out . . . Jane H. Underwood, "The Demography of a Myth: Abortion in Yap," *Human Biology in Oceania*, 2 (1973): 115–127.

158 "attributed to the American 'gods' ": Bashkow, "The Dynamics of Rapport," p. 198.

158 "I first claimed [Tannengin]": ibid., pp. 217–218.

158 Finally, the greatest irony . . . See Harold W. Scheffler, "Remuddling Kinship: The State of the Art in Oceania," Faculty seminar presentation, University of the Witwatersrand, Johannesburg, August 11, 1995 (manuscript).

5. Marshall Sahlins: History as Culture

159 "Different cultures, different historicities": Marshall Sahlins, *Islands of History* (Chicago: University of Chicago Press, 1985), p. x.

160 Marvin Harris published a polemical history of anthropology . . . *The Rise of Anthropological Theory: A History of Theories of Culture* (New York: Thomas Cromwell, 1968).

160 Leslie White wrote a ferociously dismissive essay on the Boasian heritage . . . *The Social Organization of Ethnological Theory*, in Rice University Studies, vol. 52(4), Fall 1966 (Houston: Rice University, 1966).

160 In a series of textbooks, the young men staked out a large territory for the new evolutionism . . . See Marshall Sahlins and Elman R. Service (eds.), *Evolution and Culture* (Ann Arbor: University of Michigan Press, 1960); Elman R. Service, *Primitive Social Organization* (New York: Random House, 1962); Eric Wolf, *Anthropology* (Englewood Cliffs, N.J.: Prentice-Hall, 1964); E. R. Service, *The Hunters* (Englewood Cliffs, N.J.: Prentice-Hall, 1966); Eric Wolf, *Peasants* (Englewood Cliffs, N.J.: Prentice-Hall, 1966); M. D. Sahlins, *Tribesmen* (Englewood Cliffs, N.J.: Prentice-Hall, 1968).

160 White argued that, taking the long view, human civilization had progressed . . . See Leslie A. White, *The Science of Culture: A Study of Man and Civilization* (New York: Grove Press, 1949).

160 Julian Steward was more skeptical than White . . . Julian Steward, *Theory of Culture Change: The Methodology of Multilinear Evolution* (Urbana: University of Illinois Press, 1955).

160 In his first ambitious theoretical essay, Sahlins took it upon himself . . . "Evolution: Specific and General" (this essay appeared in a collective Michigan manifesto, edited by Sahlins and Service, *Evolution and Culture* [1960]).

161 "the character of progress itself": ibid., p. 13.

161 "that Moalan culture is an adaptive organization": M. Sahlins, *Moala: Culture and Nature on a Fijian Island* (Ann Arbor: University of Michigan Press, 1962), p. 7.

161 In the small-scale, kin-based societies of New Guinea . . . Sahlins developed his view of political evolution in the Pacific in his doctoral dissertation, published in revised form as *Social Stratification in Poly-*

nesia (Ann Arbor: University of Michigan Press, 1958). The argument was developed in a very influential paper, "Poor Man, Rich Man, Big-Man, Chief: Political Types in Melanesia and Polynesia," *Comparative Studies in History and Society*, 5 (1963): 285–303.

162   Sahlins now turned his attention to . . . "stone age economics." In essays written mainly in the 1960s . . . Collected in *Stone Age Economics* (Chicago: Aldine-Atherton, 1972).

162   Its elements had been sketched out by . . . Karl Polanyi . . . See Karl Polanyi, *Primitive, Archaic and Modern Economies* (Boston: Beacon Press, 1968); Karl Polanyi, Conrad Arensberg, and Harold Pearson (eds.), *Trade and Market in the Early Empires* (New York: Glencoe, 1957).

163   "original affluent society": Sahlins's paper on the original affluent society appears in *Stone Age Economics*.

164   He launched a culturalist assault on a radical mutation of Darwinian theory . . . Sahlins, *The Use and Abuse of Biology: An Anthropological Critique of Sociobiology* (Ann Arbor: University of Michigan Press, 1976).

165   "For structuralism, meaning is the essential property": Sahlins, *Culture and Practical Reason* (Chicago: University of Chicago Press, 1976), p. 22.

165   Yet Geertz had repudiated Lévi-Strauss's fundamental premise . . . Clifford Geertz, "The Cerebral Savage: On the Works of Claude Lévi-Strauss," *Encounter*, 28(4) (1967): 25–32.

166   " 'In France,' Marc Augé remarked": M. Augé, *The Anthropological Circle: Symbol, Function, History* (Cambridge: Cambridge University Press, 1982; first published in French, 1979).

166   Lévi-Strauss had suggested even more provocatively . . . See especially C. Lévi-Strauss, *Race and History* (Paris: UNESCO, 1952).

167   "corresponds to an ideal": C. Lévi-Strauss, *Structural Anthropology* (New York: Basic Books, 1963; first published in French, 1958), p. 4.

167   "The cultivation of plants without soil": ibid., p. 28.

167   "that there is *one* human history": J. P. Sartre, *Critique of Dialectical Reason* (London: New Left Books, 1976; first published in French, 1960).

167   Maurice Godelier ventured across the Atlantic . . . and his essays of this period . . . These essays were collected as *Rationality and Irrationality in Economics* (London: New Left Books, 1972; French edition, 1966) and *Perspectives in Marxist Anthropology* (Cambridge: Cambridge University Press, 1977; French edition, 1972).

168   "The question that first inspired this book": Sahlins, *Culture and Practical Reason*, p. 1. Such explicit concern with Marx's ideas was a

new phenomenon in American anthropology. It was, however, part of a more general tendency in American academic life, as the Vietnam War polarized opinion and put in question the entrenched anti-Communism of American intellectuals. Sahlins himself continued to be reluctant to abandon the claim that he remained, in some sense, a Marxist, though his Marx came more and more to resemble the mature Sahlins.

168 "as an intervention in physical nature": ibid., p. 127.

168 "only in its capacity as the expression": ibid., p. 139.

169 "it is Marx who here criticizes Marx": ibid., p. 168.

169 "would be of the highest service to anthropology": ibid., p. 2.

169 He and others had demonstrated that there was no room . . . for the classic opposition between a material base . . . and a superstructure . . . This had been a central theme in Sahlins's essays in *Stone Age Economics*. As Godelier put it, he himself (together with Sahlins and other anthropologists) had come to realize in the late 1950s that "the distinction between infrastructure and superstructure" should not be treated any longer "as a distinction between institutions, but as one between functions which could be located in very different areas of social practice." Godelier, "Intellectual Roots," in Robert Borofsky (ed.), *Assessing Cultural Anthropology* (New York: McGraw-Hill, 1994), p. 10.

169 "In the tribal cultures": *Culture and Practical Reason*, p. 6.

169 "The so-called infrastructure": ibid., p. 39.

170 "The relation between productive action in the world": ibid., p. 3.

170 "in Western culture the economy": ibid., p. 211.

170 "what Americans do produce": ibid., p. 170.

171 "money is to the West": ibid., p. 216.

171 "Historical materialism is truly": ibid., pp. 166–167.

171 "differences in institutional design": ibid., p. 212.

173 Edmund Leach had ruminated that a model of categories of thought could not . . . model change . . . E. R. Leach, *Political Systems of Highland Burma* (Boston: Beacon Press, 1954).

173 Lévi-Strauss floated the notion that some societies were . . . static . . . See Lévi-Strauss, *Race and History; The Savage Mind* (London: Weidenfeld and Nicolson, 1966; first French edition, 1962; see especially chap. 9); and *The Scope of Anthropology* (London: Cape, 1968), pp. 49–50 (this is a translation of his inaugural lecture at the Collège de France, delivered in 1960). The master of the Annales school of history, Fernand Braudel, had famously identified two historical rhythms. One was the long-term and very slow change in structures; the other, which followed the flow of events, was quick but often su-

perficial. See F. Braudel, "Histoire et sciences sociales: la longue durée," *Annales: Economies, Sociétés, Civilisations,* 13 (1958): 725–753. But Lévi-Strauss was making a different point. What mattered was the way in which people understood history, and managed it.

173 "Of course, this is an illusion": Didier Eribon, *Conversations with Lévi-Strauss* (Chicago: University of Chicago Press, 1991; first published in French, 1988.)

173 "an open, expanding code": Sahlins, *Culture and Practical Reason,* p. 211.

174 "Some Polynesian mythologies": Lévi-Strauss, *The Savage Mind,* p. 253.

175 "a burst of enthusiasm": Sahlins, *Islands of History,* p. xviii.

175 Jan Vansina, who pioneered the new oral history in Africa... J. Vansina, *Oral Tradition* (London: Routledge and Kegan Paul, 1973). A structuralist anthropologist, Luc de Heusch, questioned whether it was possible to separate a strand of historical truth from the seamless web of Central African mythology, provoking Vansina to a furious attack on structuralism. See Luc de Heusch, *The Drunken King, or The Origins of the State* (Bloomington: Indiana University Press, 1982; first published in French, 1972); Jan Vansina, "Is Elegance Proof? Structuralism and African History," *History in Africa,* 19 (1983): 307–348.

175 "A more mythic formulation": Sahlins, *Historical Metaphors and Mythical Realities: Structure in the Early History of the Sandwich Islands* (Ann Arbor: University of Michigan Press, 1981), p. 15.

175 "The final form of cosmic myth": Sahlins, *Islands of History* (Chicago: University of Chicago Press, 1985), p. 58.

176 "think of the future": ibid., p. 55. (This comment refers particularly to the Maori.)

176 "Mythical incidents constitute archetypal situations": Sahlins, *Historical Metaphors and Mythical Realities,* p. 14.

176 "the royal heroes": Sahlins, *How "Natives" Think: About Captain Cook, For Example* (Chicago: University of Chicago Press, 1995), p. 25.

177 "the structure of the conjuncture": Sahlins offers a variety of definitions of this notion of a structure of the conjuncture. One is as "a situational set of relations, crystallized from the operative cultural categories and actors' interests. Like [Anthony] Giddens's notion of social action, it is subject to the double structural determination of intentions grounded in a cultural scheme and the unintended consequences arising from recuperation in other projects and schemes." *Islands of History,* p. 125, note.

177   "The great challenge": *Historical Metaphors and Mythical Realities,* p. 8.

177   Sahlins worked up several case studies of mythopraxis in Polynesia . . . The most important of these were collected in two books, *Historical Metaphors and Mythical Realities: Structure in the Early History of the Sandwich Islands* (1981) and *Islands of History* (1985).

178   Sir Peter Buck had rejected it completely . . . Peter Buck (Te Rangi Hiroa), "Cook's Discovery of the Hawaiian Islands," *Bernice P. Bishop Museum Bulletin,* 18 (1945).

178   "was a logical idea": Ralph S. Kuykendall, *The Hawaiian Kingdom 1778–1854: Foundation and Transformation* (Honolulu: University of Hawaii Press, 1957), p. 15.

179   "As soon as he went on shore": ibid., p. 16.

179   "the old relations were resumed": ibid., p. 17.

179   "Lono, if indeed this was Lono": ibid., pp. 18–19.

179   "treated like that of a high chief": ibid., p. 19.

180   The Makahiki, the Hawaiian New Year festival . . . On the Makahiki, see Valerio Valeri, *Kingship and Sacrifice: Ritual and Society in Ancient Hawaii* (Chicago: University of Chicago Press, 1985), especially chap. 7, and David Malo, *Hawaiian Antiquities (Moolelo Hawaii)* (Honolulu: University of Hawaii Press, 1951; first published in English, 1898).

181   "it proves possible to collate": This and the following citations in this paragraph are from Sahlins, *Historical Metaphors and Mythical Realities,* pp. 20–22.

182   "Cook was now *hors catégorie*": ibid., pp. 22–23.

182   "One might say that he invoked": ibid., p. 23.

182   Sahlins even offers a solution to the murder mystery . . . *Islands of History,* pp. 129–131.

182   "historically sacrificed as a rival": *Historical Metaphors and Mythical Realities,* p. 25.

183   "The incidents of Cook's life and death": ibid., p. 11.

183   "We need not suppose": *Islands of History,* p. 121.

183   "Captain Cook appears": ibid., p. x.

183   "the Hawaiian powers-that-be": ibid., pp. 121–122.

184   "Cook was a tradition": ibid., p. 148.

184   "The Hawaiian chief for whom 'King George' ": ibid., p. 144.

185   According to Robert Borofsky and Alan Howard . . . Robert Borofsky and Alan Howard, "The Early Contact Period," in A. Howard and R. Borofsky (eds.), *Developments in Polynesian Ethnology* (Honolulu: University of Hawaii Press, 1989). See especially pp. 258–266.

185   "When sacrifice turned into trade": Sahlins, *Historical Metaphors and Mythical Realities,* p. 53.

186 "Constituting the social nature": ibid., pp. 51–52.

186 "Hence it is not simply": ibid., p. 53.

187 "For everything that sharpens": ibid.

188 It is not evident, then, that they were intellectual prisoners of the cult of Lono . . . The historian Greg Dening made this point in a review of Sahlins's argument. See Dening, "Sharks That Walk on the Land: The Death of Captain Cook," *Meanjin*, 41 (1982): 427–437.

188 Many conflicting explanations have been offered for this remarkable event . . . They are reviewed by Malcolm Webb, "The Abolition of the Taboo System in Hawaii," *Journal of the Polynesian Society*, 74 (1965): 21–39.

189 "Once an attitude of the kind develops": A. L. Kroeber, *Anthropology* (New York: Harcourt, Brace and World, 1948), pp. 403–405.

189 According to Robert Redfield . . . See Robert Redfield, *The Primitive World and Its Transformations* (New York: Cornell University Press, 1953), pp. 128–130.

189 Sahlins deals with this episode . . . *Historical Metaphors and Mythical Realities*, pp. 56–62.

190 "a ritual act": ibid., p. 65.

190 The story is clearly open to a Machiavellian interpretation . . . Cf. William Davenport, "The Hawaiian 'Cultural Revolution': Some Economic and Political Considerations," *American Anthropologist*, 71 (1969): 1–20.

190 "Thus the set of inversions that, by *mauvaise foi*": Sahlins, *Historical Metaphors and Mythical Realities*, p. 66. *Mauvaise foi* (literally, bad faith) was a very Parisian phrase, favored particularly by the Existentialists, for whom it represented the most reprehensible form of bourgeois immorality.

190 Sahlins's account . . . was soon challenged by a Princeton-based anthropologist, Gananath Obeyesekere . . . See Gananath Obeyesekere, *The Apotheosis of Captain Cook: European Mythmaking in the Pacific* (Princeton, N.J.: Princeton University Press, 1992). Sahlins quickly published his riposte, *How "Natives" Think: About Captain Cook, For Example* (Chicago: University of Chicago Press, 1995). For a valuable, balanced review of the debate, with a full bibliography of commentaries, see Robert Borofsky, "Cook, Lono, Obeyesekere, and Sahlins," *Current Anthropology*, 38(2) (1997): 255–282.

191 "such a confrontation of cultures": Sahlins, *Historical Metaphors and Mythical Realities*, p. vii.

191 "push into view": Clifford Geertz, "Culture War," review of Sahlins, *How "Natives" Think*, and Obeyesekere, *The Apotheosis of Captain Cook*, in *New York Review of Books*, November 30, 1995, p. 4.

191 "is germane to the American culture wars": Ian Hacking, "Aloha, Aloha," review of Sahlins, *How "Natives" Think,* and Obeyesekere, *The Apotheosis of Captain Cook,* in *London Review of Books,* September 7, 1995, p. 6.

191 "Whether Obeyesekere's or Sahlins's analysis": Borofsky, "Cook, Lono, Obeyesekere, and Sahlins," p. 260.

192 "I am not unsympathetic to that theory": Obeyesekere, *The Apotheosis of Captain Cook,* p. 8.

192 "in Geertz's felicitous phrase": ibid., p. 11.

192 "can make all sorts of subtle discriminations": ibid., pp. 21–22.

193 "the Western idea of the redoubtable European": ibid., p. 177.

193 several commentators have pointed out that it was only in Hawaii . . . See, for example, Borofsky, "Cook, Lono, Obeyesekere, and Sahlins," pp. 277–278.

193 "a myth of conquest": Obeyesekere, *The Apotheosis of Captain Cook,* p. 3.

193 the eighth lineal descendant of the Ba'al Shem Tov . . . The Ba'al Shem Tov was an eighteenth-century Jewish mystic in Poland, the charismatic founder of Hasidism. Eric Wolf recalls that when Sahlins gave a paper on Polynesian exchange in France, "he remarked that no one present knew that his presentation was a discussion between the grandson of the rabbi of Strasbourg (Lévi-Strauss), the grandson of the rabbi of Marseille (Mauss), and the eighth lineal descendant of the Ba'al Shem Tov." Jonathan Friedman, "An Interview with Eric Wolf," *Current Anthropology,* 28(1) (1987): 115.

194 "It must be remembered": Obeyesekere, *The Apotheosis of Captain Cook,* p. 72.

194 The Hawaiian texts have different limitations . . . There is a useful review of the relevant Hawaiian sources in Valerio Valeri, *Kingship and Sacrifice.* See also Ben R. Finney et al., "Hawaiian Historians and the First Pacific History Seminar," in Neil Guson (ed.), *The Changing Pacific* (Melbourne: Oxford University Press, 1978), pp. 308–316.

195 "one of complete alienation": Nathaniel Emerson, "Biographical Sketch of David Malo," in Malo, *Hawaiian Antiquities (Moolelo Hawaii)* (1898), p. ix.

195 "a mythic charter": Obeyesekere, *The Apotheosis of Captain Cook,* p. 162.

195 "leaving only their names": Sahlins, *How "Natives" Think,* p. 134.

195 if one admits, with Valerio Valeri, that Hawaiians had complex and subtle ideas about gods . . . Valeri, *Kingship and Sacrifice.*

195 "no necessary contradiction": Valerio Valeri, review of G. Obeyesekere, *The Apotheosis of Captain Cook,* in *Pacific Studies,* 17 (1994):
124–136.

195 According to Herb Kawainui Kane . . . See "Comment" on R. Borofsky, "Cook, Lono, Obeyesekere, and Sahlins," *Current Anthropology,*
38(2) (1997): 265.

196 "it need not be supposed": Sahlins, *How "Natives" Think,* p. 65.

196 "Cook was a living manifestation": ibid., p. 61.

197 He is also still convinced that monarchical states everywhere evolved
from tribal chiefdoms . . . Sahlins has recently revived the old
model whereby the state evolved from kinship structures: "Everything looks as if Hawaiian society had been through a history in which
the concepts of lineage . . . had latterly been eroded by the development of chiefship. Intruding on the land and people from outside, like
a foreign element, the chiefship usurps the collective rights of land
control and in the process reduces the lineages order in scale,
function, and coherence." Patrick V. Kirch and Marshall Sahlins,
Anahulu: The Anthropology of History in the Kingdom of Hawaii, vol. 1,
Historical Ethnography (Chicago: University of Chicago Press, 1992),
p. 192.

198 Matters are not improved by the flights of neo-Hegelian abstraction in
which Sahlins indulges . . . For example: "The dialectics of history,
then, are structural throughout. Powered by disconformities between
conventional values and intentional values, between intersubjective
meanings and subjective interests, between symbolic sense and symbolic reference, the historical process unfolds as a continuous and reciprocal movement between the practice of the structure and the
structure of the practice." *Historical Metaphors and Mythical Realities,*
p. 72. (This is the final passage of the text.)
   Or again: "In the end, we must return to dialectics. I did not really
mean to ignore the interplay of structure and *praxis,* only to reserve for
it a proper theoretical place, viz., as a symbolic process. For all Hawaiian culture is designed to symbolically valorize the force of worldly
practice. It then changes precisely because, in admitting the world to
full membership in its categories, it admits the probability that the categories will be functionally revalued." *Islands of History,* p. 31.

198 "Does Friedman really think": Sahlins, "Deserted Islands of History:
A Reply to Jonathan Friedman," *Critique of Anthropology,* 8(3)
(1989): 41.

198 "If we take mythopraxis to mean": Jonathan Friedman, review of
Sahlins, *Islands of History,* in *Critique of Anthropology,* 8(3) (1989): 20.

199   "is to explode the concept": Sahlins, *Islands of History*, p. xvii.

199   A resolutely idealist conception of culture will not be adequate . . . And Sahlins has settled on an extremely idealist conception of culture. Responding to Friedman's criticism, he writes, for example: "In the perspective I just described, 'cultural' is anything that is ordered or configured by the human symbolic faculty, anything whose mode of existence is thus symbolically constituted." Sahlins, "Deserted Islands of History: A Reply to Jonathan Friedman," p. 46.

6. *Brave New World*

201   "On or about December 1910 human character changed": The passage continues: "The change was not sudden and definite . . . But a change there was, nevertheless; and, since one must be arbitrary, let us date it about the year 1910 . . . All human relations have shifted—those between masters and servants, husbands and wives, parents and children. And when human relations change there is at the same time a change in religion, conduct, politics, and literature. Let us agree to place one of these changes about the year 1910." Virginia Woolf, from a talk to the Heretics Club in Cambridge, delivered in 1924, "Mr. Bennett and Mrs. Brown." Published in her *Collected Essays*, vol. 1 (London: Chatto and Windus, 1971). Quotations from pp. 320–321.

201   David Riesman had depicted as "outer-directed" . . . David Riesman (with Reuel Denney and Nathan Glazer), *The Lonely Crowd* (New Haven: Yale University Press, 1950).

202   "a kind of Western projection": Edward Said, *Orientalism* (New York: Pantheon, 1978), p. 95.

203   "The anthropology of the 1970s": Sherry Ortner, "Theory in Anthropology since the Sixties," *Comparative Studies in Society and History*, 26 (1984): 126–166.

203   "Marxist and other discussion groups": Renato Rosaldo, *Culture and Truth: The Remaking of Social Analysis* (Boston: Beacon Press, 1989), p. 37.

203   "we are still in the process": Sherry Ortner, "Reading America," in Richard Fox (ed.), *Recapturing Anthropology: Working in the Present* (Santa Fe, N.M.: School of American Research Press, 1991).

204   "quickly moved to the deeper question": Ortner, "Theory in Anthropology since the Sixties," p. 138.

204   "internally imperialized groups": Rosaldo, *Culture and Truth*, p. 35.

204   "received notion of culture": ibid., p. 36.

204 "unable to handle": Ortner, "Theory in Anthropology since the Sixties," p. 134.

205 "It was in many ways the perfect vehicle": ibid., p. 141.

205 "Now there appears to be an apathy of spirit": ibid., p. 127.

205 "reorientation of anthropology": Rosaldo, *Culture and Truth,* p. 36.

206 This new trend announced itself in 1986, with a book . . . entitled *Writing Culture* . . . James Clifford and George E. Marcus (eds.), *Writing Culture: The Poetics and Politics of Ethnography* (Berkeley: University of California Press, 1986).

207 Clifford Geertz was recognized as the father . . . though Oedipal rivalries were freely expressed . . . For example: "Despite Geertz's occasional acknowledgments of the ineluctability of fictionalizing, he has never pushed that insight very far." Or again: "Geertz makes a bow to self-referentiality (thereby establishing one dimension of his authority) and then (in the name of science) evades its consequences." Paul Rabinow, "Representations Are Social Facts," in *Writing Culture,* pp. 243, 244.

207 "was to introduce a literary consciousness": George Marcus, "Afterword: Ethnographic Writing and Anthropological Careers," in *Writing Culture,* p. 262.

207 "What does the ethnographer do?": Geertz, *The Interpretation of Cultures,* p. 19.

207 Like any author, the ethnographers were writing "fictions" . . . Clifford Geertz had introduced the postmodernist anthropologists to the ancient, Latin root *fictio,* meaning something made up (*The Interpretation of Cultures,* p. 15). The postmodernists seized on this as a license to equate ethnographies (and other scientific writing) with novels and plays. It might be objected that if a telephone directory, for example, is a fiction in this sense, it does, nevertheless, provide you with the information you need in order to call somebody up.

209 "Culture is contested": James Clifford, "Introduction," *Writing Culture,* p. 19.

209 "A conceptual shift, 'tectonic' in its implications": ibid., p. 22.

210 "historian and critic": James Clifford, *The Predicament of Culture: Twentieth-Century Ethnography, Literature, and Art* (Cambridge, Mass.: Harvard University Press, 1988), p. 289.

210 "Ultimately my topic is": ibid., p. 9.

210 "Distinct ways of life": ibid., pp. 6–7.

210 "It is too early to say": ibid., p. 272.

211 "does not see the world": ibid., p. 5.

211 "began with a reality": ibid., p. 120.

211 "an ambiguous person": ibid., p. 6.

212 "Culture is a deeply compromised idea": ibid., p. 10.

212 "persistent hope for the reinvention": ibid., p. 15.

212 "around 1900": Clifford continues: "I want . . . to historicize the statement that the self is culturally constituted by examining a moment around 1900 when this idea began to make the sense it does today." *The Predicament of Culture*, p. 92.

213 "a hybrid activity": ibid., p. 13.

213 "a specific strategy of authority": ibid., p. 25.

213 "the truths of cultural description": ibid., p. 112.

214 "processes by which 'cultural' objects": ibid., p. 38.

214 "Paradigms of experience": ibid., p. 41.

216 "Such terms as *objectivity*": Rosaldo, *Culture and Truth*, p. 21.

216 "Analytical postures developed during the colonial era": ibid., p. 44.

216 "All of us inhabit": ibid., p. 217.

217 "For me as a Chicano": ibid., pp. x–xi.

217 "social criticism made from": ibid., p. 195.

217 "At the broadest level": George E. Marcus and Michael M. J. Fischer, *Anthropology as Cultural Critique: An Experimental Moment in the Human Sciences* (Chicago: University of Chicago Press, 1986), p. vii.

218 "affected, and even shaped": ibid., p. 44.

218 "contemporary interpretive anthropology": ibid., p. 33.

218 "interpretive anthropology fully accountable": ibid., p. 86.

219 "Ours is definitely a postcolonial epoch": Rosaldo, *Culture and Truth*, p. 44.

219 "American society, if not": Marcus and Fischer, *Anthropology as Cultural Critique*, p. 9.

220 "might be seen as a kind of replay": Ernest Gellner, *Postmodernism, Reason and Religion* (London: Routledge, 1992), pp. 26–27.

220 "Colonialism went with positivism": ibid., p. 26.

221 "If we note that the world has changed": ibid., p. 41.

221 "Is the notion of a distinct culture": Said, *Orientalism*, p. 325.

221 "mobilize passions atavistically": Edward Said, *Culture and Imperialism* (London: Chatto and Windus, 1993), p. 42.

221 "To stress . . . the paradoxical nature": Clifford, *The Predicament of Culture*, p. 145.

222 Lévi-Strauss pointed out a generation ago . . . Claude Lévi-Strauss, *Race and History* (Paris: UNESCO, 1952).

223 "only women can understand feminine experience": Said, *Culture and Imperialism*, p. 35.

223 "always entails the violence": Lila Abu-Lughod, "Writing Against Culture," in Richard Fox (ed.), *Recapturing Anthropology: Working in*

the *Present* (Santa Fe, N.M.: School of American Research Press, 1991), pp. 140, 147, 157.

223 "harassed by grave inner uncertainties": Clifford Geertz, *Works and Lives: The Anthropologist as Author* (Stanford: Stanford University Press, 1988).

223 "what is perhaps most striking": Joel Kahn, *Culture, Multiculture, Postculture* (London: Sage, 1995).

224 "These proclamations must be seen": Paul Rabinow, "Representations are Social Facts," in *Writing Culture*, p. 252.

224 "Sturm und Drang und Tenure": Ernest Gellner, *Postmodernism, Reason and Religion*, p. 27.

7. Culture, Difference, Identity

FURTHER READING

Joel S. Kahn, *Culture, Multiculture, Postculture* (London: Sage, 1995).

226 A missionary's report on the Basotho Chief, Moshoeshoe: Quoted by Leonard Thompson, *Survival in Two Worlds: Moshoeshoe of Lesotho, 1786–1870* (Oxford: Clarendon Press, 1975), p. 81.

228 "Anthropologists have been doing a lot of complaining": Terence Turner, "Anthropology and Multiculturalism: What Is Anthropology that Multiculturalists Should Be Mindful of It?" *Cultural Anthropology*, 8(4) (1993): 411.

228 "*Multiculturalism*, unlike anthropology": ibid., p. 412.

230 "The suspicion is": Stefan Collini, "Badly Connected: The Passionate Intensity of Cultural Studies," *Victorian Studies* (Summer 1993): 457. This is an extended review of Lawrence Grossberg, Cary Nelson, and Paula A. Treichler (eds.), *Cultural Studies* (London: Routledge, 1992).

230 "It is partly where hegemony arises": Stuart Hall, "Notes on Deconstructing 'the Popular,' " in R. Samuel (ed.), *People's History and Socialist Theory* (London: Routledge and Kegan Paul, 1981).

230 "All the basic assumptions": John Storey, "Cultural Studies," in Adam Kuper and Jessica Kuper (eds.), *The Social Science Encyclopedia*, 2nd ed. (London: Routledge, 1996), p. 160.

231 George Marcus specifically urged that cultural anthropology should be recast as a branch of cultural studies . . . Introduction to George Marcus (ed.), *Rereading Cultural Anthropology* (Durham, N.C.: Duke University Press, 1992).

232 Terence Turner . . . opposes a *difference* multiculturalism . . . Turner, "Anthropology and Multiculturalism."

233 "a noticeable tendency to equate cultural studies with the theory and politics of identity and difference": Lawrence Grossberg, "Identity and Cultural Studies," in Stuart Hall and Paul du Gay (eds.), *Questions of Cultural Identity* (London: Sage, 1996), p. 87.

Terence Turner notes that the development of cultural studies "directly influenced the rise of multiculturalism. Cultural studies is similarly concerned with the subcultures, media, and genres of representation of groups on the margins of the hegemonic classes and status groups of British and American society. Like multiculturalism, it represents a decentering move in the study and teaching of culture, and the working concepts of culture it has developed have had a direct influence on multiculturalism. The two movements have involved essentially the same academic constituencies (mostly English and other modern literatures) and have been similarly indifferent toward anthropology as they developed their own approaches to culture." Turner, "Anthropology and Multiculturalism," p. 420.

234 Restating the neo-Enlightenment project . . . Samuel P. Huntington, *The Clash of Civilizations and the Remaking of World Order* (New York: Simon and Schuster, 1996).

235 "arises along with an ideal": Charles Taylor, *Multiculturalism: Examining the Politics of Recognition*, edited and introduced by Amy Gutman (Princeton: Princeton University Press, 1994), p. 28. This is an expanded version of Taylor's 1992 lecture, "Multiculturalism and 'the Politics of Recognition,' " together with commentaries.

236 "Cultivation comes about": Quoted by Fritz K. Ringer, *The Decline of the German Mandarins: The German Academic Community, 1890–1933* (Cambridge, Mass.: Harvard University Press, 1969) p. 107.

236 "The concepts of identity-building and of culture": Zygmunt Bauman, "From Pilgrim to Tourist—or a Short History of Identity," in Stuart Hall and Paul du Gay (eds.), *Questions of Cultural Identity* (London: Sage, 1996), p. 19.

236 "Demanding respect for people": K. Anthony Appiah, "Identity, Authenticity, Survival," in Taylor, *Multiculturalism*, pp. 162–163.

237 "they seemed naturally grounded": Erik H. Erikson, " 'Identity Crisis' in Autobiographic Perspective," in *Life History and the Historical Moment* (New York: Norton, 1975), p. 43.

237 "in part, at least, because I think that immigrants": Michael Walzer, "Comment," in Taylor, *Multiculturalism*, p. 103.

239 "straining for a concept": Clifford, *The Predicament of Culture*, p. 10.

239 "in practice, American post-modernist anthropologists": Roger M. Keesing, "Theories of Culture Revisited," in Robert Borofsky (ed.), *Assessing Cultural Anthropology* (New York: McGraw-Hill, 1994),

p. 302. The quotations embedded in Keesing's second quote are from *Anthropology as Cultural Critique*, pp. 62 and 45.

240   "it is only when we know which race we are": Walter Benn Michaels, *Our America: Nativism, Modernism, and Pluralism* (Durham, N.C.: Duke Univerity Press, 1995), p. 15.

240   "if the Indian's culture": ibid., pp. 121–122. The quote from Sapir is from his essay, "Culture, Genuine and Spurious" (1924), p. 318.

241   "The things the African Negro used to do": Michaels, *Our America*, p. 127.

241   "The modern concept of culture": ibid., p. 129.

241   "what's wrong with cultural identity": ibid., p. 142.

241   Stuart Hall points out . . . Stuart Hall, "Who Needs Identity?" in Stuart Hall and Paul du Gay (eds.), *Questions of Cultural Identity* (London: Sage, 1996), pp. 1–17.

242   "interpretive frameworks . . . facilitate creative adaptation": David Chaney, *The Cultural Turn* (London: Routledge, 1994), p. 208.

242   "the continuing ability of groups to make a real difference": Clifford, *The Predicament of Culture*, pp. 274, 275.

243   "barbarian is first of all": Claude Lévi-Strauss, "Race and Culture" (1971); reprinted in his essay collection, *The View from Afar* (Oxford: Blackwell, 1985), p. 330.

243   "All cultures are the result of a mishmash": Lévi-Strauss, *Race and History*.

243   As Gerd Baumann has shown so well . . . G. Baumann, *Contesting Culture* (Cambridge: Cambridge University Press, 1996).

244   "I recently spent some weeks": Roger Keesing, "Theories of Culture Revisited," p. 304.

246   "A 'culture' is thus better seen": Eric Wolf, *Europe and the People without History* (Berkeley: University of California Press, 1982), p. 387.

246   "the breaking up of culture into parts": Roy D'Andrade, *The Development of Cognitive Anthropology* (Cambridge: Cambridge University Press, 1995), p. 247.

ACKNOWLEDGMENTS

This project was undertaken with some trepidation, but in the most perfect circumstances imaginable, while I was a member of the Institute for Advanced Study at Princeton. I am grateful to Clifford Geertz for inviting me to spend a year in that idyllic place, and to Anna Tsing and Stefan Collini, fellow members, who allowed me to try out my ideas on them without complaint. Anna Tsing took endless late afternoon walks with me in the Institute woods, trying to teach me something about contemporary American anthropology, and she gave my first drafts the benefit of her friendly but rigorous scrutiny. Stefan Collini tactfully pushed me to improve my account of the European traditions, and he subsequently undertook a critical reading of a draft of the whole book. To help me through the next-to-last lap, the Rockefeller Foundation generously allowed me to spend a month at its center in Bellagio. A draft summary of the argument was presented at an early stage at the Institute for Advanced Study, at Harvard University, and at York University in Toronto, and later in a more considered form at Bellagio, at the École Normale Supérieure, and at the University of Oslo. At each stage I benefited from constructive criticism.

David Schneider and Marshall Sahlins kindly provided me with background materials and copies of papers. During my year at Princeton I had regular telephone conversations with David Schneider, and his death shortly after my return to England was a sad blow. He was looking forward to what he knew would be a critical account of his work, and I was hoping to have the benefit of his response to it. The chapter on David Schneider was read by Ira Bashkow and Harold Scheffler, and was presented to a lively seminar at the London School of Economics. Robert Borofsky, Benoit d'Estoile, Gerald Gaillard, and Nicholas Thomas commented on the chapter on Marshall Sahlins, which was the basis of a paper presented at the Maison Française at Oxford. The chapter on Clifford Geertz was read by Henk Driessen and Léontien Visser, and was discussed at a seminar at Manchester University.

David Gellner, Eric Hirsch, and Christina Toren, my colleagues at Brunel University, were always ready to comment on my drafts, as were Simon Kuper, Richard Kuper, Evie Plaice, and Julie Reeves. My editor at Harvard University Press, Michael Fisher, was both encouraging and strict, so that I kept going even when I was losing heart. Mary Ellen Geer was, as ever, a sympathetic and meticulous copy editor. My wife, Jessica Kuper, provided support from start to finish. She enjoyed Princeton with me, read every chapter (sometimes more than once), and, as always, proved to be my very best editor.

INDEX

Abu-Lughod, Lila, 223
Adorno, Theodor, 29, 229
American policy in Third World, 80, 95, 125, 126, 130, 202, 204, 216. *See also* Vietnam War
anthropology, 13–14, 19; and race, 14, 61, 63, 227, 240–241; and culture concept, 15–16, 53–56, 59–60, 168–169; Parsons and, 15–16, 53–56, 68–71; cultural determinism in, 16–17, 165, 200; shifts to study of meaning, 81–82, 205–206, 224; four fields in, 129; cultural relativism in, 159, 160, 168, 206; and neo-evolutionism, 159–161, 164, 168, 200, 219–220; and postmodernism, 206–225, 227; and cultural studies, 228, 232; and multiculturalism, 232
apartheid, xii–xiv
Appiah, K. Anthony, 236–237
Apter, David, 84
Arnold, Matthew, ix, 4, 9, 36, 38, 41, 42, 43, 44, 45, 59–60; view of culture, 41, 64, 211; compared with Tylor, 59–60
Aron, Raymond, 81
Augé, Marc, 166

Bali, 14, 17, 78, 208; cockfights in, 94, 106–109, 229, 264
barbarism, 4, 5, 25, 28, 234, 243
Barthes, Roland, 166
Bashkow, Ira, 157, 266, 267, 273
Bastian, Adolf, 13, 61
Bauman, Zygmunt, 236
Baumann, Gerd, 2, 243
Becker, Howard, 69
Benedict, Ruth, 60, 62, 64, 124–125
Bentham, Jeremy, 8, 42, 106, 107
Benveniste, Emile, 28
Berkeley, University of California, department of anthropology, 78, 128
Berlin school of ethnology, 12–13, 36, 61, 62
Bildung, 8, 31
biology and culture, 11–12, 14, 125, 131
Blake, William, 40
Bloch, Marc, 24
Boas, Franz, 172, 174, 229; and Berlin school of ethnology, 13, 61, 160; and American anthropology, 13–14, 61, 67–68; on culture, 56–57, 60–62, 64, 66–68
Boeke, J. H., 85, 86
Borofsky, Robert, 185, 191
Bourdieu, Pierre, 4, 205, 247

Braudel, Fernand, 177, 276–277
Brightman, Robert, 19
British social anthropology, xiv, 58, 127, 128, 147, 148, 149–150, 204
Broder, Charles, 154–155
Bruner, Jerome, 119
Buck, Peter, 178
Burke, Kenneth, 82, 119

campus politics, 80–81, 130, 201–203, 224, 225, 231, 233
capitalism, 7, 42, 48, 51–52, 202, 208, 218, 231
Carlyle, James, 40, 42, 43, 45
Center for Advanced Study in the Behavioral Sciences, Stanford, 69, 78, 128
Chaney, David, 242
Chase, Stuart, ix–x
Chicago, University of: Geertz at, 78, 128–130; Schneider at, 128–130; anthropology at, 129; Sahlins at, 164
Chomsky, Noam, 18
Cicero, 31
civilization, 4, 5–6, 8, 10, 57, 58; French discourse on, 5–6, 10, 45, 58–59; and science, 6; and culture, 7, 8, 14, 33, 35, 37, 58, 64, 65, 66; and Catholic outlook, 8; and progress, 8, 24–27, 28, 38, 59, 63, 65, 160; Febvre on, 23–27; history of the term, 25–27; Mauss on, 27; and technology, 27; as secular substitute for religion, 28; sacred aura of, 29; Elias on, 30–33; Freud on, 33; artificial, 33–34; Coleridge on, 40–41; Arnold on, 41
Clifford, James, 209, 210, 224; *Predicament of Culture*, 210–215, 221–222, 239, 242; on difference, 210–211, 212, 221–222, 239; on culture, 211–213; on identity, 212–213, 216, 239, 242
Coleridge, Samuel Taylor, 8, 9, 38, 42, 43, 45; on culture and civilization, 40–41
Collini, Stefan, 229–230
Columbia University, anthropology at, 159, 162–163
Committee for Comparative Study of New Nations, 78, 83–84, 130

Comte, Auguste, 8
Conrad, Joseph, 213
Constant, Benjamin, 29
Cook, Capt. James, 177–188; Sahlins on, 178, 180, 181–184, 190–197; identified with Lono, 178–179, 180–184, 190, 194; death of, 179–180; Obeyesekere on, 190–197
Counter-Enlightenment discourse on culture, 5, 7, 10–11, 48, 234
cultural difference, 218, 233–234, 239; Clifford on, 210–211, 212, 221–222, 239; importance exaggerated, 242–245
cultural identity. *See* identity
cultural politics, 228, 231, 234–237, 238
cultural studies, 2, 228, 229–232; and Marxism, 230–231; anthropologists and, 231; and multiculturalism, 232–233, 286
culture: and anthropology, ix, 15–16, 53–56, 59–60, 168–169, 226–228; Lowie on, ix, 62–63, 67–68; a source of explanation, xi, 255–257; and race, xii, 11, 12–14, 61, 63, 227, 237–238; and apartheid, xii–xiv; Radcliffe-Brown on, xiv; a Western concept, 2, 3, 145; elite, 4, 5, 43, 44, 45, 229; popular, 5, 43, 44, 229, 230; mass, 5, 44, 229; German discourse on, 5, 6, 9, 10–11, 26–27, 30–36, 51, 60, 61, 62, 68; opposed to civilization, 7, 8, 14, 33, 35, 37, 58, 64, 65, 66; explains failure of development plans, 10, 83; conceived in opposition to biology, 11–12, 125, 131; depends on borrowings, 13, 61; popular usage in USA, 14, 240–241; and society, 15, 55, 69–70, 91, 92, 97, 99, 101, 116, 130; importance of, 16–17, 99, 120; how to study, 17–19; like language, 17–18, 19; science of, 17–18; no science of, 17, 19; Geertz on, 17, 76, 83, 97–100, 118, 120, 121; a text, 19; is contested, 19, 209; Elias on, 30–33, contrasting views of Alfred Weber and Mannheim on, 30; Freud on, 33; and

instinct, 33–34; Max Weber on, 35; Eliot on, 36–39; and social class, 37; world, 38–39; and religion, 38–39, 97, 100–101; Williams on, 40–45; Arnold on, 41; Leavis on, 44; anthropological ideas of, 43, 54–59, 168–169, 226–228, 231; Parsons on, 53, 55, 97–98; Kroeber and Kluckhohn on, 54–59; Boas on, 56–57, 60–62, 64, 67–68; Culture and cultures, 60–61; acquires its modern meaning, 60, 62–72; Tylor on, 64, 98, 211; Sapir on, 64–66; autonomous system, 71, 245–246; and nature, 72, 145; Schneider on, 129, 132, 136–137, 142–143, 153; Sahlins on, 165, 199; Marx on, 165, 168–169; Clifford on, 211–213; a way to speak of difference, 212; in cultural studies, 229; Michaels on, 240–241; and identity, 234–237, 238–240, 241–242; weaknesses of culture theory, 245–247; disaggregated, 246

defined: "a way of talking about collective identities," 3; refers to high art, 4; "the best that has been thought and said," 9; in opposition to civilization, materialism, animal nature, 14; Freud refuses to distinguish culture from civilization, 33; "the endowment of events with meaning," 35; "that which makes life worth living," 38; "way of life of a particular people," 37; "the consciousness of the race," 44; "that complex whole," 56; "traditional ideas and values," 58; "consists of patterns . . . of and for behavior acquired and transmitted by symbols," 58; "an integrated spiritual totality," 61; embodies "any socially inherited element," 64; "individual refinement," 64; "may be defined as civilization in so far as it embodies the national genius," 65; "a system of symbols and meanings," 71; "an historically transmitted pattern of meanings," 98; "a set of symbolic devices," 98; "extrasomatic sources of information," 98; "the fabric of meaning,"

100; "a collective cast of mind," 227; "a series of processes," 246
Culture (Kroeber and Kluckhohn), x, 16, 54, 55, 56–59, 61, 62
culture and personality, 66–67, 124–125
culture wars, 1, 191
Cuvier, Georges, 26

Darnton, Robert, 119
Darwin, Charles, 11, 12, 13
deconstruction, 19, 131, 206. *See also* literary theory
de Maistre, Joseph, 6
Department of Social Relations, Harvard University, 18, 53, 54–55, 70, 77, 80, 81, 124–125
Diderot, Denis, 28
difference. *See* cultural difference
Dilthey, Wilhelm, 35, 66, 71
Dobu, 66, 67
Durkheim, Emile, 27, 49, 50, 52, 53, 84, 89, 101, 121, 147
Dumont, Louis, 5, 114

economic development 10, 84–88
Eggan, Fred, 129
Eiselen, W. W. M., xiii
Elias, Norbert, 23, 29–34, 46, 47, 48, 58, 229; on culture and civilization, 30–33
Eliot, T. S., 36–39, 42–43, 46; on culture, 36–39
elite culture, 4, 5, 43, 44, 45, 229
English culture, 37–38
English discourse on culture, 5, 8–9, 36, 39–46
Enlightenment discourse on civilization, 5, 7, 10, 11, 13, 48, 59, 60, 219, 234
Erikson, Erik, 237
ethnography, 208, 223; Geertz on, 104–106, 110, 112, 113, 120; Clifford on, 211, 213–215; Rosaldo on, 215–216; Marcus and Fischer on, 217–218
Evans-Pritchard, E. E., 58, 207–208
evolutionism, 9, 11–14, 63, 159–161, 204; and Marxism, 160; Sahlins on, 160–164, 172–173, 197–198, 219–220

Fallers, L. T., 84, 128, 12
Febvre, Lucien, 23–27, 46, 47, 58; on civilization, 23–27
fictions, 19, 207, 283
Fiji, 161
Firth, Raymond, 127, 132
Fischer, Michael, 217–218, 219, 231, 239
Foucault, Michel, 247
Frankel, Max, 95
Frankfurt School, 29, 46
Frazer, J. G., 197, 213
French anthropology, 166–168, 200, 204
French discourse on civilization, 5–6, 10, 45, 58–59; Dumont on, 5; Febvre on, 23–27; Elias on, 30
Freud, Sigmund, 33–34, 123, 124, 192; on culture, 33
Friedman, Jonathan, 198–199

Geertz, Clifford, 16–17, 72, 228, 246; on culture, 17, 76, 83, 97–100, 120, 121; culture and social structure, 83, 91, 92, 97, 99, 116; defines culture, 98, 100, 118; critics of Geertz, 19, 118–120, 214, 259–260, 283; and Parsons, 70–71, 76, 78–79, 80–83, 89, 100, 101, 120–121; style of, 75–76, 120; education of, 76–77; and Margaret Mead, 77; research in Indonesia (see also Bali; Java), 77, 79, 83–86, 91, 94–96, 108, 121; Java, 78, 84, 85, 86, 87–88, 89–96, 99–100, 120–121; Bali, 78, 85, 94, 106–109, 114–118, 148; at University of Chicago, 78, 128–130; and Kluckhohn, 78; Morocco, 79, 103–104, 109–111, 113; Institute for Advanced Study, 79, 81, 130; and Weber, 80, 82, 88, 98, 100, 102, 105; political views, 80–81, 130; and interpretation, 81–82, 98, 104–114; and textual analogy, 82, 106, 108–114; and economic development, 83–88; on religion, 88–90, 93–94, 97, 100–101, 102–104, 176; and symbolism, 98–99, 100, 101, 113, 118, 121; local knowledge, 99–100, 263; common sense, 100, 102–103, 104, 193, 263–264; ideology, 102–104; on ethnography,
104–106, 110, 112, 113, 120; thick description, 104, 109–113; and historians, 118–119; a humanist, 119; an idealist, 120; and Schneider, 122, 128, 129, 130; on Lévi-Strauss, 165–166; on death of Cook, 191, 197; influence on American anthropology, 205, 207, 224
    works: Negara, 17, 79, 114–120, 121; Interpretation of Cultures, 79, 104–113; Local Knowledge, 79; Works and Lives, 79, 113–114, 208; After the Fact, 80, 82; The Religion of Java, 84, 89–90, 90, 104; Agricultural Involution, 85–87, 261; Social History of an Indonesian Town, 90–91; "Deep Play: Notes on the Balinese Cock-fight," 94, 106–109, 264; Islam Observed, 103–104; "Thick Description," 104, 109–113; Kinship in Bali, 148
Geertz, Hildred, 77, 78, 148
Gellner, Ernest, 147, 220–221, 224
German culture, 7, 8, 29–32; Jews and, 13, 29–30
German discourse on Kultur, 5, 6, 9, 10–11, 26–27, 30–36, 51, 60, 61, 62, 68; Elias's account of, 30–32
globalization, 10, 27, 231
Godelier, Maurice, 2, 167–168, 177, 276
Goethe, Johann Wilhelm, 40, 45
Goldenweiser, Alexander, 63–64; and involution, 86
Goodenough, Ward, 18, 139
Gorer, Geoffrey, 124
Gouldner, Alvin, 81
Gramsci, Antonio, 46, 229
Grossberg, Lawrence, 233
Guizot, François, 26

Hacking, Ian, 191, 192
Haeckel, Ernst, 12
Hall, Stuart, 230, 241
Harris, Marvin, 159, 160, 168
Harvard University. See Department of Social Relations
Hawaii, 17, 161, 162, 175; death of Cook in, 177–188, 190–197; historiography of, 178, 194–195; gods in, 178–179,

180–181; makahiki festival in, 179, 180–181, 185, 278; British sailors in, 180, 184–186, 193, 196; tabu in, 184–186; abrogation of tabus in, 188–190
Hegelianism, 34, 35, 198
Heidelberg University, 30, 48
Herbert, Christopher, 11–12, 16
Herder, Johann Gottfried von, 31, 36, 60, 229
hermeneutics, 10, 17, 82
Herskovits, Melville, 240–241
history, 17, 118–119, 156, 157, 174–175, 178; Lévi-Strauss on, 173; Sahlins on, 173–175, 177, 178, 179
Homans, George, 128, 267
Howard, Alan, 185
humanist view of culture, 56, 72
Humbolt, Alexander von, 26–27, 36, 60
Huntington, Samuel, 3, 234

idealism, 19–20, 34, 47, 72, 81, 120, 236; in European sociology, 48–49, 50–51, 81
identity, 10, 210, 211, 234–237, 238, 239, 240, 241, 242; Clifford on, 212–213, 216, 239, 242; Rosaldo on, 216–217; identity politics, 224–225; defined, 234–235; in the USA, 237–238, 241; Michaels on, 240–241; culturally constructed, 241–242; multiple, 247
ideology, x, 15, 102–104, 167, 168, 169, 203, 231
Indonesia, 77–78, 79, 80, 83–88, 91, 102, 103–104; coup in 1965, 94–96, 108. *See also* Bali; Java
individual, 67, 68, 144
individualism, 48, 237
Inglis, Fred, 4
Institute for Advanced Study, Princeton, 79, 81, 130
interpretation, 17, 19, 72, 214, 218; Geertz on, 81–82, 98, 104–114
Islam, 79, 103–104; in Java, 87, 89, 91–93, 101, 103–104

Jakobson, Roman, 18
James, Henry 6

Jaspers, Karl, 30
Java, 78, 84, 85, 86, 87–88, 89–96, 99–100, 101, 120–121

Kahn, Joel, 223–224
Kane, Herb K., 195–196
Kant, Immanuel, 50, 51
Keesing, Roger, 239, 244
Kimball, Roger, 3–4
Kinsey, Alfred C., 134
kinship, 17, 125, 126–128, 245–246; kin terms, 127, 139–140; Schneider's critique of theory, 130–132; American, 134–145; Parsons on, 143–145; nature of, 146–149; Geertz on, 148; Sahlins on, 163–164, 169, 171
Kirch, Patrick, 197
Kirkpatrick, John, 154–155
Klemm, Gustav, 62
Kluckhohn, Clyde, x, 15, 70, 72, 228; *Culture* (by Kroeber and Kluckhohn), 16, 54–55, 56, 57, 58, 59, 61, 62; and Parsons, 68–69; and Geertz, 78; and Schneider, 124–125, 127, 128–129, 132
Koentjaraningrat, 93
Kroeber, Alfred, x, 15, 64, 72, 128–129, 188, 228; *Culture* (by Kroeber and Kluckhohn), 16, 54–55, 56, 57, 58, 59, 61, 62; and Parsons, 68, 69, 70
Kuykendall, Ralph S., 178–180
Kwakiutl, 66, 67, 227

Labby, David, 153–154, 155–156, 157
Lacan, Jacques, 166
Lamarck, Jean-Baptiste de, 25
Lancing, J. Stephen, 116
Langer, Susanne, 82
language, 17, 18, 19, 72, 245
Lawrence, D. H., 42
Leach, Edmund, 147–148, 173, 175
Lévi-Strauss, Claude, 128, 136, 165, 177, 198, 200, 222, 229; on linguistics, 17–18; Sahlins on, 165–166; Geertz on, 165–166; influence in France, 166–167; on Marxism, 166–167, 168, 169–170; on progress, 167; on history, 173; on myth, 174–175, 176, 200; on cultural difference, 242–243

Lingenfelter, Sherwood, 155
linguistics, 17–18, 19, 71
Linton, Ralph, 60
literary theory, 19, 206, 207, 224. *See also* fictions
Lono, 178–179, 180–184, 190, 194
Lounsbury, Floyd, 18
Lowie, Robert, 61, 64, 172, 254; on culture, ix, 62–63, 67–68
Lynd, Robert and Helen, 44

Macaulay, Thomas Babington, 9
Malinowski, Bronislaw, 47–48, 151, 175, 213, 215, 229
Malo, David, 195
Mann, Heinrich, 8
Mann, Thomas, 8, 30
Mannheim, Karl, 29, 30, 32, 33
Marcus, George, 206, 207, 231, 239; *Writing Culture*, 206–210, 224; *Anthropology as Cultural Critique* (by Marcus and M. Fischer), 217–218, 219, 231, 239
Marshall, Alfred, 49–50
Marx, Karl, 48, 121, 172, 177, 217; and the culture concept, 165, 168–169; and ideology, 168; anthropological critique of, 169–170
Marxism, 5, 20, 29, 44, 84, 131, 155–156, 160, 162, 163, 225, 230–231; Sahlins on, 162, 163, 164–170, 171, 172, 198, 200; in France, 166–167; and structuralism, 166–170; in anthropology, 166–167, 203, 205, 209, 169–170; cultural, 169
mass culture, 5, 44, 229
materialism, 7, 8, 34
Mauss, Marcel, 27, 32, 213, 215; on civilization, 27
Mead, Margaret, 60, 62, 67, 77, 124, 125, 229
Michaels, Walter Benn, 240–241
Michigan, University of (Ann Arbor), anthropology at, 159
Mill, John Stuart, 8, 42, 45, 47
Mintz, Sidney, 159
Mirabeau, Victor, 28, 29
modernization, 10, 83, 86, 87, 94, 101–102, 103–104, 143, 212, 221

Moffatt, Michael, 14
Morgan, Lewis Henry, 13, 160, 172
Morita, Aikia, 2–3
Morocco, 79, 80
Morris, William, 42
Moshoeshoe, Basotho chief, 226
multiculturalism, 228, 232–234; and difference, 242
Murdock, George Peter, 123–124, 125–127, 149, 155
myth, 174–177; Lévi-Strauss on, 174–175; Malinowski on, 175; Vansina on, 175; Sahlins on, 175–177, 183, 184, 187–188, 196, 197–198; Obeyesekere on, 192, 193
mythopraxis, 176–177, 184, 192

nationalism, 34, 80, 222
nature and culture, 72, 145
Needham, Rodney, 148, 267
Newman, John Henry, 38
Nietzsche, Friedrich, 7–8, 66, 211
norms, 71, 143

Obeyesekere, Gananath, 193; on Cook, 190–197, 199; on myth, 192, 193
organicism, 9, 48, 49
Orientalism, 202–203
Ortner, Sherry, 203–205

Pareto, Vilfredo, 49, 50, 53
Parsons, Talcott, 15, 47–56, 68, 71, 81, 84, 144, 205, 228, 246, 247, 255; and the anthropologists, 15–16, 53–56, 68–71; on culture, 53, 55, 97–98, 129; and Kluckhohn, 68–69; and Kroeber, 68, 69, 70; and Geertz, 70–71, 76, 78–79, 80–83, 89, 97–98, 100, 101, 120–121, 122; and Schneider, 70, 71, 122, 124, 127, 132–133, 136, 143–145, 156; on symbolism, 71, 133; on love, 136, 268; on kinship, 143–145, 271
Pecora, Vincent, 118
Peirce, Charles S., 133
person, 137, 144
Polanyi, Karl, 162–163, 167, 168
popular culture, 5, 43, 44, 229, 230
positivism, 10, 47, 48–50, 51, 59, 81, 220

postmodernism in anthropology, 18, 19, 206–225, 227; and romanticism, 10–11, 219–221; and relativism, 206, 216, 217, 218, 220–221; criticized, 218–223; reasons for success, 223–225. *See also* Clifford; Marcus; Rosaldo

progress, 8, 11, 24–27, 28, 38, 44, 160–161, 227; and civilization, 8, 24–27, 28, 38, 59, 63, 65, 160; Lévi-Strauss on, 167

psychoanalysis, 71, 109, 129

Rabinow, Paul, 224
race and culture, xii, 11, 12–14, 61, 63, 227, 237–238, 240–241
Radcliffe-Brown, A. R., xiii–xiv, 58, 128, 129, 147, 215–216
Rappaport, Roy, 159
rational choice theory, 10, 48
rationalism, 5–6, 27, 48, 50, 192
Redfield, Robert, 129, 189
relativism, 10, 19–20, 27, 38–39, 62, 204; cultural, 58, 211, 227–228; and postmodernist anthropology, 206, 216, 217, 218, 220–221
religion: and culture, 38–39, 50, 90, 100–101, 176, 245; and social change, 84, 93–94, 101, 102–104; Geertz on, 88–90, 93–94, 97, 100–101, 102–104. *See also* Islam
Richards, Audrey, 127, 128
Ricklefs, M. C., 117
Ricoeur, Paul, 82, 106, 109
Riesman, David, 201
Rimbaud, Arthur, 29
Ringer, Fritz, 34
Rivers, W. R., 147
Romantic view of culture, 10–11, 13, 34, 40, 235
Rorty, Richard, 82, 119
Rosaldo, Renato, 203, 204, 215–216, 219
Rostow, W. W., 95
Rousseau, Jean-Jacques, 40
Ruskin, John, 42
Ryle, Gilbert, 82, 109, 110

Sahlins, Marshall, 2, 16, 246; anthropological training, 159; on evolution, 160–162, 164; political evolution, 161–162, 163, 172–173, 197–198, 281; fieldwork in Fiji, 161; on Polynesia, 161–162, 197; on exchange, 161, 163, 184–186; on Big Men, 161–162, 163; on economics, 162–163, 170–171; and Marxist theory, 162, 163, 164–170, 171, 172, 198, 200; on kinship, 163–164, 169, 171; in Paris, 164; on structuralism, 164–171, 199; on culture, 165, 199, 282; on sociobiology, 171; cultural evolution, 172–174; on history, 173–175, 177, 178, 197; on myth, 175–177, 183, 184, 187–188, 196, 197–198; mythopraxis, 176–177, 184; on Captain Cook, 177–188; on structural transformations, 186–188, 190; on tabu, 186, 188–190; debate with Obeyesekere, 190–197, 199; descended from Ba'al Shem Tov, 193, 280; a cultural determinist, 197, 198–199, 200; debate with Friedman, 198–199; neo-Hegelian rhetoric, 198, 281
    works: Evolution and Culture, 160; *Moala*, 161; *Social Stratification in Polynesia*, 161; *Stone Age Economics*, 162–163; *The Use and Abuse of Biology*, 164; *Culture and Practical Reason*, 164–165, 168–172, 173–174; *Islands of History*, 175, 177, 182, 199, 281 (reviewed, 198); *Historical Metaphors and Mythical Realities*, 176, 181–187, 189, 190, 281; *How "Natives" Think*, 176, 190, 195, 196 (reviews of, 191); *Anahulu*, 197–198, 281
Said, Edward, 202–203, 221, 223
Saint-Simon, Claude-Henri de Rouvroy, 8
Samoa, 14
Sapir, Edward, 62, 64–66, 67–68, 71, 72, 240
Sartre, J.-P., 167
Saussure, Ferdinand de, 133
Schneider, David, 16, 70, 71, 72, 78, 246; and Parsons, 70, 71, 122, 124, 127, 132–133, 136, 143–145, 156; early years, 122–123; relationship with father, 122, 125, 131, 148; and

Schneider, David (*continued*)
  Geertz, 122, 128, 129, 130; and Murdock, 123–124, 125; at Dept. of Social Relations, 124–125, 128; and Kluckhohn, 124–125, 127, 128–129, 132; on kinship, 125, 126–128, 130–132, 146–149; and biology, 125, 131, 145, 147–148; on Yap, 126–127, 128, 149–158, 272; and Firth, 127, 132; on kinship terms, 127, 139–140, 146, 155; at University of Chicago, 128–130; on culture, 129, 132, 136–137, 142–143, 153; psychoanalyzed, 129, 267; on sexual intercourse, 131, 134–135, 143; on American kinship, 132–146; on symbols, 132–135, 144; on love in America, 135–136, 137, 143; culture and nature, 136–137, 138, 145; on the person, 137, 144, 158; religion and kinship, 141; defines culture, 142–143, 153; criticizes kinship theory, 146–149
  works: American Kinship: A Cultural Account, 132–146, 147 (criticized, 136, 138, 141–143); *The American Kin Universe*, 141; *A Critique of the Study of Kinship*, 146–153 (criticized, 153–157)
Schulte Nordholt, H., 116–117
Schutz, Alfred, 105
Service, Elman, 159
Sharp, R. Lauriston, 123
Shelley, Percy Bysshe, 8, 40
Shils, Edward, 55, 78, 81, 84, 100, 101, 130
Shweder, Richard, 10–11
Simmel, Georg, 235
Skinner, Quentin, 114, 117
Smith, Raymond T., 142
Smith, Woodruff D., 35–36
social structure, 15, 54, 55, 69–70, 91, 92, 97, 99, 101, 116
Sombart, Werner, 48
South Africa, xii–xiv, 222
Spengler, Oswald, 34, 66
Starobinski, Jean, 28
Steward, Julian, 159, 160
Stocking, George, 59–60
Storey, John, 230

structuralism, 17–19, 98, 164–168; Sahlins on, 164–171, 186–188, 190, 191, 199; and Marxism, 166–170
Suharto, 94–95
Sukarno, 94–95
symbols, 16, 17, 18, 19, 50, 81, 82; culture as a system of, 53, 57, 58, 62, 71, 93, 132–135, 144, 227; Parsons on, 71, 133; Geertz on, 98–99, 100–101, 113; Schneider on, 132–135, 144

Tahiti, 161, 162, 181, 194
Tambiah, Stanley, 117
Taylor, Charles, 235–236
Tax, Sol, 129
technology, 8, 27, 65
textual analogy, 19, 82, 106, 108–114, 214, 224. *See also* fictions
Thompson, E. P., 39
Tonga, 161, 162
Trilling, Lionel, 119
Turner, Terence, 228, 232, 238, 285–286
Tylor, E. B., 37, 56–57, 59–60, 62, 63, 160, 164, 213; compared with Arnold, 59–60; definition of culture and civilization, 64, 98, 211

University of Chicago: Department of Anthropology, 78, 128–130
Updike, John, 80, 260
Utilitarianism, 10, 48, 49, 106, 107, 171, 192, 198, 199

Valeri, Valerio, 195
values, 35, 57–58, 70, 71, 227, 245
Vansina, Jan, 175, 277
Vernant, J.-P., 166
Vietnam War, 80, 95, 130, 178, 201
Virchow, Rudolf, 12–13, 36, 61

Wagner, Roy, 15–16
Waitz, Theodor, 62
Wallace, Antony, 136, 138, 139
Walters, Donald, 118, 119
Walzer, Michael, 237
Warner, W. Lloyd, 129
Weber, Alfred, 29

Weber, Max, 17, 34, 48, 71, 80, 84, 97, 192; on culture, 35; Parsons's account of, 51–52, 53, 121; Geertz and, 80, 82, 88, 98, 100, 102, 105
Wertheim, W. F., 88
White, Leslie, 159, 160, 165, 198
Williams, Raymond, 1, 39–46, 47, 229, 230
Williams, William Carlos, 211, 212
Wittgenstein, Ludwig, 82, 119
Wolf, Eric, 159, 246
Woolf, Virginia, 201, 219, 282

Wordsworth, William, 40, 45
World System Theory, 202, 209
Writing Culture, 206–210, 224

Yale University: anthropology at, 18, 123–124, 127
Yap, 70, 126–127; kinship system of, 126–127, 128, 149–158; population decline in, 126, 157–158; ideas about paternity, 151, 153, 154, 157, 158, 272; adoption in, 151, 154–155; colonial rule in, 157–158